CREATING
BLOCKBUSTERS!

CREATING BLOCKBUSTERS!

How to Generate and Market Hit Entertainment for TV, Movies, Video Games, and Books

Gene Del Vecchio

PELICAN PUBLISHING COMPANY
GRETNA 2012

The word "Pelican" and the depiction of a pelican
are trademarks of Pelican Publishing Company, Inc.,
and are registered in the U.S. Patent and Trademark Office.

ISBN 9781455615292
e-book ISBN 9781455615308

Printed in the United States of America
Published by Pelican Publishing Company, Inc.
1000 Burmaster Street, Gretna, Louisiana 70053

This book is dedicated to storytellers.
Thank you for your wild imaginings.

In memory of Dr. Milburn Calhoun,
publisher of Pelican Publishing Company.
He generously gave wings to my words.

Contents

Acknowledgments

Many people provided information as well as wonderful insights to shape this book.

I am grateful to the talented, experienced executives who provided their thoughts regarding the principles that lead to blockbuster entertainment. They are Ann Andrade, Raf Berardinelli, Jocelyn Christie, Cherie Crane, Elie Dekel, Jill E. Dowless, Alan Fine, Jay Fukuto, Danny Kaye, Ken Kauffmann, Anne Parducci, Monika Salazar, Bill Stenton, Meredith Roberts, and Sandy Wax.

An added thank you goes to Bill Stenton, who reviewed and critiqued an early draft of the entire manuscript, and to Cherie Crane and Danny Kaye, who provided valuable help on various sections of the book.

I am appreciative to the companies that provided information and permission to use data, which helped provide a foundation for industry insights. These included Ira Mayer, publisher of the *Licensing Letter*; Ed Mintz, president of CinemaScore; Jacob Mazel of VGChartz; Bruce Nash, president of Nash Information Services; Ray Subers, an industry analyst for Box Office Mojo; and Brian Szaks at TEA (Themed Entertainment Association).

I am also gratified for the excellent, highly professional research conducted specifically for this book by C+R Research in Chicago, Illinois. Specific thanks go to Robbin Jaklin, president, and Erika Willig, senior research analyst. They do great work.

I wish to thank Rod Fong for the illustration he created within the book.

I am greatly appreciative of Pelican Publishing for its continued support, and a special thank you goes to my editors, Nina Kooij and Heather Green.

9

I'd also like to thank Ken Goldstein for his guidance.

A final thank you goes to my wife, Linda; daughter, Megan; and son, Matt, for their support and commentary.

Introduction: Why This Book?

This book is more insightful than any other book you might have previously read on the subject of creating, developing, and marketing entertainment. The knowledge comes from my thirty years in the entertainment business, working alongside some of the largest entertainment companies in the world. Authors of other books have provided an excellent foundation of the skills needed to write a decent screenplay or novel. This book builds upon that foundation and goes well beyond it. My emphasis is on creating that special class of entertainment known as blockbusters, which capture the attention of huge audiences and make fortunes. I will explain in detail how blockbusters succeed in hopes that yours can too.

My book goes even further, providing guidance on how to create Multi-Category Franchises that dominate all business categories ranging from film, television, toys, video games, publishing, music, and even apparel. The importance of this is profound; unless you build essential elements into your entertainment while it is in an embryonic state, it will never become a blockbuster let alone a full-fledged franchise. I will also show you how to effectively market blockbusters in ways that keep them *Ever-Cool!* No other book goes the distance as this one does.

Other books don't provide actual tools to help you generate ideas for new entertainment. This book does. It is chockfull of techniques to help you produce the next potential big idea, backed up by principles that will help you refine, develop, and market it.

To my knowledge, no other author demonstrates the principles he espouses by generating and articulating his own new story ideas. This book does. Within these pages, you will find twenty story ideas that I generated myself. I then outline the pros and cons of each idea and invite you to do the same. It's incredibly instructive. Don't miss it!

Many of the previous books on the subject give advice on what is needed to sell an idea to industry executives who have the authority to green-light projects. If you are developing a screenplay, for example, previous books provide guidance on how to come up with the kind of characters, drama, and story structure that executives look for. Many of these books also describe the importance of creating a "hook" that can get your idea noticed by executives. The advice they provide is quite good. However, despite the great intentions of previous authors, a great many ideas for entertainment that are generated, selected, and produced eventually lose money. The entertainment is not sufficiently motivating to put enough butts in seats at the movie theater or enough noses in front of television sets for high ratings or enough traffic in stores to sell books. They fail!

While this book is also about creating and nurturing ideas for entertainment, my frame of reference is *not about how you can sell an idea to entertainment executives.* Instead, my book is about *how you can create entertainment that audiences will want to buy!* Great storytellers from Jeffrey Katzenberg to John Lasseter instinctively know that the audience is ultimately in charge, so it's highly advisable to give the audience what it wants.

By focusing on the end consumer of entertainment, this book provides invaluable tips, which will help creators and executives increase the odds of creating, producing, and marketing entertainment that audiences will flock to experience. After all, entertainment executives may give permission to proceed on projects, but they don't actually turn them into blockbusters. Audiences do that by either giving or withholding their interest. While previous authors do discuss some aspects of audiences' needs and interests, this book is far more audience-centric than any previous book you might have read on creating entertainment.

I am a weird hybrid, a cross between consumer researcher and storyteller. That, too, is rather unique among others who have written previous books on this topic. It allows me to bridge the gap that often exists between what audiences want (audience research) and how to create it for them (storytelling). My career started in consumer research. Overtime, I have conducted more than one thousand consumer research studies, most of which have been for the largest entertainment companies in the world. I have tested films, TV shows, and story-based video games and toys. My research has included both large-scale quantitative studies conducted around the world and small-scale, local focus groups where I have sat face to face with audiences. Audiences have told me why they love some entertainment and hate others. They have told me about the elements of stories and characters that they cherish and the elements that they think suck. Audiences have not been shy. All told, I have heard the voices of approximately 100,000 audience members. When added to my three decades of general industry observations, this research provided more input into the creation of effective principles.

To demonstrate my appreciation for audience research, I conducted a new study among four hundred respondents across the nation specifically for this book. They tell us their preferences for storylines and character types and the elements of execution they dislike. I also asked the respondents to evaluate my story ideas as a way to demonstrate the value of research in deciding which ideas to pursue. No other author has done that! It shows the benefit of scientific research as a way to help inform the development of art.

I am also a professional writer and novelist. My first novel for young adults, *The Pearl of Anton*, received a starred review in *Booklist* in 2004, which is the bible for the American Library Association. The sequel, *The Sword of Anton*, received the Young Adults' Choices Award by the International Reading Association in 2008. In addition, I've written two books on youth marketing—*Creating Ever-Cool: A Marketer's Guide to a Kid's Heart* and *The*

Blockbuster Toy! How to Invent the Next BIG Thing. Both of these marketing books did well and helped executives understand what's in the heart of the child so that they can apply the concepts to television shows, films, toys, and packaged goods.

Given my background in consumer research and storytelling, I have developed knowledge-based tools and insider tips to help you create blockbusters. No other author has those credentials.

In summation, this book provides insights that build upon the knowledge of other books but goes far beyond them. Unlike other books written on the entertainment industry, this book provides insights and advice to help you create and market not just any entertainment, but *blockbuster* entertainment that might even jump into the realm of franchise . . . forever!

This book provides concrete tools to help you generate ideas, right now, for the next blockbuster. I even offer my own ideas as a way to demonstrate how the tools work.

This book is written from the point of view of what audiences want to buy, not from the point of view of what you can sell to Hollywood.

This book provides new research on what audiences want, thus offering a fresh perspective. I even threw my own ideas into the research in order to demonstrate how the process should work.

This book is from an author who is both a researcher and a writer/novelist; this allows me to bridge the gap between audience research and storytelling.

Whew!

It's a widely known fact that most of the people who traveled west seeking gold during the California Gold Rush did not strike it rich. The same is true for most writers and inventors of today. The great majority will not be able to support themselves on their efforts, and it can be frustrating to witness the prominence of those few that do. Success always feels so close, but in actuality, it can be miles away. The people who, as a class, were the most successful during the California Gold Rush were those who sold merchandise such as shovels, pans, and food to the miners.

For the great part of my research career, I have sold shovels (tools) to those looking to make it rich in entertainment. But here's the critical difference between me and the merchants during the Gold Rush days; the merchants didn't tell miners where to dig for gold. I do. And there's lots of gold in them thar hills. They are called blockbusters. Let me help you find them; but not by explaining how to *sell* something to Hollywood executives, but rather, by explaining what your consumer audiences are extremely anxious to *buy*.

Let us begin.

Chapter 1

Blockbusters . . . for the Kid in All of Us!

Blockbusters are easy to find. They are the best-selling novels, best-selling video games, toys that become *must haves* at Christmas, the comic books whose heroes become aspiring worldwide role models, the television shows with impressive ratings, and the movies that achieve at least $100 million in domestic box office receipts, though accounting for inflation and the higher price of 3-D movies that hurdle is rapidly increasing to $150 million (in 2011 dollars).

Not All Blockbusters Are Created Equal

There are three types of blockbusters. *Single-Event Blockbusters* are those that have great success but do not continue from there. If it's a movie, for example, it might do very well at the box office but the story might be too close-ended to allow for a sequel. Some blockbusters are extendable enough to become *Linear-Franchise Blockbusters,* which are successful and open-ended enough to warrant on-going installments in their original category. This occurs when a successful novel becomes a book series, a successful video game has added versions, or a successful movie leads to sequels. Some blockbusters are so immense that they transition into *Multi-Category-Franchise Blockbusters.* This denotes a blockbuster that is an on-going success in its category and is able to hop from business category to business category to become a movie, video game, book series, apparel, concert, and more.

Any blockbuster type (Single-Event, Linear-Franchise, Multi-Category Franchise) is to be cherished.

Winners and Losers

It's not easy to create a blockbuster of any type. The majority of entertainment projects fail. Either they are never bought by entertainment executives or they never survive the development process. Even if they make it through the development process, a great percentage of them fail once they are launched into the marketplace of entertainment options.

In June of 2011, the *Hollywood Reporter* noted that "only 23 percent of past season's new broadcast series were picked up for the fall, the lowest rate in the past five years." According to Bruce Nash, president of Nash Information Services, a special analysis of his database of 625 movies released since the beginning of 2006 revealed that only 30 percent of studio films end up making money after accounting for studio overhead. He notes that "one interesting observation from the numbers is that less than 5 percent of the films account for all of the profits."

Success and failure are based upon numbers. A TV show will be deemed a failure if it did not achieve high enough ratings to bring in sufficient advertising dollars. A film will be deemed a failure if it did not put enough butts in theater seats to justify the cost. A first novel is deemed a failure if it did not attract enough readers to justify the advance. The reasons for the failure are plentiful. It may be a result of a poor concept, a lousy execution of that concept, inadequate and unimaginative marketing, or a lack of support from senior management.

The unfortunate fact in the entertainment world is that blockbusters are vital not just because they make money for their own sake, but because they pay for the great percentage of projects that fail miserably and lose fortunes. As a March 2011 headline in the *Los Angeles Times* read, "Theater owners and studio chiefs put their finger on the cause of a ticket slump: Most of today's films stink." It went on to quote Michael Lynton, chief executive of Sony Pictures Entertainment, who added, "So far there is just nothing terribly compelling about what we're delivering as an industry."

The objective of this book is to help entertainment executives and creative types increase the odds of creating, selecting, and launching blockbusters. The scope is broad and will include key venues where storytelling is central, most notably in film, television, and publishing. But it will also discuss related fields that have become reliant upon storytelling, particularly in video game and toy arenas. Effective storytelling will continue to make its way throughout many manufacturing venues as I discussed in my earlier marketing books— *Creating Ever-Cool: A Marketer's Guide to a Kid's Heart* and *The Blockbuster Toy! How to Invent the Next BIG Thing.*

Industries and Blockbusters

But let's begin our voyage in the industry that is at the heart of the entertainment beast, in the venue where storytelling is most prominent in terms of generating both mass awareness and mass financial trepidation—film. Exhibit 1 shows the top ten films from 2008. Assuming you did not live in a cave that year, it's probably not a surprise to you that *The Dark Knight, Iron Man,* and *Indiana Jones and the Kingdom of the Crystal Skull* made it to the top of the list with domestic grosses exceeding $300 million each. You might argue that these films topped the list because they were based upon already proven storylines, and in two cases, they were based upon already proven film franchises. That's fair enough. It's always harder to invent something entirely new than it is to take something old and contemporize it for today's audiences. But a closer look at the top films reveals a deeper truth.

Exhibit 1: Top Ten 2008 Films	
Films	**Domestic Grosses**
1 The Dark Knight	$533,345,358
2 Iron Man	$318,412,101
3 Indiana Jones and the Kingdom of the Crystal Skull	$317,101,119
4 Hancock	$227,946,274
5 WALL-E	$223,808,164
6 Kung Fu Panda	$215,434,591
7 Twilight	$192,769,854
8 Madagascar: Escape 2 Africa	$180,010,950
9 Quantum of Solace	$168,368,427
10 Dr. Seuss' Horton Hears a Who!	$154,529,439

Source: Box Office Mojo, permission granted

Notice that the highest-grossing blockbuster films in 2008 were not intended only for the older crowd with mature drama subject matter. Instead, the bulk of the most successful films had their origins in youth culture. Most importantly, they did not just appeal to kids, they appealed to the *kid in all of us*. It's by attracting the kid in all of us that helps stories appeal to as many of the "four audience quadrants" as possible—younger males, older males, younger females, older females.

(Courtesy Rod Fong)

Born from the grand imaginations of Bob Kane and Bill Finger, *The Dark Knight* (aka Batman) originated as a superhero in comic books read by kids and teens in 1939. However, the 2008 film version would not have attained more than $500 million in domestic box office sales by attracting kids and teens alone. It did more than that. Batman connects with the kid in all of us who desires to have the power to right the wrongs that exist in crime-infested Gotham City. Through Batman, the kid in all of us can imagine he wears the cool costume, fights with the cool gadgets, and drives the cool car. The film added touches of realism that are dark, edgy, and action packed, exactly what was needed for adults to line up for their own sake. In effect, the film teased the child up from the depth of our adult souls and rocketed it to the surface long enough to watch a great film while tossing buttered popcorn pass our lips at a rapid pace. It's kid stuff, made enticing for adult tastes, too.

Similarly, *Iron Man* was born in 1963 at Marvel Comics. It came from the genius of story plotter Stan Lee, scripter Larry Lieber, story artist Don Heck, and character designer Jack Kirby. Read by millions of youth the world over, *Iron Man* gave us a fantasy that we could not achieve in our own lives; the fantasy to build and wear a suit that can save and protect us from evil. What kid wouldn't want that? And what adult couldn't appreciate the same? Even better, the war-related themes used in the early *Iron Man* comics connected with America's involvement in the Cold War. It was on trend. But the film went one better. It was brought to the screen with a great story, well told, and executed in an edgy, realistic, action-packed way, thus giving permission for adults to seek out the film in order to feel like kids again.

Indiana Jones connects us to our kidlike wonder. Who among us hasn't dreamed of finding ancient treasures and unraveling ancient mysteries? Who doesn't want to wear Indy's hat and crack his whip?

Films like *WALL-E* and *Kung Fu Panda* appear on the surface to be solely "kid stuff," but beneath the surface, these films contain themes that touch the childlike wonder within all of us; themes that adults and children can easily admire and love. *WALL-E* connects us to tender romance, overcoming evil, and a great desire to save Earth from environmental calamity (on trend). *Kung Fu Panda* connects us to characters that, like us, have great, hidden potential.

To be clear, when children love films, they will drag their parents along with them, which enhances box office receipts. That happens all the time. I suspect that the film *Dr. Seuss' Horton Hears a Who!* did that because children who went to see this movie were likely to be younger. Nevertheless, with the right storytelling, adults will desire to see a film with kidlike icons independent of their children's desires. And some (this author included) will even use their children as the excuse to see a film that they wanted to see. We never quite grow out of the kidlike wonder of our youth. We hold onto fantasies and revisit them when those fantasies are served up in more mature, realistic ways.

In 2008, the films that were much more adult-oriented showed up as numbers 11 and 12 on the list (*Sex and the City* and *Gran Torino*). Both did well but were dwarfed in size by those films that targeted the kid in all of us.

As a child, a girl might love the story of a commoner who marries a prince in the classic tale of *Cinderella*. As a teen and young adult, she might love *The Princess Diaries,* a story about a teen who discovers she's a princess of a small European country. As an adult, she might love *Pretty Woman,* a story about a prostitute who falls in love with a successful businessman who hires her as his escort. In all three cases, the princess's slipper fits perfectly. About two billion of these same girls . . . young and old . . . were glued to the television set in May 2011 to watch the Royal Wedding of Prince William and Kate Middleton. It's a real life story of a commoner marrying royalty. The fantasy lives in all of us!

Adults might say that they are not kids, but who are they kidding? Our interests betray us and demonstrate that our childlike fantasies never die. Why else would a thirty-five-year-old man plunk down $12 for a theater ticket to see *Transformers*, a story based upon a toy line that he played with when he was about ten years old? Answer: part of him never grew up, and he looks to relive his childhood in ways that feel more realistic, even gritty, so as to be acceptable to adult sensibilities. The cliché is true—the bigger the kid, the bigger the toys.

As Robert A. Iger, president and chief executive officer for the Walt Disney Company, stated in the company's 2010 annual report, "*Toy Story 3* is at once a gorgeous work of art, a great example of how new technology can make entertainment even more compelling, and a story that speaks to all of us. It shares the DNA of Disney classics like *Snow White*, *Pinocchio* and *Beauty and the Beast*; deeply human stories that appeal to people across cultures and ages and are enjoyed every day the world over."

In a similar fashion, providing appeals that connect to the kid in all of us has resulted in the tremendous success of *Star Wars*, *Harry Potter*, *Shrek*, and more. My intent throughout this book is to explain why.

This book will help you to craft entertainment that millions of adults will rush to see because it entices that aspect of their psyches that demands to be a kid—their kid's heart. The added bonus is that the principles I impart will entice children as well.

You might say that the year 2008 was just a fluke. Not so. Exhibit 2 shows the top 10 domestic grossing films for 2009 and 2010. Once again, you will note that nearly every film on the lists has fundamental themes that appeal to adults who are kids at heart. Also notice that the films with adult themes such as *The Hangover* and *The Blind Side* are further down the list.

You might argue that the biggest blockbusters are simply "family-friendly films." That description belittles what is really happening here. The term "family-friendly film" often implies that the movie has a sweet story, that there's something for everyone, and so the kids might bring mom and dad, too. First, there's nothing sweet about the battle inherent in *Avatar*. Second, the theaters for many of these blockbusters are filled with adults with and without their kids.

Exhibit 2: Top Ten 2009 and 2010 Films

	2009 Films	Domestic Grosses
1	Avatar	$749,766,139
2	Transformers: Revenge of the Fallen	$402,111,870
3	Harry Potter and the Half-Blood Prince	$301,959,197
4	The Twilight Saga: New Moon	$296,623,634
5	Up	$293,004,164
6	The Hangover	$277,322,503
7	Star Trek	$257,730,019
8	The Blind Side	$255,959,475
9	Alvin and the Chipmunks: The Squeakquel	$219,614,612
10	Sherlock Holmes	$209,028,679

	2010 Films	Domestic Grosses
1	Toy Story 3	$415,004,880
2	Alice in Wonderland	$334,191,110
3	Iron Man 2	$312,433,331
4	The Twilight Saga: Eclipse	$300,531,751
5	Harry Potter and the Deathly Hallows: Part 1	$295,001,070
6	Inception	$292,576,195
7	Despicable Me	$251,513,985
8	Shrek Forever After	$238,736,787
9	How to Train Your Dragon	$217,581,231
10	Tangled	$199,634,414

Source: Box Office Mojo, permission granted

I have not yet addressed the issue of profitability. A film may have domestic box office receipts of a very respectable $150 million and a total worldwide gross of $300 million, but it would be considered a tremendous flop if it cost more than that to produce and market. It happens all the time but has more to do with bad production decisions and expectations than with consumer interest, which is best exhibited by consumer measures like box office receipts.

Now let's jump way down the box office list. Exhibit 3 shows 2010 films that ranked 141 to 150 by box office receipts. They are predominantly films directed toward an adult audience, featuring more dramas, foreign titles, and R ratings. None of the themes were for the kid in all of us. The documentary *Waiting for "Superman"* received considerable press for its analysis of the failures of the American public education system. Such films have an important place, but they are not the topic of this book.

The immense distance between top-grossing films and bottom-grossing films is staggering and represents the difference in potential between developing adult-oriented films and developing entertainment that targets adults who possess a kid mindset. To be fair, each of the films on the bottom list could have had any number of issues that resulted in their lower performance, including poor marketing, a crowded premiere date, or inadequate distribution. Some might have still been profitable depending upon their production and marketing costs. However, just a quick glimpse at Exhibits 1, 2, and 3 provides at least one inescapable conclusion; films that target the kid in all of us have far more massive appeal than those that don't. Yet, the industry still creates an abundance of films that end up at the bottom, financial failures that must be subsidized by those films at the top.

Similarly, some of the most enduring TV shows are those that connect with the childlike aspects of our psyche. *The Simpsons* is a standout example. It debuted on FOX in 1989 and has become the longest-running American sitcom, lasting nearly twice the number of seasons as other comedies (see Exhibit 4). Adults and children alike are enthralled by this seemingly childlike *cartoon*. But it's not just for kids. In 2009, it even became the longest-

Exhibit 3: Lower-Ranking 2010 Films		
Films	Genre/MPAA Rating	Domestic Grosses
141 City Island	Comedy/PG-13	$6,671,036
142 The Last Station	Historical Drama/R	$6,617,867
143 Winter's Bone	Drama/R	$6,531,503
144 Waiting for "Superman"	Documentary/ PG	$6,417,135
145 The Secret in Their Eyes	Crime Drama/R	$6,391,436
146 It's Kind of a Funny Story	Drama/PG-13	$6,363,628
147 The Warrior's Way	Western/R	$5,666,340
148 The Girl Who Kicked the Hornet's Nest	Foreign/R	$5,190,196
149 I Am Love	Foreign/R	$5,005,465
150 Mao's Last Dancer	Drama/PG	$4,817,770
Source: Box Office Mojo, permission granted		

running American primetime entertainment series by surpassing the adult-oriented, live-action series *Gunsmoke*. After all these years, the animated series still lands on the list of the top shows. It won twenty-seven Primetime Emmy Awards, *Time* magazine once named it the twentieth century's best television series, and the Simpson family received a star on the Hollywood Walk of Fame. It consistently delivers wide audiences because it speaks to all of us through the characters of Homer, Bart, Marge, Lisa, and Maggie. Kids and adults can identify with them, albeit in different ways, which is a key concept that will be explored in this book as well. That is, how to create entertainment that is layered with characters, humor, action, and nuances in such a way that both kids and adults can find some aspect of it to enjoy.

It's also worth noting that of all television shows, one of the longest-running is *The Wonderful World of Disney* with fifty-two seasons under its belt. It touched the childlike wonder in all of us.

Exhibit 4: Longest-Running Television Sitcoms as of September 2010	
Sitcom	Seasons on Air
The Simpsons	22
The Danny Thomas Show	18
South Park	15
The Adventures of Ozzie and Harriet	14
King of the Hill	13
My Three Sons/The Lucy Show (I Love Lucy)	12
Happy Days, Married . . . with Children, The Jeffersons, 7th Heaven, Fraiser, Cheers, M*A*S*H	11
Source: Various	

Exhibit 5 shows an assortment of best-selling *single-volume* books. *A Tale of Two Cities* is the only book with higher sales than *The Lord of the Rings* and *The Hobbit;* both of which are giants compared to more adult-themed books like *Gone with the Wind* and *The Godfather. The Lord of the Rings* and *The Hobbit* have achieved such great success because they appeal to the childlike mindset in all of us. It's pure fantasy. The four-hundred-pound gorilla in the bookstore isn't on this list because it's not a *single* book. It's a series. If you add all the Harry Potter books together, they total more than 400 million copies sold! One of the few books to have greater total sales than the *Harry Potter Series* is *The Holy Bible.*

How could that be possible?!

The world of Harry Potter satisfies deep emotional needs within all of us . . . young and old. We rushed into stores to buy the books. We waited in long lines to see the films. We purchased merchandise to *look* and *feel* like the characters. What is it about this franchise that makes us act so? This book will explain all of this in the hopes that you, too, can achieve even a fraction of that success.

Exhibit 5: Assorted Best-Selling Single-Volume Books

Title	Author	Copies Sold
A Tale of Two Cites	Charles Dickens	200+ million
The Lord of the Rings	J. R. R. Tolkien	150+ million
The Hobbit	J. R. R. Tolkien	100+ million
And Then There Were None	Agatha Christie	100+ million
The Lion, the Witch and the Wardrobe	C. S. Lewis	85+ million
The Da Vinci Code	Dan Brown	80+ million
Gone with the Wind	Margaret Mitchell	30+ million
The Godfather	Mario Puzo	21+ million

Source: Various

Let's jump to theme parks. Exhibit 6 shows that Disney-related theme parks dominate top attendance. Why? In part, the overall theme and related rides and parades are predominantly based upon stories and adventures we all grew up with! At Disneyland, you can visit Cinderella's Castle, experience the Indiana Jones-themed ride, and visit Tom Sawyer's Island. We can all feel like youngsters again.

Video games show a similar pattern. Of the top best-selling video games from 2000 to 2009 (see Exhibit 7) several are based upon childlike fantasies, such as *Super Mario Bros.* and *Pokemon*. Importantly, the average age of a game player is thirty-seven according to industry statistics. Thirty-seven! Many gamers born in the 1970s, with the introduction of Atari and Nintendo, never left their games behind. They continued to play video games well into adulthood. Why? At their core, video games appeal to the kid in all of us by providing a good dose of childlike fantasy fulfillment.

Exhibit 6: Top Fifteen Amusement/Theme Parks

	Amusement/Theme Parks	2010 Attendance
1	Magic Kingdom at Walt Disney World (Florida)	16,972,000
2	Disneyland (California)	15,980,000
3	Tokyo Disneyland	14,452,000
4	Tokyo DisneySea	12,663,000
5	Epcot at Walt Disney World	10,825,000
6	Disneyland Park at Disneyland Paris	10,500,000
7	Disney's Animal Kingdom at Walt Disney World	9,686,000
8	Disney's Hollywood Studios at Walt Disney World	9,603,000
9	Universal Studios Japan	8,160,000
10	Everland (South Korea)	6,884,000
11	Disney California Adventure	6,278,000
12	Islands of Adventure at Universal Orlando (Florida)	5,949,000
13	Universal Studios at Universal Orlando	5,925,000
14	Lotte World (South Korea)	5,551,000
15	Hong Kong Disneyland	5,200,000

Source: The Global Attractions Attendance Report, 2010. Themed Entertainment Association (TEA) and AECOM, permission granted

Exhibit 7: Best-Selling Video Games from 2000-09 (Multiplatform)

	Game	Units Sold
1	Wii Sports	58.40 million
2	Wii Play	26.53 million
3	Nintendogs	23.43 million
4	Wii Fit	22.50 million
5	New Super Mario Bros. DS	20.92 million
6	Mario Kart Wii	20.71 million
7	Grand Theft Auto: San Andreas	20.15 million
8	Brain Age	18.73 million
9	Pokemon Gold/Silver	18.02 million
10	Pokemon Diamond/Pearl	17.35 million

Source: VGChartz, permission granted

Uncovering and Applying Principles Are Key

This book will outline the principles that made these blockbusters successful. Not all great films, novels, toys, comic books, or video games are financial blockbusters. There are countless offerings that we hold dear that never enjoyed huge financial success. Not all financial blockbusters are deemed to be great by the critics. But the only critics that matter for the purpose of this book are audiences who have voted with their dollars.

There are many books that teach you how to write and sell your screenplays or novels to the entertainment industry, most notably to entertainment company presidents, publishers, or producers. Given the failure rate, many executives appear to be picking the wrong material. If you are a writer/developer, this book will show you how to create entertainment that audiences *want to buy*. If you are an executive, this book will provide a system of principles that you can employ to evaluate and market that entertainment.

The knowledge and insights within this book come from several sources. They are derived from my thirty years of making general observations in the entertainment industry regarding what works and what has not. They come from working on a slew of research and consulting projects for films, TV shows, video games, and toys. They come from my experience as a storyteller and novelist. They come from many successful entertainment executives whose helpful tips you will find within these pages. And they come from a new research project that I commissioned specifically for this book in order to provide fresh audience opinions. This research discovered the types of emotional satisfaction audiences seek through entertainment, the types of iconic characters they desire to see, the challenges and fears they want these characters to face, the emotional and physical ways they wish these characters would transform in the context of the story, and the dislikes they have of current entertainment offerings. This research shows, for example, that when asked for chief dislikes of entertainment, 44.5 percent of the respondents said that today's offerings don't interest them from the start. Among other things, many of today's entertainment offerings lack relevant and aspiring stories and characters. All of this and more created a foundation for the key principles you will find within. I will demonstrate these principles with examples old and new, spanning many decades of observations, to provide both a historical and contemporary context.

William Goldman once famously said that "nobody knows anything," in reference to whether anyone could predict if a particular film would be a success or a flop. With due respect, he's wrong. Immensely creative, Goldman knew that he was onto something when he wrote the Academy Award-winning screenplay for *Butch Cassidy and the Sundance Kid* as well as *The Princess Bride*. George Lucas must have known something, deep down, or else he would have given up on *Star Wars* long before the final edit. Stephen King must have thought that *Carrie* had potential or he would have succumbed to the plethora of rejection letters he received.

It seems that *somebody knows something,* and some very successful storytellers have proven that they do time and again. These writers have an instinct that is not magic. Their instinct is rooted in sound principles. This book will explain these principles and how you can immediately apply them in order to help you create, develop, and market blockbusters.

Then you will be *somebody who knows something,* too.

Chapter 2

The Key Success Principles

Most people never get their screenplay produced, their TV show picked up, their novel published, or their toy idea sold. To be honest, many times it's because the ideas are crap. Sometimes it's because the people responsible for making the decisions are clueless to the actual strength of the idea. Even when the gods smile upon the idea and it gets produced it typically gets battered, beaten, and broken on its death march to failure.

Welcome to the entertainment industry.

Failure is the norm. The guys who never get their ideas produced are saddened and frustrated because they never got the chance, and so they continue to wait on tables in Hollywood restaurants or in bars in New York City.

The one hit wonders come next. These are the guys who had one great triumph and then are dumbfounded that they can't do it again. Most of these "accidental" creators never looked at what they did critically enough to draw conclusions as to why it worked the first time, and so their next efforts are as much luck as was the first.

A string of successes is so exceedingly rare that we can count the famous people who have done it on our fingers without ever getting to our toes. Some of those who have had a string of successes might mistakenly think they have a supernatural *feeling* as to what works and what doesn't, a feeling that can't be quantified or specified. They just know. They give credit to their gut when in fact it's science. They have the soul of a researcher. They've seen what audiences crave, applied what they observed, experienced that success again, and then duplicated the key principles. They know stuff; stuff that they have ingrained into their subconscious.

They apply their knowledge repeatedly and may not even be aware that they are doing it. It's natural.

This book is not so much a text as it is a working battlefield manual. Its intent is to help you know what others have already learned and to help you immediately apply it.

This chapter is the primer. It provides the overview for the rest of the manual and can be used as a short cut summary once the rest of the text has been consumed. The purpose is to give you a fast checklist of the step-by-step principles you must follow in order to increase the odds of inventing the next blockbuster.

This chapter is also dangerous if you think that by reading the summary of core principles you don't need to read the rest of the book. You would be wrong. Success is not only guided by overall principles, but in the detailed execution of those principles. So read and understand the principles in this chapter as they will provide a nice overview, but don't skip the details in the rest of the book. That would be like reading a pamphlet about aviation and then jumping into the cockpit of a jet fighter and expecting to win an aerial dogfight at twenty thousand feet. You'll be blown out of the sky by far more experienced and deadly pilots.

Consistent success stems from the rigorous, consistent application of following the eleven guiding principles. These principles may appear obvious, but I assure you that they are not obvious to those who have failed. It's also true that while we claim to know certain principles, we don't always apply them consistently or well enough.

Principle 1: Satisfy Deep Emotional Needs

It seems as if this observation should go without saying, but it can't. Of all the entertainment ideas I have been paid to review or test over the past three decades, and there have been many hundreds, this is where most ideas fail. They never make the emotional connection with audiences. It's not unusual for executives to get excited about an idea and then jump into product or screenplay development without answering a basic question: how do we want our entertainment to make the audience *feel* when they play with our toy or when they are watching our movie? What exactly is the emotional connection we are trying to make? This is the crux of all great ideas.

The basic needs that we strive to satisfy are many, and most of them are the same for adults and for children—that kid in all of us. Blockbusters tap into our common needs for survival, safety, love, belonging, acceptance, friendship, self-respect, achievement, independence, power, creativity, control, mastery, and attractiveness to name a few. Satisfying these basic needs provide a sense of fulfillment, discovery, and excitement.

Achieving "emotional transformations" is an important element of need satisfaction. It includes our desire to transform from cowardice to bravery, shy to bold, unconfident to confident, and loser to winner. Physical transformations are often critical as well, such as transforming from weak to strong, ugly to pretty, and rags to riches. If we cannot achieve these transformations in reality, blockbuster entertainment delivers them in fantasy.

Our collective fears are also fodder for successful entertainment. We fear monsters, divorce, loneliness, injury, and even ourselves. Some fears are shared by many ages and genders; other fears are experienced by smaller segments of the population. Crafting a story that names our fears and then helps characters resolve them gives us hope that we could do the same. It allows audiences to feel triumphant over external and internal demons.

Our weaknesses are revealed by the seven deadly sins. People are forever enticed by greed, sloth, anger, envy, lust, gluttony, and pride. These make great underpinnings for the weaknesses in heroes and the motivations for villains.

Creators and entertainment executives who seed their entertainment with deep emotional drivers are on their way toward success. The intense desire for power, as one example, has led to such ageless icons as Hercules and such contemporary ones as Superman. The timeless fantasy to rise from rags to riches has led to such brilliant stories as *Cinderella* and the board game *Monopoly*.

If you miss by an "emotional inch" when your idea is in the conceptual stage, you'll be off by a mile by the time your project is done. Knowing the details of the key needs to satisfy, and all the deviations thereof, will be the topic of chapter 3.

Principle 2: Align with Contemporary Culture and Trends

Blockbusters often reflect contemporary culture and trends. This includes entertainment-based pop culture (pop stars, music, fashion, literature, etc.) as well as issues-based culture (religion, politics, environment, crime and punishment, etc.). New story twists can be found by associating culture with different eras, locales, characters, or plots. For example, a pop rock group theme was crafted as a boy band in the 1960s (*The Monkees*), a family in the 1970s (*The Partridge Family*), and as a high-school's glee club in 2009 (*Glee*). In each case, contemporary pop culture was used as a platform for television entertainment.

Blockbusters also reflect trends. The *Harry Potter Series* was introduced during a time when magic and mysticism was growing. The *Monopoly* board game was invented during the Great Depression when people needed the get-rich fantasy. The Barbie doll was introduced at a time when girl empowerment was on the verge of exploding. The film *Home Alone* was launched when the so-called "latchkey" kid segment was growing, referring to children who return to an empty house because both parents work. It's probably not a coincidence that Disney-Pixar's brilliant film *Up* was a success due, in part, to an aging population, thus reflecting the central character of the film.

Today's cultural elements and trends are plentiful, and any one can be used as a foundation for the next blockbuster. Chapter 4 will help you see a whole world of possibilities.

Principle 3: Create Relatable, Aspiring, Memorable Characters

The kid in all of us loves to see specific character archetypes. Each story will have its own needs, but the key characters we often desire to experience include the aspiring character (the hero I want to be), the relatable character (the character that I am), the nemesis (the one I must thwart), the ultra-stupid character (the one I can feel superior to), the friend character (the one I share my trials/secrets with), the dateable character (for romance scenarios), and the nurturer/mentor character (the one who protects and teaches). I'm often surprised when character types that could have been used in a specific story are missing, much to the disappointment of audiences.

Importantly, audiences want character types to "fit" together in "conflict." Honest characters must battle dishonest ones; smart characters work best when they must suffer dumb ones; shallow, beautiful characters are more fun to watch aside the smarter, deeper, more beauty-challenged ones. Each character's persona shines most when it is matched against its opposite. For this reason, audiences often want character personas pushed to the extreme. Extreme characters faced with extreme situations are more likely to be successful. Many times, entertainment fails because the character and situation are not extreme enough.

Iconic characters are the stuff of childhood dreams that we all love, such as warriors, princesses, adventurers, rock stars, astronauts, and secret agents to name a few. Iconic characters matter because audiences live through them as a means to fulfill their emotional needs. Indiana Jones, Wonder Woman, and James Bond are all fulfillment of fantasies. We live through them. Blockbusters are often based upon the iconic characters that we loved as children and then never tossed away when we became adults. This will be further explained in chapter 5.

Principle 4: Generate Compelling Story Ideas

The previous principles, when used well, form the basis for unique story ideas. The key components that make up a story idea are simply as follows: *a story is about a specific character who has a burning need to meet an important goal and must overcome a great challenge or series of challenges to reach it.*

Ideas that are too generic cannot be owned by you. Ideas

that are more detailed and provide specifics regarding the character, the burning need, the goal, and the challenges can be owned. I term these Intellectual Property (IP) Story Ideas. An example is the character Superman. Superman is a great hero who comes from the planet Krypton; has great physical powers; has disguised himself as Clark Kent, a mild-mannered reporter; and needs to save the world from devilish villains, particularly Lex Luthor. This idea can be owned and protected. A generic version of a story is as follows: this is the story of a powerful hero who must overcome great odds to save the world from the forces of evil. This description fits every superhero story and is not the basis of an IP Story Idea.

When considering story ideas, it is helpful to insert the emotional needs, iconic fantasies, cultural components, trends, and key character types and twists found throughout this book. The more unique your combinations, the more likely you will find an IP Story Idea that audiences will appreciate. Chapter 6 will provide several tools to help you actually generate ideas.

Principle 5: Add Broad Audience Appeal

Once you have the embryonic idea, it needs to be shaped to maximize audience appeal because massive blockbusters typically attract a wide audience. This can be done by enticing the kid in all of us. When I'm tasked with evaluating scripts, pilots, toys, etc., I'm often asked if the entertainment has the potential to appeal to a broad audience of males and females, younger kids and older kids, and adults. Too often the question is asked late in the development process when very little can be shifted.

The implications are dramatic. If you think of your audience as divided into four simplified quadrants—older males, younger males, older females, younger females—then each quadrant represents only 25 percent of the potential. Thus, if you have an idea that only targets younger males, you have cut off 75 percent of your potential audience. The best time to address widening the audience is during the early stages of concept development when many elements are flexible enough to change. Here's how.

Gaining Males: If your story currently skews toward a female audience and you desire to gain more males, then you must add themes that males care about. This might include themes related to power, dominance, winning, good vanquishing evil, gadgets and weapons, and related action.

Gaining Females: If your story currently skews toward a male audience and you desire to gain more females, then you must add themes that females care about. This might include themes related to beauty, fashion, building relationships, romance, and female empowerment (power, being tough, etc.). I know; this all smacks of sexism, but it doesn't make it false.

Expanding Age Appeal: If you think your original story is handicapped by appealing to younger audiences only, you might add greater realism, grittiness, or older themes and character types. If you think your story appeals to older audiences only, you might add a lighter tone or more age-accessible story elements and characters.

Gaining the largest audience typically entails satisfying the emotional needs we all appreciate but served up with an edgier sense of heightened realism. There are many nuances to employ to help executives reap the maximum audience size. They are covered in chapter 7.

Principle 6: Build in Elements That Make It a Franchise

If you want your entertainment to become a huge franchise, you need to add specific ingredients while the project is in development. Some ingredients lead to Single-Event Blockbusters that do extremely well but never spin-off sequels or extend beyond the category of origin. Adding other ingredients turn a Single-Event Blockbuster into a Linear-Franchise Blockbuster, which is an on-going financial success that is limited to its category of origin (e.g., a successful film leads to sequels but little else). Adding all necessary ingredients leads to a Multi-Category-Franchise Blockbuster, which is an on-going success that is able to move from business category to business category (e.g., a successful film leads to sequels, a video game, a toy line, and apparel). There are six key ingredients for success. The more you add, the more likely your entertainment will become a Multi-Category-Franchise Blockbuster. The six key ingredients are as follows: 1) the entertainment must satisfy audiences' deep emotional needs, 2) include a theme or story that is at least minimally open-ended, 3) have characters worth emulating (persona/possessions/fashions), 4) have components that are vastly playable (playable toys, playable music, etc.), 5) have fanciful, exciting environments, and 6) include unique iconography.

Writers and creators need to think about these ingredients when generating ideas. Why? Because sometimes subtle changes in storyline, characters, events, or features can provide a basis for a vast array of venues from toys, video games, apparel, food and beverage, CDs and concert tours, publishing, stationery, and theme parks. The unfortunate thing is that may creators think too narrowly. A writer might pitch her idea as a movie alone with little regard to potential merchandise. A toy inventor might pitch his idea only as a toy, not realizing that he could have attached a storyline, which would allow it to become a book series.

When I'm hired to evaluate ideas, I always address whether the ideas have the potential to become more than they appear. Can the lead character in a TV show be given a distinct fashion sense to lead to an apparel line? Can a musical component be central to the toy idea? Many veteran writers and inventors should do this routinely. Many novices don't. Chapter 8 will provide insights to help you turn a blockbuster idea into a blockbuster franchise.

Principle 7: Fix Common Execution Problems

Blockbusters are constructed to avoid common problems of execution. Their fundamental ideas are translated into splendid tales on television series, films, or novels in ways that avoid common pitfalls. The creator needs to set up an engaging premise, lead the protagonist through increasing challenges, help him or her positively evolve in ways to overcome the challenges, and then resolve the story in an emotionally satisfactory way. A misstep at any of these critical points will doom the entertainment. Common audience complaints are these:

- It's not relevant enough. This means that the premise of the story and/or the central character was not relatable or aspiring, a fundamental problem that often cannot be fixed with bandages alone.

- It doesn't have enough action. Sometimes audiences are at the edge of their seats and sometimes they nod off. The action that maintains their attention puts central characters in peril using devices such as a ticking clock (time pressure to save the world), an engaging battle (when forces collide), a challenge larger than the hero (creates doubt that he will succeed), great character relationship friction (interpersonal battles), and suspense in all of the above.

- It's not funny enough. If the entertainment is supposed to be funny, it needs to be truly hilarious. Memorable humor is often created with extreme characters in conflict, utilizing embarrassing, humiliating, and pain-inducing circumstances, which often create character empathy.

- It was confusing. Some stories are just too convoluted, with many twists and turns. They need to be streamlined.

- It's not unique enough. By adding key adjustments to characters and storylines the familiar becomes different. This can include switching character demographics, psychographics, villain types, the era/locale, style/tone, and more.

Nuances in execution can make or break a potential blockbuster. Chapter 9 can help you to avoid the major pitfalls.

Principle 8: Create Marketable Artistry

Great entertainment is *marketable artistry*. It starts with a great product, adds a great name/title, includes extreme marketable scenes, inserts marketable dialogue, and oftentimes is newsworthy due to its subject matter or the way it was produced. By inventing entertainment that is marketable, it helps the marketing team create advertising, publicity, consumer promotions, and viral marketing efforts that stem organically from the entertainment itself. The entire effort from entertainment to marketing will then entice, cajole, and ultimately motivate audiences to action. That might include buying, watching, listening, joining, or playing. Check out Chapter 10. It will help you add elements to your entertainment that make it marketable artistry.

Principle 9: Apply the Ever-Cool Formula
If you are lucky enough to create a blockbuster, you want it to last. Make it eternal by using the Ever-Cool Formula: *To become and stay successful, your entertainment must satisfy your audiences' timeless emotional needs, but routinely dress itself up in contemporary clothing . . . particularly in popular culture and trends.* This is a combination of Principles 1 and 2 cited earlier but now applied to extend a blockbuster indefinitely. This is how fashion dolls stay "cool" year after year; they satisfy a girl's desire for glamour, beauty, and fashion, but they are flexible enough to be updated each year to reflect the current trends (e.g., Nurse Barbie eventually became Doctor Barbie to reflect changing aspirations).

A similar approach accounts for the longevity of *The Simpsons;* it wraps itself, season after season, in the controversies of the moment, including timely takes on celebrity, environment, politics, and religion, to name a few. But it stays true to the timeless emotions we all experience. Chapter 11 will detail the many ways that your entertainment can be constructed to achieve ever-cool.

Principle 10: Use Research to Optimize Decisions
Many creative types shun research. I get that. Research is often used to tell the creator if their baby is beautiful or ugly,

worthy of nourishment or deserving of suffocation. That's scary. Nevertheless, research can turn a mediocre idea into a blockbuster. I have seen this many times and have been fortunate enough to be part of the teams that did so. It can also give you the courage to kill an idea early, before fortunes are spent and reputations are damaged.

A full research program surveys the environment for consumer and cultural trends. It is used to assess the potential of an entertainment idea at critical junctures from concept to rough product to near final. It can be used to pick potential winners from potential losers and to refine marketing components. Research can also be used to track the results once the baby is tossed into the world. Most importantly, it can tell you whether your idea is broad enough to entice the kid in all of us, and if not, how adjustments might make it so. Chapter 12 will help.

Principle 11: Launch an Idea Quest

We sometimes fall in love with an idea too early. We see its flaws but downplay them. We struggle to make it better, but it drains our resources in the process. Then it typically fails any way.

In my experience, it is best to routinely conduct a full-fledged *Idea Quest* in which you generate and evaluate many ideas before you narrow them down to those worthy of your attention, which is easier said than done. So in chapter 13 you will find ideas that I have generated myself using the tools and principles found in this book. I provide my personal evaluation of their strengths and weaknesses. I narrowed them down to the top ten and submitted them to audience research to find the most promising. My hope is that the analysis will help you generate and evaluate your own ideas.

Don't peek at the ideas yet (I know you want to). They will make more sense after you read the book.

Key Takeaway

The following core principles will help you to invent, select, develop, and market blockbusters.

- **Principle 1:** Satisfy Deep Emotional Needs
- **Principle 2:** Align with Contemporary Culture and Trends
- **Principle 3:** Create Relatable, Aspiring, Memorable Characters
- **Principle 4:** Generate Compelling Story Ideas
- **Principle 5:** Add Broad Audience Appeal
- **Principle 6:** Build in Elements That Make It a Franchise
- **Principle 7:** Fix Common Execution Problems
- **Principle 8:** Create Marketable Artistry
- **Principle 9:** Apply the Ever-Cool Formula
- **Principle 10:** Use Research to Optimize Decisions
- **Principle 11:** Launch an Idea Quest

Everyone wants a unique idea. There are no truly unique ideas, so we play with variations. This book will help you to search for and find variations of characters, needs, and challenges, while applying trends and culture in ways that make for different approaches.

This book is structured to provide insights bit by bit as outlined in this chapter, focusing on each principle. This "layering" approach will help us examine each critical element individually as we build to the greater gestalt of blockbusters.

The general principles are now behind you and the details anxiously await.

Chapter 3

Satisfy Deep Emotional Needs

It's about EMOTION, stupid!

Of all the ideas I have been asked to review or test through the years, this is where most ideas fail. They never make the emotional connection. It's not unusual for writers or executives to get excited about an idea and then jump into development without answering one basic question: how do we want the audience to *feel* when sitting in the darkened theater, gazing at a TV screen, reading a novel, or playing a video game. Yet it's all about emotion. Or more specifically, it's about identifying a specific emotional connection that we are trying to make and then doing a deep dive into it.

"Screenwriting's purpose is first and foremost to provoke intense, passionate feelings," states Richard Walter, longtime professor and screenwriting chairman at UCLA's famed film school, in his superb book *Essentials of Screenwriting*. He goes on to say, "There should arise within each member of the audience a sense that what has transpired on the screen is really about him."

In an interview appearing on TheDabblingMum.com, John Lasseter, the chief creative officer at Walt Disney and Pixar Animation Studios said, "It's the heart of the movie that makes audiences remember how a film made them feel. . . . The thing that always drives me is that emotion is a key part of storytelling. . . . The heart is not something you can add at the end of the movie."

The basic needs audiences strive to satisfy are many, and most of these needs are the same for adults and for kids— the kid in all of us. That's key, because it means that if the entertainment we create satisfies emotional needs in both the child and the adult, then we have a chance of motivating both. James Cameron, writer and director of the blockbuster *Avatar,* is quoted on jamescamerononline.com as saying, "The reason we made the film was really to connect people back to an almost child-like sense of wonder." That's precisely the underpinnings of a blockbuster that is apt to please us all.

I have been involved in many studies and can attest that the core emotional needs are universal. If your entertainment idea superbly satisfies a core emotional need in one country, chances are it will work elsewhere unless there are cultural issues embedded within the execution of the idea.

The Basic Needs

Our basic human needs were the playthings of ancient storytellers and philosophers. While much has been written on the topic throughout the centuries, the matter became more widespread in 1943 when Abraham Maslow categorized our needs into a hierarchical framework. Exhibit 8 outlines the basic hierarchy of needs with some added twists. Physiological needs are at the bottom and include fundamental human survival. Higher-level safety needs add personal and financial well being. While these first two appear to be "physical" needs, they have deep emotional consequences. Higher still are the needs for love and belonging. The need for esteem comes next. At the top is the need for self-actualization, which relates to being the best *you* that you can be. While later theories challenge that these needs are not necessarily hierarchical (i.e., no need to fulfill lower level needs before moving up the chart) or in the correct order (some dispute that sex is fundamental), the needs themselves are not in dispute.

With due respect to Maslow and others, the additions I made reflect the ways in which the child within us gravitates toward entertainment. This is particularly important in the specific context of storytelling. For example, I added thwarting evil under the safety needs; romance under love and belonging; and power, redemption, revenge, winning, control, rebelliousness, beauty, and bravery under the esteem category.

You can quibble with my placement of these additions. You might also argue that the need that some feel to attain beauty and power are not needs in themselves, but merely ways for some to achieve the deeper need for self-esteem. Align them where they make the most sense to you. They are essential regardless of placement. Satisfying these basic needs provide a sense of fulfillment, discovery, and excitement.

Exhibit 8: Human Needs	
Basic Needs	Elements
Self-Actualization	Fulfilling your full potential
Esteem	Respect, appreciation, recognition, status, fame, glory, mastery, independence, freedom, power, redemption, revenge, control, winning, rebelliousness, beauty, confidence, bravery
Love and Belonging	Social needs for family, friendship, intimacy, romance
Safety	Personal health and well being *vis-à-vis* accidents, illness, financial, thwarting evil
Physiological	Human survival: air, food, water, clothing, shelter, sex

Satisfying these needs has led to wonderful blockbusters. As Syd Field observed in his classic book *Screenplay, the Foundations of Screenwriting,* "When you think about it, underneath this skin of ours we're really the same, you and I; certain things unite us. We share the same needs, the same wants, the same fears and insecurities; we want to be loved, have people like us, be successful, happy and healthy."

The desire for power and the ability to thwart evil led to such icons as Superman, Wonder Woman, the Power Rangers, and Iron Man. Said J. K. Rowling, author of the Harry Potter series, in a June 1997 article titled "Happy ending and that's for beginners" by Anne Johnstone of the *Herald* (permission granted), "The idea that we could have a child who escapes from the confines of the adult world and goes somewhere where he has power, both literally and metaphorically, really appealed to me." It also appealed to millions of people the world over.

The quest for survival and vanquishing evil can be found in an array of storylines from the hit film *Home Alone* to the more recent *Avatar*. Our innate need to satisfy the desire for rebelliousness has led to such characters as Fonz from the hit TV show *Happy Days* to the more recent Cartman, Kenny, Stan, and Kyle from *South Park*.

Through the entertainment we create, we allow audiences to satisfy the emotional needs they might not be able to fulfill as easily in real life. The character Bart Simpson allows us to feel rebellious in the animated world because we cannot do so in our real world. Spiderman allows us to feel that we can right all wrongs. The *Twilight Saga* allows teen girls to taste a dangerous, forbidden love that most would otherwise not be able to partake in. The video game *Halo* allows gamers to feel empowered as they destroy evil. The computer game *RollerCoaster Tycoon* allows players to feel creative by building their own roller-coaster park.

The emotions that entertainment incites often need to be more intense than those we experience in real life. They need to be exaggerated, allowing people to reach beyond their grasp and fulfill emotional needs in grand ways.

Identify the Emotional Drivers

When I ran the planning and research department at Ogilvy & Mather advertising in Los Angeles, my role was to craft strategies for advertising. The position entailed developing an astute description of the consumer's life, a key emotional need, and a key benefit the brand could promise that would satisfy that need. The best debates I had during those years were with Bill Stenton, the executive creative director at the time. Brilliantly creative, deeply intelligent, and a fun debater, Bill would challenge every strategy I devised. While I was accustomed to writing a creative strategy that consisted of sentences, Bill would challenge me to boil it down to ONE WORD! He'd say, "Gene, . . . just give me ONE WORD that tells me what you want the consumer to FEEL when they use the brand."

It was an immense challenge, but it always worked. One brand might provide power above all else, another might provide mainly mastery, one might offer love first and foremost, another may promise attractiveness, one might offer freedom, and another might aid survival. That was advertising. You often had, at best, thirty seconds to convince a consumer to buy your product. The task was to promise one big benefit that satisfied one big emotional need.

The more I became involved with entertainment and storytelling, the more I realized that the same dynamics apply. All great blockbusters often hang their success on satisfying one big emotional need of its audience, though they often fulfill many smaller emotional needs as well. If you can boil your entertainment idea down to one key emotional need your main character must fulfill, your audience will be fulfilled vicariously. Your idea will have focus and force. Then satisfy other core emotional needs that fit with your original idea.

If you are not sure what core emotional needs your idea satisfies, then you are lost. Your entertainment idea will become unfocused and will unravel as it proceeds in development. Different executives will read different things into it and will toss it down different paths. If your idea gets launched into the world, someone in your marketing department will eventually need to make a thirty-second spot and provide key art. If you can't condense your idea down to an emotional essence, don't expect your marketing team to be able to do it either. As a mentor told me long ago, "If you don't know where you are going, any road will get you there."

Exhibit 9 puts this into a more powerful, relatable context by adding a column of highly successful entertainment that satisfied core emotional needs. Admittedly, where I have placed the examples is subjective and open to debate. My point is to demonstrate that these examples dominated at least one core emotional driver. Many satisfy more than one, but we will get to that in a moment.

I placed the novel/film *Jurassic Park* under physiological and safety needs. The story allows us to experience the sheer terror of being hunted by dinosaurs. Sure, there were undertones of belonging and even self-esteem, but they took a backseat to the fear of being eaten alive. The film *Alien* fits here as does the novel/film *Jaws*.

Under love and belonging, I placed novel/movie *The Princess Bride*. Though it makes departures into various emotional needs, the centerpiece is the protagonist's quest to find true love and what he will endure to achieve it.

I think that the best examples of entertainment that addressed esteem are from the late writer/director John Hughes. His outstanding portrayals of teen angst and need for respect, understanding, and recognition are brilliantly displayed in several films, most notably in the 1985 film *The Breakfast Club*. The story is about five teenagers from different cliques in high school who spend Saturday in detention. The film also connects with the need for belonging irrespective of stereotypes. The 2004 film *Mean Girls* fits mainly under the esteem category as well (the title says it all; no description necessary). You might place the book series/films *Diary of a Wimpy Kid* primarily in this category too because of the underdogs need for respect.

Under self-actualization, I placed the 1970s television series *Kung Fu* because it featured a protagonist (a Shaolin monk) with an enlightened approach to life in the Wild West. Though there were elements that would also place the show in the safety/survival needs category, the story arc was more about the monk's lifelong efforts to reach his full spiritual potential. On the lighter side, I think the classic film *The Bad News Bears* fits here. The central theme depicted an underdog Little League team and its quest to reach its full potential in the final championship game. We all self-actualize differently, but striving to achieve our potential binds us. It's about discovery, enlightenment, and achievement.

Exhibit 9: Human Needs and Entertainment		
Basic Needs	Elements	Entertainment
Self-Actualization	Fulfilling your full potential	Kung Fu, The Bad News Bears
Esteem	Respect, appreciation, recognition, status, fame, glory, mastery, independence, freedom, power, redemption, revenge, control, winning, rebelliousness, beauty, confidence, bravery	The Breakfast Club, Mean Girls
Love and Belonging	Social needs for family, friendship, intimacy, romance	The Princess Bride
Safety	Personal health and well being *vis-à-vis* accidents, illness, financial, thwarting evil	Jurassic Park, Alien
Physiological	Human survival: air, food, water, clothing, shelter, sex	Jurassic Park, Alien

As I mentioned previously, great stories do a superb job of satisfying a key emotional need while nibbling at others. So there's a case to be made that each of the aforementioned stories satisfies, at least partially, other needs on the list as well. Fair enough. Some stories go beyond that. They do a tremendous job of satisfying multiple needs simultaneously and in a big way. Hence, while one need is central for each, they do more than just nibble at the others. They dominate. Exhibit 10 reveals the ways in which some blockbusters have satisfied multiple needs.

Star Wars meets the central need for self-actualization via Luke Skywalker's efforts to command the Force and become a full-fledged Jedi Knight. The movie fulfills our desire for self-esteem through the character's personal achievement and growth (i.e., his efforts to conquer fear). It satisfies our need for love and belonging by using the strong friendship theme displayed among the rebels and the potential for romance between Han Solo and Princess Leia. The need to achieve safety and survival is satisfied by thwarting the Empire's plans to kill the protagonist rebels. Firing on all cylinders, the original *Star Wars* film grossed roughly $775 million

Exhibit 10: Human Needs and Entertainment		
Basic Needs	Elements	Entertainment
Self-Actualization	Fulfilling your full potential	Star Wars, Avatar, the Harry Potter Series, The Lion King
Esteem	Respect, appreciation, recognition, status, fame, glory, mastery, independence, freedom, power, redemption, revenge, control, winning, rebelliousness, beauty, confidence, bravery	Star Wars, Avatar, the Harry Potter Series, The Lion King
Love and Belonging	Social needs for family, friendship, intimacy, romance	Star Wars, Avatar, the Harry Potter Series, The Lion King
Safety	Personal health and well being *vis-à-vis* accidents, illness, financial, thwarting evil	Star Wars, Avatar, the Harry Potter Series, The Lion King
Physiological	Human survival: air, food, water, clothing, shelter, sex	Star Wars, Avatar, the Harry Potter Series, The Lion King

worldwide on a reported production budget of $11 million.

A central theme in the 2009 film *Avatar* is saving the indigenous Na'vi natives on the planet of Pandora. It is basic survival. The story is a strong adventure combined with a romance between Jake Sully (a paraplegic former marine) and a female Na'vi named Neytiri. Jake also needs to master the Na'vi ways (esteem) and win the approval and acceptance of the Na'vi people (love and belonging). Ultimately, he has to find it within himself to turn away from his human leaders and lead the Na'vi into battle (self-actualization). To date, the film holds the record for the biggest box office success, grossing $2.78 billion worldwide.

In the *Harry Potter Series,* the central character must survive the resurrection of the evil wizard Lord Voldemort, who is bent upon killing him (survival/safety). Harry's strong friendships provide the love and belonging while his continuing growth in power and confidence makes way for self-esteem and ultimate self-actualization. The movie based upon that first book made nearly $975 million at the worldwide box office. All seven books combined have sold more than 400 million copies.

The character Simba in *The Lion King* faces many overt challenges. The cornerstone is his self-actualization. Simba realizes he cannot run from his responsibilities and must take his rightful place as king in the circle of life. He fulfills his full potential and, vicariously, our own. Along the way, he struggles to survive, struggles with his relationships with others in the pride of lions, and battles his own self-esteem. The 1994 film took in $783 million worldwide, a staggering sum for that year.

I could have easily added many other great blockbusters to this list, such as *Beauty and the Beast, E.T.: The Extra-Terrestrial,* and *Toy Story.* They are all great adventures about discovery and enlightenment that satisfy multiple emotional needs.

You might be wondering which needs are the most important from the audience's perspective. To answer this, I commissioned a research project exclusively for this book. Among other questions, I asked four hundred respondents across the nation to tell me the needs/challenges they most want to see story-based characters achieve. Exhibit 11 shows the top twenty results. At the top of the list, most audiences want characters to face life and death situations, to be brave when doing so, to reach their full potential along the way, to find love of family and/or friends, to thwart evil, and to gain respect while doing all of the above. This chart is amazing for two reasons. First, the top challenges fit perfectly into each of the basic needs we have been discussing. Second, they are all satisfied by the four mega-blockbusters just cited.

Do not dismiss needs that fall lower on the list. With the right story and character, they can be successfully utilized to create audience engagement. This is because the ones that fall lower on the list (beauty and glamour, rebelliousness) can be used as a means to satisfy more important audience needs (romance, respect).

The more entertainment satisfies broad needs, the more it will entice broad audiences. Still, deeper insights can also be found when delving into the responses by gender and age (see appendix for complete list of needs by audience segments).

- Male audiences show higher interest in characters being brave and stopping evil
- Female audiences show greater interest in finding love and gaining respect
- Kids ages eight to twelve show more interest in characters who strive to be winners
- Teens show slightly more interest in characters who want to achieve their full potential and be rebellious
- Audiences ages twenty to thirty-five are slightly more interested in characters who gain respect
- Audiences ages thirty-six to fifty-five have a slightly greater interest in characters achieving love of family and redemption

If you think of the life stage that each audience segment is in, it makes perfect sense that they want their characters to achieve what they themselves desire most! I am not aware of any other book that has researched and ranked core needs as they relate to characters and stories. This information is invaluable for those who create and market entertainment.

What can we learn from this? First, the greatest blockbusters have extremely overt, undeniably strong emotional underpinnings that broad audiences care about most. They don't dabble on the subtle surface of its audiences' emotional needs. Instead, they go deep down, right to the jugular by pushing the emotional driver to the extreme—life or death, success or failure, all or nothing. Everything is at risk. When people come to see films, read books, or play video games, they imagine that they would triumph over similarly dire circumstances. Second, if entertainment is crafted to connect with a core emotional need, with strong fulfillment of secondary needs, there is an increased chance of reaching greater emotional satisfaction for audiences since each of us has many emotional needs to satisfy. By satisfying an array of emotional needs extremely well,

Exhibit 11: Top Twenty Character Goals/Needs Desired by Audience

	Goals/Needs	Total Nationwide Sample* (Males and Females Ages 8 to 55)
1	Survive life and death situations	52.8%**
2	Be brave	48.8
3	Fulfill full potential	45.0
4	Find love of family and friends	44.8
5	Stop evil	42.8
6	Get respect	39.8
7	Redemption	39.5
8	Be appreciated	39.3
9	Be creative	37.8
10	Find romance	36.0
11	Achieve mastery of some ability	35.8
12	Become a winner	35.0
13	Get freedom or independence	33.8
14	Get control of a situation	32.8
15	Increase his or her power	24.5
16	Get recognition	22.5
17	Get health back	19.8
18	Get to be rebellious	17.8
19	Get fame/glory	17.0
20	Get beauty and glamour	13.8

*Sample size equals four hundred
**Percent of respondents who enjoy characters to face this challenge/goal
(Limited number of responses allowed. See appendix for complete list by
audience segment.)
Source: 2011 Study of blockbuster entertainment, conducted by C+R Research,
Chicago, Illinois, exclusively for the book Creating Blockbusters!

entertainment will capture different people in the same way and different people in different ways. For example, subtle, more sophisticated emotional nuances can be "layered" into a story so that there is something extra for adults. *The Lion King* has emotional elements related to Simba's redemption. He mistakenly thinks he is responsible for his father's death but returns to Pride Rock nonetheless. The redemption nuance is great for older adults, but many younger kids are unable to understand the depth of it. For all audiences, though, the emotional satisfaction comes from Simba's return in order to kick Scar's big, nasty butt! I will further discuss capturing various audiences with overt and subtle nuances in chapter 7.

Transformational Needs

We all want to transform ourselves into the people we would like to be. This is also central to great storytelling; the main character must change or grow by the end of the tale in order to meet a personal challenge or goal. When audiences see characters transform, they imagine what it would be like to experience it too

Exhibit 12 shows the key ways many of us desire to transform. The list includes both emotional transformations in which a character might change from unconfident to confident, shy to bold, or cowardly to brave, as well as physical transformations in which a character might change from weak to strong, ugly to pretty, or rags to riches. All great stories depict a character's emotional journey. Many great stories also include a character's physical alteration. In *Star Wars*, Luke Skywalker transforms emotionally by facing his fears and gaining confidence. He transforms physically by mastering his light saber and fighting skills. Both were made possible by mastering the Force. Audiences fantasize that they might be able to transform as well, leading to the satisfaction of the basic needs we discussed earlier. Sadly, I have reviewed many screenplays, TV scripts, and story-based toys and games that had no discernable transformational fantasy whatsoever! Swing and a miss!

Exhibit 12: Transformational Needs	
Emotional transformations	**Physical transformations**
Unconfident to confident	Weak to strong
Shy to bold	Ugly to pretty
Cowardice to bravery	Rags to riches
Selfish to selfless	Dumb to smart
Unloved to loved	Novice to master
Pessimistic to optimistic	Younger to older to younger
Sad to happy	Small to big to small
Evil to good	Sick to well
Unpopular to popular	Mortal to immortal
Alone to companionship	Inhuman to human to inhuman
Boring life to exciting life	Etc.
Loser to winner	
Helpless to survivor	
Etc.	

Blockbuster entertainment often displays extremely overt transformations. Rags to riches provided the foundation for *Cinderella*. The desire to rise from weak to strong includes *The Karate Kid* and the *Harry Potter Series*. It also provided the foundation for the story of Captain America in which a scrawny young man tries to enlist in the military during World War II but is judged unfit; therefore, he volunteers for a secret experiment that visibly transforms him into a super soldier. Transforming from selfish to selfless provided a foundation for Charles Dickens' *A Christmas Carol* as well as Dr. Seuss' *How the Grinch Stole Christmas!* In the above examples, each character's transformation was oftentimes both emotional and physical.

The "etc." at the bottom of Exhibit 12 is there for you to insert your own observations about transformational needs. You will see "etc." at the bottom of most exhibits. I want this book, your battlefield manual, to be highly usable and tailored to your needs. Add to them!

Many of us, young and old, at some point in our lives, have the same transformational fantasies. These are universal. So by overtly selecting a transformation that connects with a broad audience you will be on your way to creating a blockbuster for the kid in all of us.

So, what are the most important ways to show a character transform? While the nature of the story will dictate that, audiences can tell us the character transformations they like best (see Exhibit 13). In the study conducted exclusively for this book, audiences said that the transformations that excite them most are when characters transform from weak to strong, helpless to survivor, loser to winner, and cowardly to brave. These are universal across all audiences. Note that all of these character transformations are inherent in many of the greatest blockbusters, and they support the core needs as found in the earlier exhibits.

Once again, don't completely dismiss transformations that fall lower on the list. Going from small to big (younger to older) led to the success of the films *BIG* and *13 Going on 30* in which kids wake up one day and are adults. These lower-level transformations often support higher-level transformations (e.g., weak to strong, loser to winner, boring life to exciting life). This list simply tells us where the audience begins in terms of their innate appeal of transformations, but it can't tell us how much appeal a great story can bring to those transformations. That's up to the skill of the writer.

The rank order of transformations varies a bit by gender and age. For example, kids and teens care more about characters who transform from unpopular to popular than other audience segments do. Older audiences care more about transforming from helpless to survivor. That makes sense given their personal life stage. They can relate. See the appendix for the entire list broken down by audience segment.

Exhibit 13: Top Twenty Desired Character Transformations

	Transformations	Total Nationwide Sample* (Males and Females Ages 8 to 55)
1	Weak to strong	52.8%**
2	Helpless to survivor	44.0
3	Loser to winner	42.5
4	Coward to brave	40.0
5	No love to love	39.5
6	Boring to exciting life	39.0
7	No friends/family to friends/family	37.0
8	Selfish to selfless	35.5
9	Beginner to a master	35.0
10	Evil to good	35.0
11	Poor to rich	33.5
12	Unpopular to popular	27.5
13	Not so smart to smart	26.8
14	Not in charge to in charge	26.0
15	Sick to well	25.5
16	Unknown to famous	23.0
17	Mortal to immortal	21.0
18	Ugly to pretty/handsome	19.8
19	Younger to older or from older to younger	15.5
20	Small to big or from big to small	12.3

*Sample size equals four hundred
**Percent of respondents who enjoy seeing characters transform in this way (Limited number of responses allowed. See appendix for complete list by audience segment.)
Source: 2011 Study of blockbuster entertainment, conducted by C+R Research, Chicago, Illinois, exclusively for the book Creating Blockbusters!

Our Innermost Fears

Fears are primal. We all have them. They are derived from our reactions to a perceived threat. It's a survival mechanism sparked by the threat of danger. Fears are rooted in our belief that any number of our basic needs are at risk, including our need for survival, safety, love and belonging, esteem, or our hope for self-actualization. Our two options are fight or flight.

Exhibit 14 reveals the most popular fears that audiences want protagonists in a story to face, as found in the study conducted exclusively for this book. I intentionally did not ask respondents what their personal fears were because many people are hesitant to state what frightens them. But by asking audiences what fears they want characters to face, we can arrive at fears that are not only top of mind with audiences, but they are ones that audiences want to see in the context of a story. Researchers and writers have one important thing in common; we are psychologists.

Overall, audiences most want characters to face the fear of death, personal injury, war, kidnapping, and the loss of friends and family. These fears are once again highly related to the core needs discussed earlier (survival, bravery) and to the way they desire their characters to transform (weak to strong, helpless to survivor). It all fits.

The rank order of some fears varies by gender and age (see appendix). For example, males are more interested in characters facing fear of war and monsters than are females. Females are more interested in characters facing fears related to kidnapping, intimacy/romance, and gossip. Kids ages eight to twelve are more interested in characters facing fears of public humiliation, fierce animals, being alone in the dark, failing at school, and being beat up by bullies. Teens are more likely to want their characters to face social rejection and criticism. Older audiences want characters to face being alone and terrorism. It all makes sense given each audience segments' life stage. The fears that audiences want characters in stories to face are highly related to what we would expect their own fears to be. Be sure to check out the appendix.

Exhibit 14: Top Twenty Desired Character Fears

	Fears	Total Nationwide Sample* (Males and Females Ages 8 to 55)
1	Death	35.3%**
2	Personal dangers/injury	35.0
3	War	30.3
4	Kidnapping	30.0
5	Losing friends, family or girl/boyfriends	29.0
6	Being Alone	28.5
7	Intimacy/romance	28.5
8	Rejection of friends, etc.	28.5
9	Getting lost	27.8
10	Losing all of their money	27.0
11	Public humiliation	26.3
12	Plane and car crashes	26.3
13	Terrorism	26.3
14	Monsters	26.0
15	Police	25.8
16	Fierce animals	25.5
17	Burglars/robbers	23.5
18	Criticism	22.8
19	Making big mistakes at school or work	22.8
20	Spiders or snakes	21.5

*Sample size equals four hundred

**Percent of respondents who enjoy seeing characters face this fear (Limited number of responses allowed. See appendix for complete list by audience segment.)

Source: 2011 Study of blockbuster entertainment, conducted by C+R Research, Chicago, Illinois, exclusively for the book Creating Blockbusters!

Once again, don't completely dismiss fears at the bottom of the list. Monsters ranked number 14, but if that monster tries to kill the protagonist, it supports higher-level fears that broad audiences love to see.

For the storyteller, exploring and resolving fears is a commonly used device. The audience experiences triumph when the story's central character finds the bravery to face a fear that audiences share. In that context, Exhibit 14 is the storyteller's playground. Many blockbuster films, TV shows, novels, video games, and even toy lines are based upon a fundamental fear. Some notable examples include

- *Jaws:* Underwater terror came to the theaters in 1975 in the form of a great white shark, based upon a novel of the same name. The novel and the film kept lots of us out of the water for a long time.

- *The Exorcist:* This novel and subsequent film demonstrated that you can't stay home either. Demonic possession can follow you anywhere.

- *The Lord of the Rings:* In this grand trilogy, Frodo Baggins must muster the bravery to leave the comfort of his shire to travel across Middle-earth under constant threat of death from an array of monsters in order to destroy the One Ring before it falls into the hands of the Dark Lord Sauron. The realism of the films was haunting.

- *Monsters, Inc.:* This Disney/Pixar film confirmed our worst childhood fears—that monsters do live in our closets. These monsters sought to terrorize us in order to extract energy from our screams. The movie made fears fun and funny for audiences of all ages!

- *The Twilight Zone:* This masterful 1950s television show touched our deepest fears. It had elements of fantasy, science fiction, drama, and horror, always dipped in suspense. Interestingly, the shows didn't always have a happy ending, but they always made us think.

- *Fear Factor:* This reality TV show, introduced into the United States in 2001, pitted contestants against each other in order to discover the bravest among them. The contestants confronted an array of personal dangers from jumping in a vat of snakes to jumping from one building to the next. Actual injuries may have been few, but the threat of injuries (and disgust) was always front and center.

Stories that become blockbusters often feature overt fears that are the most universal. That explains why many characters often face death and injury. But to reach the kid in all of us, it's often most successful to create a tonality (degree of scariness) that entices older audiences while still being acceptable for younger audiences. This will be explained in a later chapter.

Seven Sins of Emotion

The seven deadly sins are greed, sloth, anger, envy, lust, gluttony, and pride. Talk about emotional underpinnings! These sins are a part of us and can be the focus of great storytelling. They are used to give a hero flaws that must be overcome. They provide motivation for villains. They are also used to give a secondary character a humorous vice.

Greed: The excessive desire for the pursuit of riches, power, or status. This can lead to betrayal, theft, bribery, hoarding, and trickery. This character flaw applies to the villainous Scar. He killed his brother Mufasa in *The Lion King* so that he could have the throne for himself. In the film *Indiana Jones and the Last Crusade,* there's a great scene at the climax when Jones, dangling above a crevice, must decide between reaching for the coveted Holy Grail or reaching toward his father and safety. His father told him to let the Grail go (emotionally and physically). Indiana chose wisely.

Sloth: Excessive laziness. This can lead to missed opportunities or the lack of care for oneself or others. I regard the Shrek character as a bit of a sloth at first, not wanting to be bothered, wanting to be left alone, which made it fun when he was thrust into adventures.

Anger: Uncontrolled hatred or rage. This can lead to sudden outbursts, feuds, and revenge. This sin is a key villain trait but is oftentimes also found in heroes. Darth Vader from *Star Wars* used his anger to become powerful, but it also led him to the dark side. In contrast, Luke Skywalker needed to control his anger to avoid being consumed by the dark side; yet in that control, he attained greater power.

Envy: Resentment for what other people have. *"If I can't have it, no one can!"* The characters in *Mean Girls* revealed many envious undertones, along with a good dose of revenge and spite. It was beautifully ugly.

Lust: An excess of sexual desires. You wouldn't think this vice would make its way into a film enjoyed by both young and old. Yet the *Austin Powers* films have captured this vice in a way that made it acceptable. "Oh, behave!"

Gluttony: Overindulgence and overconsumption of anything. It is often associated with food and drink but can extend to possessions, experiences, and lifestyles. This can be the vice for a villain or a humorous character trait for a sidekick. *Charlie and the Chocolate Factory* was a lesson in childish gluttony, among other sins.

Pride: The quality of being proud. In small doses, this is a positive trait and denotes feeling good about your achievements or those of others. But when pushed to the extreme, pride is considered one of the most serious of the deadly sins because it can lead to excessive love of self and elevated importance over others. Pride before the fall.

This is your ugly list, which is central to many blockbuster plots and character development. Adult audiences understand all of these sins. Kids as young as preschoolers understand most of these sins. They are told not to hog toys (greed), eat too much sugar (gluttony), be lazy (sloth), worry about what others have (envy), and lose their temper (anger). Overtly incorporating the sins that we all understand into a central story or character can help create the basis for a blockbuster for audiences of all ages. It makes for simple themes that we can all understand and appreciate.

Multiple Heartstrings

Throughout this chapter, I have emphasized not only the emotional needs, but also the importance of addressing as many needs as possible without losing your central focus. Importantly, the more universal the emotional needs you select and the more overt you feature them, the more likely it is that you will create a blockbuster desired by the young and the old.

In the classic *The Wonderful Wizard of Oz*, Dorothy's central need is to return home and into the arms of loved ones (love and belonging), which is her overt, core emotional journey. Through this journey, she eventually learns that there is no place like home. Along the way, she collects friends that become her surrogate family (pseudo belonging). Each friend also has a need. The Cowardly Lion wants courage. The Tin Woodman desires a heart. The Scarecrow wishes for a brain. Each feels the need to be transformed in these ways, and yet they have these qualities from the start. The Wicked Witch is greedy and envious in her need to recover the slippers. The Wizard of Oz character is a bit of a scoundrel and a sloth.

Wonderfully conceived and constructed, the story of Dorothy in Oz works on multiple levels, with overt needs prominently displayed so that audiences of all ages can understand and appreciate them. The historians among you might say, "Hey . . . but the 1939 movie *The Wizard of Oz*, based upon the 1900 novel, was a box office flop!" True, however, some things must simmer before they boil. The film has become one of the best known. It won three Academy Awards and was nominated for Best Picture of the Year. The money it has reaped since its introduction is testimony to its continued audience interest.

Cake vs. Frosting

I realize that story ideas are not initially born with emotional drivers, what I call the *cake*. Instead, they often start with *frosting*:

"Let's write a comic book about a guy who gets bitten by a tarantula and then becomes a superhero tarantula."

Or

"Let's do a TV show about a teenage girl who's like Indiana Jones."

Or

"Let's make a science fiction movie about a president who turns out to be an alien from outerspace."

Or

"I have an idea for a comedy about zombies who are daddies."

The frosting defines the idea and makes it unique and attention getting (hopefully). However the idea starts, it needs to get pulled onto emotional drivers (cake) quickly. This is vital. Unless the cake beneath the frosting is satisfying, the frosting won't be enough to keep the audience nourished. I have worked with many story ideas (frosting) that simply could not find the right cake (emotional drivers). And to be honest, I think 80 percent of the films, TV shows, books, and video games I have experienced as an audience member never found the right cake either. Executives can easily get bedazzled by the frosting and green light the project. Perhaps this is the reason so many entertainment projects eventually fail. It is also why I started this book with emotions in the beginning. The cake is harder to make than the frosting.

Key Takeaway

To create entertainment that will connect to the kid in all of us, writers and entertainment executives need to satisfy a large, common emotional need we all share, which will give the project focus and force. The list to choose from include the needs for safety/survival, love and belonging, esteem, self-actualization, and all of the variations thereof. The need selected should be expressed in an overt way so that kids and adults alike can consume the experience equally. In Freudian terms, entertainment needs to showcase the Id, the part of the personality that strives to satisfy basic needs and desires. It operates on the pleasure principle. Young audiences will understand that, so will the child that exists within adults.

Beyond identifying a central need to satisfy, entertainment should also strive to satisfy secondary needs in order to provide a well-rounded entertainment experience. More sophisticated, subtle storylines can be layered in for adults as an added bonus.

In addition, entertainment should overtly satisfy audiences' need to transform for the better, emotionally and, sometimes, physically.

Now that we have discussed the cake (emotional drivers), the next chapter will be about frosting (culture, trends, fads, etc.) in preparation for creating well-rounded ideas for blockbuster entertainment.

Chapter 4

Align with Contemporary Culture and Trends

The previous chapter was about creating entertainment that astutely satisfies timeless emotional needs, especially those we all share. While essential, it is not yet sufficient. This chapter is about aligning the entertainment with contemporary culture and trends, which will help you to create blockbusters that are opportunistically timely. Using contemporary culture and trends is also one of many ways to make universal storylines feel unique. This is vital as we continue our quest to create blockbusters that connect with the kid in all of us.

Culture

Exhibit 15 contains a sampling of the cultural issues we are exposed to almost daily. Some cultural issues are based upon entertainment. These include pop stars/music, the fashion world, movies/TV shows, literature, and toys/video games. I would estimate that more than 90 percent of our *pop* culture comes from these five categories. Pop culture is particularly valuable because it has become multigenerational. Baby Boomers still wear their denim blue jeans "fading up to the sky" as the lyrics of a song by Cat Stevens points out. Boomers love to take their kids (and grandkids) to venues like concerts and theme parks as a way to still enjoy these places themselves. They appreciate their adulthood but think of themselves as youthful. Targeting youth culture is more valuable than ever because writers and entertainment executives are apt to interest multiple generations in ways that never occurred before.

Exhibit 15: Cultural Components	
Entertainment Based	**Social Issues Based**
Pop Stars/Music/Concerts	Religion
Fashion World	Ethnicity and Equality
Movies/TV	Politics
Literature/Novels	Sex
Toys & Video Games	Sexual Orientation
Internet	Illegal Aliens
Social Networking	Gender and Age Equality
Comic Books	Prejudice
Sports/Athletes	Education
Malls/Shopping	War and Peace
Theme Parks	Law and Order
Carnivals/Circus/Zoos	Crime and Punishment
Cruises/Oceans	Health and Well Being
Camps/Ranches/Farms	Economy and Employment
Toy/Candy Stores	Wealth Distribution
World Travel	Poverty and Homelessness
Jungles/Islands	Family Happiness and Angst
Picnics/Summer Vacations	Parenting
Cooking/Food, Collecting	Out of Wedlock Moms
Inventing/Repairing	Marriage and Divorce
Pet Care	School Violence
Parties (e.g., Prom)	Drugs
Fascination with History, Nostalgia, Genealogy	Suicide
Etc.	Peer Pressure
	Etc.

Entertainment-based culture also includes the social networks we participate in, the sports teams and athletes we cheer for, the theme parks we visit, the malls we shop at, the candy stores we frequent, the vacation spots where we spend our summers, the pets we care for, our fascination with nostalgia, and even our interest in genealogy. Many of us, young and old, are intrigued by all of these things; our collective interests can help creators generate ideas for entertainment with broad built-in appeal.

Audiences are also pushed and pulled by social issues, which are an important part of our culture. These include the big four: religion, ethnicity, politics, and sex. Other social issues affecting our culture are prejudice, gender and age bias, education, law and order, family happiness, angst and divorce, drugs, and peer pressure. All of these and more impact us.

When developing and refining entertainment ideas, creators and executives can utilize current cultural elements as contemporary "wrappers" to encompass stories that satisfy timeless emotional needs. They can make old ideas feel new again by aligning these cultural components with different eras, locales, characters, plots, platforms, or challenges. Here are some examples of how they have already been used.

A **Rock Group** theme was the focus of the Monkees, a 1960s pop group created specifically for a comedic TV series by the same title. The TV show gave us a fun inside glimpse of a boy band. *The Partridge Family* was a 1970s series about a musical family comprised of a widowed mother and her five talented children. Premiering in 2009, the television series *Glee* became a blockbuster by using a different setting (school), different character types (underdog members of the glee club), and music from contemporary artists such as Lady Gaga and Britney Spears. Pop music, applied in these three ways, gave each show a contemporary twist that was right for its time.

Our interest in **Nostalgia** helped the film *American Graffiti* became a hit. It depicts coming of age youth culture in 1962 and features an array of different teens at the precipice of change. The TV show *Happy Days* encompassed a similar era (life in the mid-1950s to mid-1960s) but focused on a teen within a nuclear family (the Cunninghams). *The Wonder*

Years took a similar family-focused approach, but shifted the era to the late 1960s to early 1970s. In each case, stories using nostalgia were made contemporary by shifting character focus and eras.

Divorce was the central theme in the 1961 Disney film *The Parent Trap* about teenage twins who try to reunite their divorced parents. The theme was novel in entertainment. Divorce jumped into television in a series titled *One Day at a Time* that aired from 1975 to 1984. It portrayed the life of a divorced mother and her two teenaged daughters. Divorce was also an underlying theme in the movie *E.T.: The Extra-Terrestrial* in which a boy from a broken home befriends an alien from outer space. Divorce as a subject and subtext can be fodder for contemporary twists on storylines.

The **Internet** provided the context for the 1995 thriller *The Net* in which a systems analyst discovers that her entire life has been electronically erased and replaced with a new one. A much more contemporary look at the Internet was utilized in 2007 with the premiere of the Nickelodeon series *iCarly* in which a girl named Carly creates her own Web show. The film *The Social Network* was a blockbuster 2010 movie. It was based upon the real-life account of the birth of Facebook and its related lawsuits. Each of these examples was based upon our Internet culture. To make each feel new, the setting, character, tonality, and target audience were shifted to create something decidedly different.

The **Neighborhood Mall** was central to the 2009 comedy *Paul Blart: Mall Cop*. This film gave us an inside peek into the life of a mild-mannered security guard who must defend his mall. It had the same feel as the 1990 film *Home Alone* in which a boy defends his house from burglars. The locales were different (mall vs. home) as were the characters (cop vs. kid) but the underlying story plot was similar and both were culture-based.

A **Theme Park** was the foundation of the 1983 comedy *National Lampoon's Vacation*, featuring the Griswold family and their hilarious, ill-fated trek across the country to reach the amusement park Walley World. A theme park was also the foundation of the computer game *RollerCoaster Tycoon*. Released in 1999, the game allows players to build and operate a roller-coaster park. The former example used a theme park as the basis of a film, whereas the latter used it for the basis of a game. Both were derived from a contemporary cultural component that audiences love. The twist in this case is the platform (film vs. game) and the emotional needs they each satisfied among their respective audiences.

Like all the lists in this book, Exhibit 15 can help you to create and refine ideas. Entertainment professionals need to keep key elements of our culture readily visible at all times. Pin this chart up. Review it often. Add to the list. Cross some items off. Find unique combinations by adjusting eras, locales, characters, plots, platforms, or challenges.

Some social issues were too mature for their era to be used as entertainment, but creative minds could not be suppressed. The *Star Trek* series was launched in 1966 at a time when network television was heavily censored. Creator Gene Roddenberry was able to use the science-fiction format of the show to insert opinions on social issues in far away planets that he would not have been able to do in a straightforward fashion here on Earth. As he said during an interview with *Penthouse* magazine, "I was working in a medium, television, which is heavily censored, and in a contemporary show I found that I couldn't talk about sex, politics, religion, and all the other things I wanted to talk about. It seemed to me that if I had things happen to little polka dotted people on a far-off planet, I might get past the network censors . . . and indeed that's what we did. . . . *Star Trek* took points of view on tolerance . . . against the petty nationalism that's destroying our planet . . . it talked about meaningful things."

In today's world, many creators have found ways to address heavy cultural issues with humor (think *The Simpsons*). When done well, it leads to thought-provoking entertainment that is also fun for our collective, childlike nature.

Trends

Blockbuster entertainment is often derived from trends. Similar to the culture elements referenced earlier, trends can be used to provide a contemporary wrapper for stories that deliver timeless emotional satisfaction. Some examples:

- The Great Depression was an economic trend, albeit a devastating one. Yet the *Monopoly* board game was invented during that time and did well. Why? The populace was in dire need of a get-rich fantasy. The game perfectly fit the times.
- Introduced in 1959, the Barbie doll arrived when girl empowerment was about to explode. The brand expanded rapidly when Barbie dolls were created to reflect girls' broadening aspirations. Barbie became a doctor, veterinarian, astronaut, and business woman to name a few. The girl empowerment trend eventually led to more contemporary icons, such as Buffy Summers of the WB series *Buffy the Vampire Slayer,* secret agent Sydney Bristow of the ABC TV series *Alias,* and the video game and film *Tomb Raider,* featuring Lara Croft.

In each case, trends allowed the storyteller to paint a contemporary, timely portrait in ways that fulfilled timeless emotional needs. Therefore, trends matter. Exhibit 16 lists some of the key trends as of June 2011. Some have been with us for years and are likely to remain for quite some time while others are more current. This list will help you generate ideas for stories and can be used to arrive at contemporary ways to develop, deliver, and market that entertainment.

Technology/Virtual Reality: Technology will continue to weave itself through the lives of the young and old. Today's children and adults are bound together by their common need for cell phones, computers, Internet access, digital video recorders, and LCD and 3-D experiences. Glasses-free 3-D is weaving its way through video games, smart phones, and television sets. Stories will be derived from technology trends. Technology will also shape how stories are delivered.

Total Immersion: Our entertainment has become more

Exhibit 16: Trends

Technology/Virtual Reality

Total Immersion

Social Networking

The Great Recession

Obesity/Health and Wellness

World Awareness and Altruism

Environmental Sensitivity

Family Composition Shifts

Greater Ethnicity

Spirituality/Alternate Realities

KGOY (Kids Growing Older Younger)

Pop Star Madness

Premium on Time

Where's the Story?

Just for Me/Personalization

"DO Something" Products

Sensory Explosions

Magical/Mystical Mania

Soaring Science

Forever Fame

Girl Power

Terrorism/Patriotism

Good to Be a Kid

Natural Disaster, Doomsday Beliefs

immersive than ever before. 3-D technology makes us feel closer to the action. Role-play video games allow us to enter fantasy worlds where we control the story by the actions we choose. Interactivity allows for a more immersive experience. Expect more of this.

Social Networking: This is a cultural component and a trend.

We will continue to connect to people at an unprecedented rate because we need social connections. We will continue to make friends who are only known to us through their avatars. We will buy a plethora of merchandise because of the online advice we get from acquaintances and strangers. We will meet, date, have sex, marry, and breakup online. The success of the film *The Social Network* is testimony to the importance that this trend plays.

The Great Recession: The Great Recession has many implications: parents without jobs, kids having to help in ways they have not had to since the Great Depression, scarcity of money and personal possessions. While the Great Recession may pass, the lessons that we learn are apt to stick with us. Consumers will have a sustained need to be frugal, more strategic than carefree in their spending, and more modest than conspicuous. Entertainment-wise, it may provide a fertile ground for stories that reflect this frugality as well as for entertainment that suits audiences' shrinking pocketbooks.

Obesity/Health and Wellness: As the incidence of adult and childhood obesity has increased, the need for healthier diets and lifestyles has increased as well. The 2001 romantic comedy *Shallow Hal* is a story of a man who cared only for a woman's personal appearance until he was hypnotized to see the physical manifestations of a person's inner beauty. This allowed him to fall in love with an obese woman who possessed a beautiful heart. The TV show *The Biggest Loser,* which premiered in 2004, relies on this trend as well, being a competition between overweight contestants.

World Awareness and Altruism: Mass, instant communication has made us all much more aware of the world around us. With immediate awareness of worldwide tragedy (e.g., earthquake and tsunami in Japan) comes instant altruism. We will continue to send instant donations via text. Expect more entertainment based upon stories of altruism in a world of troubles.

Environmental Sensitivity: Growing for decades, this trend includes concern for global warming, destruction of rainforests, overfishing of the oceans, and extinction of animals. An animated television series titled *Captain Planet and the Planeteers* was introduced in the 1990s and featured superheroes bent on saving Earth from environmental calamity. The film *Wall-E* used this as a foundation of its story, as did the film *Avatar,* written and directed by James Cameron. In it, Cameron tells the story of indigenous people who are highly connected to their environment and have to contend with its potential destruction at the hands of a technologically advanced and greedy culture. We can expect more storylines like this.

Family Composition Shifts: More children are growing up in one-parent households. The population is aging. More kids are being raised by grandparents. More children have step-families. Entertainment options that understand these shifts are highly relatable to audiences. Pixar Animation Studios introduced *Up,* a comedy-adventure about an elderly widower on a great voyage with a young wilderness explorer. It tapped into the aging population trend and received Academy Awards for Best Animated Feature and Best Original Score in 2010. ABC's highly successful *Modern Family* puts the trials and tribulations of today's contemporary family structures on display. One family consists of an older patriarch who divorced and remarried a sexy, much younger Columbian woman. Another is a more traditional family with a dad who works and a mom who stays at home. The third family is comprised of a gay couple and their adopted Asian baby. The series has won both critical acclaim and impressive ratings.

Greater Ethnicity: The U.S. has become less of a "melting pot" and more of a cultural mosaic. Ethnicity will continue to dominate headlines around the world. Entertainment that can tap into this has the potential to do well. The classic TV series *All in the Family* shattered many taboos by tackling the issues of race and prejudice head on. This topic is now ever-present in our entertainment and is likely to remain so. It has been heightened with concerns over illegal aliens and terrorism.

Spirituality/Alternate Realities: Is there an afterlife, and if so, what is it like? While traditional organized religions are alive and well, they have seen a decline in attendance whereas the belief in less rigid spirituality has witnessed an increase. Spirituality refers to the desire to understand the essence of existence, connect with your own inner values, find ways to live a good life, and align with a larger reality of the cosmos and Supreme Being. TV shows such as *Touched by an Angel* connected with this trend early on. I also suspect that films about alternate realities are part of this as well, including *The Matrix* and *Inception*. Expect this to continue.

KGOY (Kids Growing Older Younger): Kids at younger ages are being exposed to more sophisticated and mature content. This does not make children any smarter, only more aware. A ten year old in 1950 is probably about as sophisticated as a seven year old is today. This, in part, led to the addition of the PG-13 rating, which allows for more aggressive content to be shown to children, providing that parents approve. This has had a profound impact on the success of blockbusters, as we will discuss in chapter 7.

Pop Star Madness: We are obsessed with pop stars. It's not just a cultural obsession, but a trend as well. Audiences care about what these stars sing, what they wear, who they are dating, who they have dumped, how they rise to fame, and how they fall into oblivion. Our interest has led to popular reality TV shows (e.g., *American Idol*), scripted mainstream TV series (e.g., *Glee*), and youth-directed entertainment (e.g., *Hannah Montana*). It always makes sense to consider adding a musical component to your entertainment idea, assuming it can fit naturally.

Premium on Time: We are overscheduled and thus time starved. Today's kids, parents, and single adults have far more activities than ever before, and we try to squeeze them all in. Multitasking is how we cope. We eat dinner while watching TV, while reading a text from friends at a concert, while checking our Facebook page, while thumbing through a magazine. Entertainment-wise, this overscheduled theme can be the foundational context for storylines. Business-wise, overscheduled audiences create a nightmare for any company trying to gain that audiences' attention.

Where's the Story?: I've been talking about this trend for years. Early toys were not story based, nor were the first video games. The toy industry finally woke up decades ago and realized that if they create a story around their toy lines they have the opportunity to create a larger franchise that includes films, TV, and publishing. Mattel's introduction of the *Masters of the Universe* toy line in 1981 was one of the first lines born with a story attached. Video-game publishers learned early and profited because of it. Whenever I get the chance, I also recommend inserting storylines for product introductions in a variety of industries. The right story provides a platform for a franchise.

Just for Me/Personalization: Over the years, more manufacturers have started to tailor individual products to individual users. This recognizes that each of us has different needs and desires. Role-playing video games allow gamers to personalize their adventures via the decisions they make. Some movie-based DVDs have offered the opportunity to use your own voice in place of a character's voice. It's an interesting start, but that barely touches the surface of what might come. Imagine a story constructed to have different beginnings, middles, and endings to suit your desire. That may be the future of entertainment. At a minimum, it might be the foundation for a story concept.

"DO Something" Products: Decades ago, all plush animals just sat there, doing nothing. Now they can talk, walk, giggle, obey commands, pee, and even learn. Opportunities can arise by adding "do something" qualities to entertainment products. Publishers of preschool books have turned literature into broader experiences by adding sound/audio. Greeting card companies now create cards that allow you to add your own audio greeting. A related issue is how executives can make their entertainment more of an active rather than a passive experience. Video game companies already create interactive stories. When will movies and TV shows do the same?

Sensory Explosions: Related to the previous trend, efforts to satisfy all five audience senses have value. Old and new examples abound. Cereals make sounds (Kellogg's Rice Krispies), dolls smell (Strawberry Shortcake), and television sets have 3-D capability. It is a valuable exercise to ask "How can we entice our audiences to see, hear, taste, smell, and touch our entertainment in ways they could not before?"

Magical/Mystical Mania: This theme is not likely to decline any time soon. It has led to the continued appeal of the Harry Potter and Twilight series and the TV show *Supernatural*. It's a deep-seeded desire to experience the unexplained. The key will be to combine this with other elements, trends, or genres to find unique avenues. We will explore this soon.

Soaring Science: Science-related themes will expand with each new discovery in space, on Earth, in alternate dimensions, or within our own DNA and embryonic stem cells. Eastern-based medicine is part of this as well. Science-based entertainment has been popular since modern literature began. The key will be to find unique combinations when applied to other trends, iconic fantasies, or new cultural components. One of the most notable successes is the X-Men superhero team from the Marvel Universe. X-Men are mutants who possess special powers because of the "X-Gene." The use of genetics and DNA in storylines fits perfectly with society's increasing awareness and interest in these subjects. The 2000 film *X-Men* brought in $296 million worldwide in box office sales. The 2006 film *X-Men: The Last Stand* did $459 million worldwide. The 2009 film *X-Men Origins: Wolverine* did $373 million worldwide.

Forever Fame: It was once noted that each of us would get our fifteen minutes of fame. Now it's Forever Fame. The Internet allows our opinions, pictures, and personas to last forever. We can feel quasi famous in perpetuity. Can you devise an element of entertainment that will make your audience truly famous? Reality TV shows have tapped into this by fostering hyper reality, the belief that every man, woman, and child can become an American idol or have a super sweet sixteen on TV. We can also forever damage our reputations if youthful online indiscretions follow us as we seek jobs in later years. Figuring out how a piece of entertainment can help people become more famous than ever has the potential to be successful, as does efforts that help audiences manage their online reputations.

Girl Power: For the past several decades, girls have been on an extremely steep empowerment trajectory. Up and up and up. They have been rewarded with real life and entertainment icons from Hillary Clinton to Xena, Warrior Princess. Entertainment that features girl-empowering characters will continue.

Terrorism and Patriotism: Terrorism is, unfortunately, apt to continue in the world, and with it, American patriotism may rise. These trends may make their way into entertainment via the plight of both the superhero (e.g., Iron Man) and the everyday hero (e.g., policeman).

Good to be a Kid: With all the craziness in the world, kids often say they like being kids, and many adults wish they were still kids. We yearn for a simpler time; at least we delude ourselves into thinking they were simpler. Entertainment options have readily explored this, but there are plenty of other options to be explored.

Natural Disaster/Doomsday Beliefs: Recent natural disasters will be a topic of conversation for some time to come, most notably due to massive earthquakes and tsunamis around the world. This will inspire many to believe that doomsday is near, particularly since 2012 marks the end of the Mayan calendar, which for some portends the end of the world. This belief has already led to many doomsday scenarios in films, TV shows, and books. Expect this to continue.

Fads

Unlike culture and trends, which are long-lived, a fad is a short-lived but intense craving for something that appeals to a wide audience. Such crazes typically arrive fast, reach a frenzied pitch as lots of people participate, and then they suddenly die. Many times the original, positive interest turns not just to boredom, but to disdain. Still, they can be useful in certain circumstances. Fads typically originate from a couple of key categories.

Music and Music Artists: The music artists and their music can be fads if their appeal is short-lived. This typically happens when a group has one big hit and then fades away. Even if the musical group does well over time, a hit song may run aground once people grow tired of hearing it. I would put the song "Who Let the Dogs Out?" in that category. On a positive note, the TV show *Glee* relies on musicians to create an aura of continuous cool.

Film/TV/Literature and Their Celebrities: Popular films and TV shows are *mostly* a fad business because *most* of them are fleeting. Many celebrities are in the spotlight only for a short time (sorry). If stories and celebrities are successful enough, they can extend through multiple years. But by and large, most are fads, unless you know the secrets that can turn them into long-running blockbusters. Keep reading!

Fashion: Fashion comes and goes each season. By definition, it is a fad business because the fashion industry is designed to be perishable. Each year/season brings new designs. People want to be "in" fashion instead of "out" of fashion. Bell bottoms, hip huggers, and even the color purple have all had their moments of craze, as did pants that fall below the butt crack.

Playthings: This is a fad business. Most playthings are meant to last one year and then are replaced the following year by either an entirely new toy or a new version of an old toy. Parents rush to the toy store to get the latest craze so as not to disappoint their kids, and then interest wanes once the supply meets demand. Who can forget the crazes surrounding Furby, Tickle Me Elmo, POGs, Beanie Baby, and the Pet Rock? Some playthings have found ways to stay cool year after year like the Barbie doll. However, generally, many new toys are fads.

Dance: Dance moves are crazes. The Swim, the Twist, the Macarena, Moshing (Mosh Pit) run their course. When cool becomes saturated, it's deemed un-cool.

Self-Help: This is often a fad category. It is typically pushed and pulled by the latest nonfiction book that offers advice. Health and nutrition, spirituality, financial success, and parenting have all had their crazes. Some have greater longevity than others, depending upon the strength of their general acceptance. They include the Atkins Diet (based upon a book by Dr. Robert Atkins in the 1970s), the book *Battle Hymn of the Tiger Mother* (a 2011 book on parenting by Amy Chua), and just about any book on Eastern spirituality and yoga.

The aforementioned categories are the genesis of most fads. The music category stands out in terms of its impact. When pop stars reach the stratosphere in terms of popularity, audiences begin to dissect them. Audiences will listen to their music and be inspired by the lyrics of love or rebellion or angst. This may impact the way people behave. Audiences will examine the fashions that the pop star wears and may begin to wear the same. Audiences will hear about the latest diet program that the pop star is using and may try it. They might also hear about some far-flung religion that the pop star has adopted and might look into that too. If the pop star adopts children from faraway places, it might lead others to do the same. If the pop star becomes altruistic and supports the rights of underprivileged peoples around the world, audiences may support those causes with donations and time. Think Madonna.

By associating itself with rising fads, entertainment might have a leg up because it could be deemed cool by association. It can make older entertainment appear cool again (this will be explained in chapter 11). Fads are also dangerous because they are fleeting. If the foundation of a story is based upon the fad, that fad may disappear by the time the entertainment is actually introduced into the world. More importantly, the creator's and executive's jobs are to invent the next big thing (blockbuster) that becomes part of our long-term culture and trends. That's what this book is about.

Current Culture/Trends/Fads

Other and related culture/trends/fads include the increase playability of marketing efforts used to engage audiences (online contests, etc.); the need for more face-to-face contact as technology electronically distances us; the digital connective-ness of everything (remote control of home systems); brick and mortar retailers going interactive to combat Internet shopping; the increased use of digital combinations (bracelets as phones); the desire for nostalgia and retro; businesses ability to satisfy audiences need for instant gratification; covert luxury (affluent consumers appearing more frugal than they are); body paint; sexting; baby food diets for celebrities; flash mobs that suddenly assemble to perform in public places; super foods (genetically altered); hyper-food indulgences (specialty cupcakes); mobile technologies; cashless payments; participative buying (Groupon); people power (word-of-mouth via Facebook); rise of entrepreneurs (laid-off workers starting their own businesses); explosion of micro-gaming (games on smart phones, etc.) and hyper vending (vending machines dispensing technology and candy bars).

These examples are all fodder for inventing storyline ideas.

Idea Creation

A theme throughout this book is how you can use this knowledge to create ideas for stories. Here are some examples of rudimentary thoughts I had while mixing and matching elements in Exhibits 15 and 16 while thinking back to emotional drivers from the last chapter. Key elements that relate to culture, trends, or emotional drivers are in bold.

To become more attractive to boys, a nerdy **technology** wiz wants to join a **rock band** but gets **rejected** because she's a mediocre guitarist (ouch!), so the brainy kid devises a way to inject her body with a **rock star's DNA.** Working title: *Nerds Rock!*

A **grandparent** switches bodies with his bratty, estranged grandson in order to get out of the retirement home and **be young again.** Youth is wasted on the young anyway! But in the end, the **love of his grandson** won't allow him to leave his grandchild locked up and old. The grandson's experience also gives him **greater appreciation** for his grandfather's condition. Working title: *Young Again.*

A fib-telling, mischievous boy steals the **3-D glasses** he got from a movie theater and realizes when he gets home that they enable him to **see disasters before they happen.** Now he has to use them to **save the world from doomsday. But will anyone believe him?** Call it *The Future, in 3-D.*

On the product front, perhaps a sci-fi, horror TV series can be developed in which the series (and your television set) literally emits a frequency capable of lighting up letters on your Ouija game board at home (tie-in with the toy manufacturer). The letters might provide clues to a mystery, thus creating an active TV experience. Working title: *Ouija You.*

These are just quick examples of how these charts can be used to generate ideas. To take each story idea further, emotional drivers (the human story), characters, and plots need to be better explored to create greater audience experience and uniqueness. This will be further explained in chapter 6, but I hope this gave you a taste for how these charts can be used.

Key Takeaway

Culture and trends are a great first place to look for ideas. They can provide unique twists to make timeless stories new again. Business-wise, today's culture and trends can also spark ideas for ways to develop, deliver, and market entertainment.

The best way to create blockbusters for the kid in all of us is to find those contemporary elements that we all experience, and then marry them to those emotional needs that we all share. Fads can be very beneficial when used properly, but they have to be treated carefully because they are fleeting.

The greatest blockbusters do even more than satisfy emotional needs, find twists in contemporary culture and trends, and astutely utilize fads. They also create relatable, aspiring, and memorable characters. That's next.

Chapter 5

Create Relatable, Aspiring, Memorable Characters

We love relatable and aspiring character archetypes. We live our fantasies through them. To ignore them is suicide. Audiences young and old not only look for key archetypes, they readily know when some are missing, which could have made stories better.

Sandy Wax is the president of Sprout, a twenty-four-hour preschool channel. She is an outstanding senior executive who has managed and elevated some of the world's largest entertainment franchises. According to Ms. Wax, "Characters that fail to connect with audiences often do so because they are watered down. They don't generate enough passion to inspire an audience to cheer for the hero's success or root for the villain's demise. I know a character or actor is right for the part when focus group respondents call out that they "love her" or "hate him." I avoid casting those who generate broad 'I like him OK, I guess' feedback."

The key character archetypes that audiences often desire to see include those in Exhibit 17. If your story has most of these, it can be a great benefit. If your story is missing a crucial archetype, it can be at a great disadvantage. I am surprised when stories are missing key types for no particular reason. My wife and I recently saw a film produced and distributed by a major studio. The movie had a lovely protagonist but no antagonist, neither human nor otherwise. The film desperately needed one in order to maximize conflict and excitement. The movie was a flop— and from a big studio. Yet it happens all the time.

These character archetypes are not only essential for the obvious story venues of film, TV series, and literature, but also for categories like toys where new lines can greatly benefit from a story/character approach. Not all of the character examples I am about to cite are for the kid in all of us, but I hope they are instructive nonetheless.

Exhibit 17: Character Types

Hero-Type Characters

Ultimate Hero/Warrior	Hercules, Superman, Wonder Woman
Heroes-in-Training	Luke Skywalker, the Karate Kid, Harry Potter
Real Everyday Heroes	Soldiers, Police, Firemen, Doctors, Teachers
Bumbling Heroes	Maxwell Smart, Austin Powers
The Average Guy/Gal/Like Me	Richie Cunningham, Betty Suarez (from *Ugly Betty*), Bart Simpson

Nemeses

Ultimate Evil	Darth Vader, Lord Voldemort, Sharks
Bumbling Evil	Dr. Evil (from *Austin Powers*)
Bully	Biff (from *Back to the Future*)
Nagging Naysayer	Candace (from *Phineas and Ferb*)
Non-Human	Storms, Disease, Fire

Ultra-Stupid/Quirky/ Nerd Characters	Lloyd Christmas and Harry Dunne (from *Dumb and Dumber*), Sheldon Cooper (from *The Big Bang Theory*)
Friend Characters/Sidekicks	Robin (from *Batman*), Donkey (from *Shrek*)
Nurturers, Protectors, and Mentors	Mr. Cunningham (from *Happy Days*), Terminator (from *Terminator 2*), Gandalf (from *The Lord of the Rings*), Yoda (from *Star Wars*), Will Schuester (from *Glee*)
Romance Characters	Romeo and Juliet, Sam and Diane (from *Cheers*), Troy and Gabriella (from *High School Musical*)

Hero-Type Characters

This is our protagonist. This character is often crafted to be the hero that audiences aspire to be. He or she might be the ultimate powerful hero, a hero-in-training, a real everyday hero, a bumbling hero with dubious aspiring qualities, or an average guy/gal hero. In all cases, the hero is someone we can identify with in relatable and/or aspiring ways. For an interview with *Playboy* magazine, the creator of James Bond, Ian Fleming, said that "Bond is a highly romanticized version of *anybody*."

Being able to relate to the protagonist and his predicament is critical. Having worked with some of the world's largest entertainment brands, Jill E. Dowless is a highly skilled TV researcher with more than twenty years experience to her credit. She stresses the importance of crafting highly relatable entertainment. "A simple truth is that being relatable is a key element of great entertainment, either through a character or a situation. When the audience feels an emotional connection with a situation and a character it results in more engagement and investment in the product."

Ultimate Hero/Warrior: This is one of many ancient hero archetypes. They typically have great physical strength, such as Hercules. In more contemporary stories, they also have great mental powers. While they are strong, we love our heroes to have weaknesses that could lead to their doom. Without a flaw, there's no risk that they might fail. Without risk, there's no excitement and empathy for the character. The flaw allows us to relate to them as people while at the same time aspire to possess their super powers. If the hero has a secret "human" identity (e.g., Superman, Spider-Man), that's even better because audiences can relate to the "human" side of their lives. If the hero is also rich and inventive (e.g., *Batman*'s Bruce Wayne or *Iron Man*'s Anthony Stark), that's better still because it helps audiences to vicariously fulfill other emotional needs. The film *Thor* added a twist in that the title character lost his powers for a time and was banished to Earth. This plot created a fish-out-of-water scenario whereby the character Thor became more approachable . . . human . . . relatable.

Heroes-in-Training: These are emotionally powerful. Heroes-in-training are often reluctant/unlikely heroes, insecure in their abilities and afraid of the huge task facing them. Audiences can imagine themselves at the beginning of the journey being average, and then progressing slowly until they are a formidable force. Audiences can sympathize with their plight, their downtrodden beginnings, and their eventual triumph. *Star Wars'* Luke Skywalker is a perfect example of a Hero-in-Training, as are the characters from *The Karate Kid* and *Harry Potter*. They have powers, yet are relatable. Stan Lee, creator of *Spider-Man*, had a similar notion that he shared in an interview with NPR: "I thought it might be interesting to make the teenager the actual hero. What would happen if a teenage kid got a power? And then I thought it'd be even more interesting to make him a kid with the normal problems that so many teenagers have."

Real Everyday Heroes: This hero archetype is highly relatable to our everyday lives because he or she is based upon real people and professions that aid our society. TV shows, films, literature and playthings featuring police, doctors, and military personnel are commonplace. They fight for society at large and for each of us individually. The blockbuster film *Backdraft* was a story about firefighters who face the beast (fire) to save the lives of civilians and comrades.

Bumbling Heroes: These hero archetypes add humor. While we might admire their role, we laugh at their antics and personas. These include Maxwell Smart from the TV show *Get Smart* and *Austin Powers* from the film series of the same name. They are fun, funny, and a refreshing twist from heroes that are typically more serious than comedic.

Average Guy/Gal as Hero: While we admire classic heroes for various qualities, the kid in all of us also wants to relate to someone who IS them. They don't battle crime as much as they battle the challenges of day-to-day life. Truth be told, this is where 99 percent of us live. We have many faults to resolve and many mundane, daily challenges to face. The character Richie Cunningham from the popular television show *Happy*

Days reflects this. He is an ultra-average kid in the 1950s and 1960s, with an average temperament, average clothes, average hair, average intelligence, from an average family in an average neighborhood. This worked very well against the more extreme and quirky friends surrounding him. Although the series was a bit sanitized, much like classic characters in earlier sitcoms like *Leave It to Beaver* and *Father Knows Best*, the average-ness of this character type makes it highly relatable.

Even though audiences love average, relatable characters, they still have their ambitions. Those real life ambitions are less about life and death and more about livelihood and getting along. ABC's *Ugly Betty* tapped into this feeling by featuring a beautifully average young lady in the corridors of a fashion magazine. The dichotomy allowed us to see just how average she is, and what it would feel like to triumph in a setting more often reserved for the pretty people. It is a classic fish-out-of-water story in which the fish learns to swim with the sharks without having to become one of them.

Placing average characters into extraordinary situations works because we all wish we could rise to the occasion. The novel/film *The Princess Diaries* perfectly fits this scenario, as does *Cinderella* and *Spy Kids*. In each case, normal characters get extraordinary experiences and eventually triumph. Steven Spielberg has a knack for taking everyday people and giving them amazing moments. He used this theme in the blockbuster film *Close Encounters of the Third Kind* in which an ordinary husband and father has a close encounter with a UFO and is forever changed by it. That theme is repeated in the film *E.T.: The Extra-Terrestrial*. The story focuses upon an average boy in a family without a father who discovers an alien from another planet who he must save. Spielberg turned an average boy into a more-than-average hero. This formula was repeated in the 2011 film *Super 8*, which was written and directed by J. J. Abrams and produced by Spielberg. Filmmakers such as these make us believe that we ordinary folk have a chance at experiencing the extraordinary.

All of the above hero types can also include avengers,

unsung heroes, cynical heroes, broken heroes, martyrs, good Samaritans, and benefactors.

Relatable, average characters took a more controversial turn with the introduction of the show *All in the Family*. The landmark series highlighted internal family issues, like bigotry and male chauvinism, that are often hidden from public view. Depicting "average" families gave way to depicting "less-than-average" families. The hit TV show *Married...with Children* fits this description. This type of show works because the characters' personas take many of our own traits and failings and exaggerate them to make them more easily apparent. We can also appreciate these family types because we can say to ourselves, "At least my family isn't that bad!" Still, in their own way, we root for these characters to succeed. These are our downtrodden heroes that we hope will reach enlightenment.

Another highly relatable character hero is the rebel. We don't often act on our own rebellious inclinations, but we aspire to. We sometimes have disdain for elements of authority and conformity, wishing we could break loose— at least once. The rebel persona that we detect in others is greatly appreciated within us. Actor James Dean's portrayal of a troubled teen in the 1955 film *Rebel Without a Cause* provided a foundation for the Fonz character on *Happy Days*. Today we see the rebel in Bart Simpson's character on *The Simpsons* and even slightly in the Han Solo character from *Star Wars*. Audiences root for the rebel because he or she has the courage that we sometimes lack.

Other Protagonist Insights

Audiences want protagonists (heroes of all types) to be more active than passive. They prefer characters who make decisions and shape their circumstances. In *Legally Blonde*, Elle Woods decides to go to Harvard to win back her boyfriend, and then decides he wasn't worth it after all. In *The Lord of the Rings*, Frodo decides to travel to Mount Doom to destroy the One Ring. In *Star Wars*, Luke Skywalker decides to become a Jedi in order to destroy the dark forces. These characters are not dragged along for the ride; they each make several critical choices that shape their destiny. Power doesn't just exist in physical strength, but also in strength of character.

Audiences also like their protagonists to have a persona that they admire. It might be optimism (Elle Woods), surly wit (Indiana Jones), coolness (James Bond), sweetness and innocence (Cinderella), vulnerability (Forrest Gump), mischievousness (Han Solo), empowerment (Mulan), and even grumpiness (Shrek). When you think about it, at one time or another each of us expresses all of these personas and reactions. We can easily move from expressions of empowerment to mischievousness to grumpiness in any given afternoon. We love to see these traits in characters because they help us to relate, empathize, and/or aspire to possess similar qualities.

As mentioned in chapter 3, all of us want to transform in ways that we think are for the better, emotionally and sometimes physically. If we are cowardly, we want bravery. If we are physically weak, we want strength. We want our heroes to similarly transform so that they can meet the challenges facing them. It helps us to relate to them and to see ourselves in their victories.

Audiences also appreciate the hero's initial misfortunes. It makes the hero more relatable while generating audience sympathy for the character. Audiences need to feel the hero's pain as though it were their own. This will motivate audiences to root for the hero to succeed. I'm in favor of Bambi losing his mother in the classic *Bambi*. It created instant empathy. The same was true when Simba lost his father in *The Lion King* and when Joe Lamb, a thirteen-year-old boy, lost his mother at the beginning of the film *Super 8*. True heroes only become heroic when they overcome the most tragic of events.

The Nemeses (Antagonist)

We need bad guys to make the good guys look good. Harry Potter needs Lord Voldemort. George Bailey in the classic film *It's a Wonderful Life* needs the heartless and wealthy slumlord Henry F. Potter. Greg Heffley (*Diary of a Wimpy Kid*) needs bullies. Oddly, some of the entertainment ideas that I have been hired to analyze have had no formidable nemesis, and some didn't even have a discernible one. This greatly reduces tension and audience emotional fulfillment. Great heroes need great risks!

Ultimate Evil: The ultimate evil needs to be ultimate. One of the biggest complaints I have heard from audiences is that a nemesis isn't formidable enough. This started gradually over many years, but it got a huge boost with the introduction of the *Star Wars* franchise. Darth Vader became synonymous with evil at that time. An insightful scene was when Darth Vader killed his own subordinate, Admiral Ozzel, because the admiral's poor decision alerted the Rebels to an impending attack. "You have failed me for the last time, admiral!" Vader seethed. He uses the Force to telekinetically strangle Ozzel in the presence of a captain who he promotes to replace him. Cold. After that, audiences compared subsequent villains to Vader and most just didn't measure up. Truly evil villains create greater risk for the heroes. In many ways, they define the heroes. Without greater risk, the story is less compelling and the hero's triumph is less satisfying. In an interview conducted by IGN, Christopher Nolan, writer/director of *The Dark Knight,* said that Heath Ledger's portrayal of the Joker "was about a psychological concept . . . about the threat of anarchy . . . about anarchy being the most frightening thing there is . . . it's certainly the thing I'm most afraid of." That fear was shared by audiences, which motivated them to arrive at the theater in droves.

Soulless evil fits here as well. Sharks eat us. Demons possess us. Vampires kill or convert us. Similarly, mean girls need to demean us! That's what led, I think, to the success of the film *Mean Girls.* It portrayed the realities of cruel female antagonists. They might not drain your blood as vampires do, but they can empty your soul. Only through the lens of such evil can we empathize for our heroine and relish her eventual triumph.

The Bumbling Evil: This archetype is reserved for comedies. Probably the most successful in recent years is Dr. Evil from the *Austin Powers* films. He's deadly but bizarrely harmless. That description also applies to the evil Konrad Siegfried from the 1960s TV series *Get Smart*. Audiences love to see dumb villains because they make us all feel a little bit superior.

The Bully: This is a classic character. One of the best portrayals is Biff from the *Back to the Future* film series. He's the perfect archetype of the bully—mean, spiteful, contentious, prankster, having more brawn than brains, and being more cowardly than brave. He hit this note perfectly. The cheerleading coach Sue Sylvester on the hit show *Glee* is a great contemporary example of a bully. Pushing kids is not beneath her, neither is sabotaging her fellow teachers' noble efforts.

Nagging Naysayers: Some villains aren't really villains in the pure sense. They are nagging impediments or sarcastic naysayers for our hero to suffer. Their attacks are typically verbal: *You can't do it. You'll never succeed. Your odds are one in a billion. You're too stupid and talentless to make it big. You're in big trouble now. I'm telling mom.* In today's children's arena, a great example is Candace in Disney's brilliant animated TV show *Phineas and Ferb*. Her goal is to get her brothers in trouble.

Non-Human Evil: Not all nemeses are human or even human-like. Conflict comes from many sources. The nemesis of a story can be a storm (*The Perfect Storm*), a virus (*I Am Legend*), a speech impediment (*The King's Speech*), or your own mental health (*A Beautiful Mind*). Chapter 6 will further explain story ideas and the various plot conflicts that can be used to pit protagonists against varying types of antagonists.

Other Nemeses Insights: Villainous types can also include archetypes of the mad scientist, destroyer of worlds, saboteur, critics, pranksters, minions, and fake friends (those who pretend to be friends but are actually enemies). Kids young and old appreciate them all.

A lot has been said recently about the concept of the "frenemy." This character type is a friend who is also a rival. The frenemy may be our hero's friend one moment but then becomes his competitor, if it suits him, the next moment. This is not actually a new character type. A very old example is Eddie Haskell in the series *Leave It to Beaver* (airing from 1957 to 1963). He always had an angle, and it didn't always include his supposed friends. While the frenemy archetype makes for interesting storylines, this character can never replace a true enemy. Enemies add conflict, and conflict is what audiences demand.

The Ultra-Stupid/Quirky/Nerd Character

In the ancient past, the ultra-stupid characters were the jesters and clowns found in Greek stories and works of Shakespeare. These archetypes provided the foundation for contemporary versions. They make for plenty of laughs and allow the viewing audience to feel superior by comparison.

In the early days of film, these characters were ever-present. They included the hilariously funny Lou Costello from the Abbott and Costello comedy team and Curly from the Three Stooges. Always ready to fall into any manhole, to be terrorized by the slightest of fears, or to be oblivious to any insult, these characters provide a glimpse of ourselves or those around us, exaggerated to allow us to see our collective faults more clearly.

More contemporary films such as the buddy-comedy *Dumb and Dumber,* starring Jim Carrey and Jeff Daniels, have featured these characters. Homer Simpson from *The Simpsons* fits this archetype well. At one point or another, actors Steve Martin and Zach Galifianakis have played this role.

I put the nerd archetype in this category because they are often used as comic relief; as a way for cool, popular people to make fun of the brainy ones. The contemporary icon of the nerd character was solidified by the Steve Urkel persona from the hit TV series *Family Matters,* which premiered in 1989. A recent example is the character of Sheldon Cooper, a theoretical physicist in the popular television show *The Big Bang Theory.*

Having the ultra-stupid/quirky/nerd type of character is central to many comedies, but some audiences have told me that this character can be very effective when used in more serious dramas and adventures. Audiences might be saying that some films are simply too serious for their own good. If you include this character in more serious storylines, be very careful to ensure that this character's persona can be accommodated within the overall narrative. A misstep, according to some, was the introduction of Jar Jar Binks in *Star Wars Episode 1: The Phantom Menace.* The intent may have been to provide a source of humor for kids, which the character probably did, but his bumbling persona didn't quite work for adults and fan boys (enthusiasts). The more clever humor dispensed by R2-D2 and C-3PO worked better across all audiences because it was more in keeping with the tone of the larger narrative.

If the ultra-stupid character is designed for a comedy, make him truly stupid. This is especially important for youth audiences. The highest compliment a child or teen can give a character is to say that the character is "so stupid he's funny." If he's only a little stupid, they will say that "he tried to be funny but wasn't." In today's entertainment world, we are all exposed to so many idiot characters (and I mean that in a good way) that it raises the bar for stupidity. TV shows like *Jackass* have raised that bar. So audiences expect dumb to be really dumb.

The Friend Character/Sidekick

Batman needs his Robin. Shrek needs his Donkey. Audiences expect it, but it also makes for great storytelling. Why? Some sidekicks are journeymen-in-training. That is Robin's role to Batman. He is there to learn, support, and grow. Through Robin, we can also learn more about Batman—what he knows, how he handles himself, and the sacrifices he is willing to make to save his partner and friend. Robin's younger age also provides an added entry point for younger audiences.

Some sidekicks are friends that irritate: the Shrek and Donkey formula. Shrek wants to left alone, but Donkey wants to engage. Their interaction tells us about each character's persona while leading to lots of laughs.

More broadly speaking, the sidekick allows the main character to react to the antics of the friend and vice versa. The 1950s hit *I Love Lucy* TV series, starring the brilliantly funny Lucille Ball, took this approach. Crazy Lucy dragged her more responsible-minded friend Ethel into all kinds of predicaments where their personas clashed. A popular TV series of the 1980s, *Laverne & Shirley*, starring Penny Marshall and Cindy Williams, used a similar formula. But in this case, it was a buddy comedy with each character playing an equally strong role. A great example from the world of children's literature is Eeyore from the classic *Winnie-the-Pooh* series. His persona is forever pessimistic and gloomy, making for a ton of fun when he is juxtaposed against the more even disposition of Winnie-the-Pooh.

In some of the above examples, the sidekick and the ultra-stupid character merge into one.

Another sidekick archetype is the personal assistant. In the comic book *Iron Man*, the protagonist hero Anthony Stark employs Pepper Potts, who serves as both personal assistant and love interest. This character type allows for conflict and romantic sparks.

I have read and watched many stories that could have used a friend and sidekick. It is the old cliché of the affect of one hand clapping. In other instances, the persona of the sidekick was so similar to that of the protagonist that few sparks were generated. Audiences were bored. The sidekick needs a persona that conflicts with that of the hero. I'll discuss this more in a moment.

The Nurturer, Protector, and Mentor

We all need those characters who strive to nurture us, protect us, and/or mentor us. In turn, we all need to nurture, protect, and mentor others. We can relate to those characters that possess these qualities.

Nurturers provide mental, physical, and emotional sustenance. They help us grow and blossom. They listen to our needs and provide for them. Depictions of family nurturers have a long history in television and film. They include the characters Donna Stone in *The Donna Reed Show,* Jim Anderson from *Father Knows Best,* Mr. Cunningham in *Happy Days,* and Gil Buckman, a father depicted in the 1989 comedy-drama movie *Parenthood* (developed into a TV series that premiered in 2010).

The protector archetype adds another element. They are typically fierce. The reprogrammed Terminator in the second film in the *Terminator* franchise fits this archetype. It would stop at nothing to save John Connor.

The mentor archetype adds the teaching element. This character teaches real skills and provides teachable moments (e.g., glee coach Will Schuester on *Glee*).

Some characters assume all three strong roles of nurturer, protector, and mentor. They include Yoda and Obi-Wan Kenobi from *Star Wars,* Gandalf from *The Lord of the Rings,* and Mr. Miyagi from the 1984 movie *The Karate Kid* (changed to Mr. Han in the 2010 remake).

Audiences love these characters. Kids adore them and adults never outgrow them. We can identify with them on two levels. Younger children wish they had a nurturer and protector to help guard them from the evils of the world while adults imagine they are the nurturer or protector aiding those who need assistance. Younger audiences place themselves in the role of hero-in-training Luke Skywalker or Princess Leia. Older audiences think of themselves as Obi-Wan Kenobi or Yoda. Stories structured in this fashion give different audience members different entry points, allowing them to experience those characters they can best relate to.

The Romance Character

Here's an obvious point; if your story doesn't have a romance scenario, your female audience will ask for one. By providing a romance scenario, it doubles the potential size of your audience. Duh! Not so obvious is this; many men secretly like romance scenarios, too, especially if the woman is hot.

Male and female characters who come from vastly different

backgrounds, have vastly different personas, and begin the story by hating each other but then fall in love is terribly cliché. However, it works. The Sam and Diane characters from the 1980s TV show *Cheers* fit this duo archetype perfectly. Their overt bickering fit atop simmering mutual attraction. Audiences still love that. Another example is good girl Sandy Olsson and bad boy greaser Danny Zuko from the Broadway musical and subsequent 1978 film titled *Grease*.

While female audiences are sometimes attracted to men portrayed as the strong, straight-arrow, silent types, they also appreciate male characters who are a tad mischievous and downright a bad boy. Male audiences can appreciate sweet and shy female characters, but they are also attracted to tough, gun-slinging female types. The rough and tumble female archetype has made its way into classic comics (e.g., *Batgirl*), film (e.g., Ellen Ripley from *Alien*), and even video games (Lara Croft from *Tomb Raider*). While this hard-edged heroine seems new, the character is actually ancient. The Greek goddess Artemis was goddess of the hunt.

Characters in Conflict

As several examples already cited attest, audiences love to pair up characters with opposite personas. This pairing leads to exciting clashes. Exhibit 18 is comprised of the character opposites that I have seen work well. Extreme heroes must battle extreme villains, the innocent must suffer the unscrupulous, responsible characters work best when paired with irresponsible ones, brave characters should be paired with cowards, the optimist must suffer the pessimist, the brainiac must suffer the dimwit, and so forth. The examples are plentiful.

Character "fit" is one of the most serious "misses" I have seen. Audiences do not view characters in a vacuum; they view them in the context of the characters that surround them. A protagonist might be extremely brave, but unless she is matched with someone more cowardly, it's sometimes hard to see her bravery. For the TV series *Star Trek*, creator Gene Roddenberry invented the character of Spock to use cold logic above emotion, whereas Dr. McCoy would often place warm, human emotions above logic. When he wasn't playing referee between the two, Captain Kirk was much more action oriented than either of them. The three personas were often at odds, which added greatly to the storyline for both entertainment value (fun to watch the sparring) and intellectual value (logic vs. emotion vs. action).

It's also the case that some stories have too many characters. Audiences can quickly point out that some characters are not needed at all. This is true when a character plays no important role and doesn't push the story along or provide a key counterpoint to an important character.

As discussed in chapter 3, key protagonists need to grow and change by the end of a story in order to meet their greatest challenge. Audiences love to witness emotional and physical transformations because they imagine that they might transform positively as well. Exhibit 18 can be used to generate ideas for the transformational paths a character can take. Our hero might travel from extreme evil to extreme good or from extreme stupidity to extreme intelligence or from extreme conformity to extreme rebelliousness or from extreme poverty to extreme riches. In that context, Exhibit 18 is not just a list of what is. It's what can be. This is a companion to an earlier exhibit in chapter 3. Both can help you find the right emotional and physical transformation for your protagonist.

Characters also need to fit together seamlessly by motivations and goals. In particular, the hero and villain must be locked together in a cross purpose in order to keep the story viable. For example, the villain might kidnap a woman out of lust and threaten to kill her if she won't consent to marriage, and the hero must strive to save her out of love. They are all locked together in the heat of conflict until the final resolution. The above example is rather cliché, but you get the idea. In storytelling, it's called creating a crucible.

Exhibit 18: Characters in Conflict

the hero vs. the nemesis

the good/nice/naïve/innocent vs. the bad/evil/unscrupulous

the striver vs. the detractor

the smart underling vs. the stubborn authority figure

the rascal/prankster vs. the easy target

the moral compass vs. the morally challenged

the conformist/conservative vs. the rebel/liberal

the responsible vs. the irresponsible

the beauty vs. the beast

the grumpy master vs. the challenging student

the sweet vs. the nasty

the brave heart vs. the coward

the optimist vs. the pessimist

the strong vs. the weak

the brainiac vs. the dimwit

the extrovert vs. introvert

the athletically skilled vs. athletically challenged

the pretty vs. the ugly

the popular vs. the unpopular

the wild vs. the sedate

the rich vs. the poor

the high and mighty vs. the lowly and weakly

the older vs. the younger

the men vs. the women

Etc.

Character Uniqueness

Another audience complaint I sometimes hear is that characters are not unique enough. It is not because of the use of common archetypes, which are essential. Rather, the complaint stems either from not pushing the archetypes to the extreme or from not offering a contemporary perspective.

An example of an extreme hero, albeit in more adult fare, is the character Gregory House from the TV show *House*, which premiered in 2004. The show portrays the antics of a brilliant but physically and emotionally damaged, often-drug-dependent doctor. House is a classic broken hero, but he is "broken" in a contemporary, extreme way. The same formula applies to the TV series *Monk* in which the main character, Adrian Monk, is a brilliant private detective nearly crippled by compulsive behaviors and phobias.

In both cases, these heroes have extreme flaws that contribute to their contemporary uniqueness. Extreme character traits are another way to create unique story ideas.

Well-Rounded Characters

Audiences appreciate characters that feel real and are well rounded. Such characters display emotional range and depth. They may experience fear, bravery, hate, love, great pessimism, great optimism, and more throughout the story. Care has to be taken not to make a character a "single note," whereby they express only one key element of persona. Those characters are thin and cartoony. To help round out characters, develop their backgrounds, which might entail what their childhood was like, why they drive the car they do, why they live where they do, why they selected the college they attended, what early event in their lives made them stingy, cowardly, distrusting, or pessimistic. Do they have any significant talents, physical traits, interesting social skills, or quirks? These kinds of insights will lead to a set of motivations that become the foundation of emotional depth.

Monika Salazar is a senior marketing strategist with experience spanning worldwide brands including the Walt

Disney Company, MTV Networks, and McDonald's. She stresses the importance of creating a clear vision for each character along with core character conflicts. "Maintain a clear and thorough vision of each character. Not all characters need to be aspiring. Group dynamics and organizational psychology are two disciplines that need to be considered as you develop the cast of characters. Conflict will be necessary to show growth, change, and personal POV's from each character's perspective."

Iconic Characters

Exhibit 19 includes a list of the key iconic characters. They include warriors, adventurers, movie stars, space aliens, secret agents, and many more. I distinguish these from the earlier "archetype" characters because that term infers the *essence* of a character (the *good* hero, the *bad* villain, the *loyal* friend, etc.). Instead, the iconic characters in Exhibit 19 are not necessarily good or evil, friend or foe. We make them good or bad with the tales we tell. Their presence sometimes delineates stories as fantasy (e.g., elves), science fiction (e.g., aliens), horror (e.g., monsters), and so on. Some of the iconic characters are also related to character professions (e.g., doctor). The story you craft will turn them into archetypes of good or evil, friend or enemy.

Audiences young and old gravitate toward these iconic characters. We grew up with them and never left them behind. So using these iconic characters is a great way to capture the kid in all of us. This list not only includes characters we want to see at theaters, on television, and read about in novels, but it also reflects the characters we fantasize about becoming or thwarting. We live vicariously through them.

Audiences love these icons because they have easily identifiable emotional drivers that excite us. I have listed the most common emotional drivers in the exhibit. Warriors tend to satisfy our own needs for survival, power, bravery, and good vanquishing evil. Rock stars help us to live the life of fame, fortune, and status. Being a bride, groom, boyfriend, or

Exhibit 19: Iconic Characters and Emotional Drivers	
Iconic Characters	**Some Common Emotional Drivers**
Warrior/Soldier	Survival/Power/Bravery/Good vs. Evil
King/Prince/Ruler	Fortune/Power/Status
Queen/Princess/Ruler	Fortune/Power/Status/Beauty/Romance
Adventurer/Treasure Hunter/Pirate	Survival/Discovery/Riches/Bravery
Mythic Gods (Zeus, Odin, etc.)	Power/Control/Good vs. Evil
Folklore (Elf, Dwarf, Ogre, Fairy)	Power/Good vs. Evil
Billionaire/Rich	Fame/Fortune/Status
Rock Star	Fame/Fortune/Status
Movie Star	Fame/Fortune/Status
Fashion Designer/Model	Creativity/Fame/Fortune/Status
Dancer	Mastery/Creativity/Fame
Famous Athlete/Olympian	Mastery/Power/Fame/Fortune
Astronaut/Pilot	Survival/Discovery/Bravery
Wizard/Witch/Genie (Magician)	Power/Good vs. Evil
Vampires/Werewolf/Monsters	Power/Bravery/Good vs. Evil
Space Aliens	Power/Discovery/Good vs. Evil
Doctor/Vet	Survival/Respect/Self Esteem
Historical (Gladiators, Cowboys, etc.)	Survival/Power/Good vs. Evil
Racecar Driver/Daredevil	Survival/Fame
Teacher/Principal/Student	Respect/Recognition/Nurturing
Scientist/Inventor	Mastery/Creativity/Discovery
Mom/Dad/Parent/Kids	Nurturing/Love/Independence
Martial Arts Master	Mastery/Power/Bravery
Prize Fighter	Mastery/Power/Bravery
Policeman/Fireman	Survival/Power/Bravery/Good vs. Evil
Spy/Secret Agent	Survival/Power/Bravery/Good vs. Evil
Bride/Groom/Girl-Boyfriend	Romance/Love & Belonging/Sex
Native Peoples	Survival/Discovery
Circus/Carnival Performers	Mastery/Fame
Etc.	Etc.

girlfriend allows us to experience romance, love, belonging, and sex (for older audiences). I encourage you to add to the list and to make different connections. It's helpful to keep these icons up and visual at all times because they prompt the creation and refinement of ideas.

Exhibit 20 shows the same iconic character list, but it now includes stories and/or characters that have been created to address them. While not all of the examples are broad enough to capture a wide audience, nor are all blockbusters, they are instructive nonetheless. Some notable examples include the following:

- Most of us have fantasized of being rock stars, movie stars, or dancers. Both adult and children's entertainment features these iconic characters prominently. *A Chorus Line* gave us a look behind the scenes of a Broadway musical. The blockbuster TV show *Glee* allows us to imagine that any high-school student can strive to achieve greatness by tapping into their raw talent.
- Supernatural characters have exploded onto the pop culture scene. While this began many years ago with such works as Mary Shelley's novel *Frankenstein* and Bram Stoker's novel *Dracula,* a resurgence into pop culture probably began with the prominent arrival of the movie and subsequent TV series *Buffy the Vampire Slayer,* which brought us a steady stream of highly relatable and aspiring characters from slayers to vampires to werewolves (I'm not forgetting the animated *Scooby-Doo*). The great twist was that Buffy was an unlikely hero—a petite teenage girl with great unexpected powers and responsibilities, which oftentimes interfered with her pursuit of romance. The blockbuster hit 1965 TV show *I Dream of Jeannie* was perfectly crafted to appeal to the kid in all of us. It was based upon a childhood fantasy of a genie in a bottle. The premise was that of an astronaut (a newly popular icon in the 1960s) who becomes the master of a genie and eventually falls in love with her. It used two iconic characters intertwined in a comedic love story.

- Despite the range of warriors, performing pop artists, and supernatural characters, the more traditional, realistic fantasies are still prevalent. These include being a police officer, doctor, and parent. A nice twist on the doctor character from decades past was the late-1980s, early-1990s TV show called *Doogie Howser, M.D.* It starred Neil Patrick Harris as a sixteen-year-old physician. He faced both medical emergencies (aspiring) and the problems of being a normal teenager (relatable). It captured a wide audience when first introduced.

Other iconic character categories that could be added to the list include animal kingdom characters (*The Lion King, Madagascar*), mythic beasts (Bigfoot—*Harry and the Hendersons*), robots (*Transformers*), ghosts and spirits (*Casper, Beetlejuice*), advocates (lawyers or social cause champions), angels and devils, healers, judges, pioneers, thrill seekers, revolutionaries, and a whole slew of student types (jocks, cheerleaders, prom queens, nerds, Goths, schemers).

Gary Marsh is president and chief creative officer for Disney Channels Worldwide. He, along with an expert team including Adam Bonnett who is the senior vice president of Original Series, is responsible for a string of blockbuster successes in the children's arena for more than a decade. They are amazingly superb at understanding children's core iconic fantasies and then selecting and guiding stories that are both highly aspiring and highly relatable to their audiences' everyday lives. These have included iconic pop stars (*Hannah Montana*), wizards (*Wizards of Waverly Place*), dancers (*Shake It Up*), martial arts experts (*Kickin' It*), inventive kids on a summer vacation (*Phineas and Ferb*), and many more. The expert use of iconic characters, combined with outstanding casting and story development, not only makes each TV show successful, but it also enhances the image of the larger Disney brand. This string of massive successes is nearly unparalleled in children's television entertainment.

Exhibit 20: Iconic Characters and Entertainment Examples	
Iconic Characters	**Entertainment Examples**
Warrior/Soldier	Halo, Avatar, Conan the Barbarian
King/Prince/Ruler	King Arthur, The Prince and the Pauper
Queen/Princess/Ruler	The Princess Diaries, Cinderella
Adventurer/Treasure Hunter/Pirate	Indiana Jones, Capt. Jack Sparrow
Mythic Gods (Zeus, Odin, etc.)	Hercules, Thor
Folklore (Elf, Dwarf, Ogre, Fairy)	The Lord of the Rings, Shrek
Billionaire/Rich	Richie Rich, Iron Man
Rock Star	The Monkees, Glee, The Bodyguard
Movie Star	A Star is Born (1954 version)
Fashion Designer/Model	The Devil Wears Prada, Project Runway
Dancer	A Chorus Line
Famous Athlete/Olympian	She's the Man
Astronaut/Pilot	The Right Stuff, Apollo 13
Wizard/Witch/Genie (Magician)	Harry Potter Series, I Dream of Jeannie
Vampires/Werewolf/Monsters	Buffy the Vampire Slayer, Monsters Inc., Jurassic Park
Space Aliens	The War of the Worlds, E.T., Super 8
Doctor/Vet	Grey's Anatomy; Doogie Howser, M.D.
Historical (Gladiators, Cowboys, etc.)	300, Cowboys & Aliens
Racecar Driver/Daredevil	Talladega Nights
Teacher/Principal/Student	Glee; Welcome Back, Kotter
Scientist/Inventor	The Time Machine, Back to the Future
Mom/Dad/Parent/Kids	The Simpsons, Modern Family
Martial Arts Master	The Karate Kid, Kung Fu
Prize Fighter	The Fighter, Rocky, Real Steel
Policeman/Fireman	Paul Blart: Mall Cop, Backdraft
Spy/Secret Agent	James Bond, Spy Kids
Bride/Groom/Girl-Boyfriend	Cinderella
Native Peoples	Pocahontas, Avatar
Circus/Carnival Performers	Dumbo
Etc.	Etc.

The basic human needs that I originally associated with each iconic character in Exhibit 19 are the most common and expected. Looking for unexpected combinations of iconic characters and emotional drivers can lead to unique entertainment ideas. This is one way to create so-called fish-out-of-water stories. The animated film *Despicable Me* is about a super villain who falls in fatherly love with three orphan girls. The story takes the audience on a fun ride from evil villainy to love and nurturing.

Exhibit 21 can help storytellers find other twists by overtly associating an iconic character with unexpected emotional needs as found in chapter 3. It's one of the many tools I provide throughout this book that I hope you find useful.

Rock Star Thrust Into Survival Mode: While a rock star is typically imbued with fame, fortune, and status, we could switch needs by altering circumstances. Perhaps a pampered, rebellious rock star (fame/fortune/status) is shipwrecked on a deserted island filled with cannibals (safety/physiological needs). She needs to *survive* without her entourage, or die trying. It's Lady Gaga as Robinson Crusoe. The natives may become more terrified of her than she is of them. Layer in a love story with a native prince and some cool, realistic battle sequences to keep men happy, and it could be fun. Working title: *Lady Crusoe.*

Exhibit 21: Mixing Iconic Characters and Needs	
Iconic Characters	**Basic Needs**
Rock Star	**Self-Actualization:** Fulfilling your full potential
Military/Soldier/Warrior	**Esteem Needs:** Respect, appreciation,
Mom/Parent/Kids	recognition, status, fame, glory, mastery, independence, freedom, power, redemption, revenge, control, winning, rebelliousness, beauty, confidence, bravery
	Love and Belonging Needs: Social needs for family, friendship, intimacy, romance
	Safety Needs: Personal health & well being *vis-à-vis* accidents, illness, financial, thwarting evil
	Physiological Needs: Human survival: air, food, water, clothing, shelter, sex

Warrior Thrust in Nurturing/Romance Role: A Navy Seal (warrior/soldier) is typically used to search and destroy (thwarting evil). Perhaps after our hero is sent to annihilate a supposedly ruthless space alien, he discovers that the beast is not as evil as he had been told. Perhaps the alien is peaceful, female, and beautiful, which sets up other emotional needs (romance, nurturing); therefore, he decides to rescue her instead of kill her. Working title: *Alien Search and Rescue.*

Mom Thrust Into Military Role: Perhaps a loving mom of three children (love and belonging) is also a sergeant in the marines and is deployed overseas and goes into battle (power/bravery/thwarting evil). Her three kids miss her dearly, and so they leave home to search for her, only to be captured by the enemy terrorists. Now she must save her kids, or die trying. Or we might turn it around by having the mom captured, and then the kids secretly entering a war-torn country to save her. Working title: *Sergeant Mom.*

These are simply rough examples of how you can use these tools to find interesting combinations. In a later chapter, I'll discuss the construction of ideas more fully. I encourage you to add your own ideas to the lists. Make your own connections. I want this battlefield manual to be as useful to you as possible.

Any iconic character can form the basis of an entertaining story, but if you are interested in each character's innate appeal among audiences, examine Exhibit 22. In the study conducted exclusively for this book, we asked audiences across the nation which iconic characters they enjoy most. We did not associate the characters with any particular franchise. Topping the list are spy/secret agent, various monster types (vampires, werewolves, etc.), wizards/witches/genies, and adventurers/treasure hunters. Because of this rank, I don't think it's a coincidence that James Bond, Jurassic Park, Harry Potter, and Pirates of the Caribbean are among the all-time largest franchises. They were each based upon iconic characters that had innate prominence across the millennia. During the thirteenth and fourteenth centuries, the Mongols relied heavily on spies and espionage to conquer Asia and Europe; the mythological dragon was as deadly as any monster in *Jurassic Park;* Merlin from Arthurian legend is the wizard that all other wizards are patterned after; and the ancient Greek story of Jason and the Argonauts is a splendid tale of an ancient adventurer in search of a great treasure—the Golden Fleece.

Ranking fifth on the list are mom, dad and kids! I put them in the mix to see where they would fall, and they did extremely well. *We* are iconic characters. When we combine ordinary people with extraordinary icons, it's powerful. That's why when a boy faces an alien monster in the movie *Super 8* we all take notice. Similarly, we take notice when a woman battles robots (*The Terminator*), when a kid sees ghosts (*The Sixth Sense*), and when dad encounters aliens (*Close Encounters of the Third Kind*).

Rankings do differ slightly by age and gender, so peek in the appendix for the larger list of icons, split by demographic appeal. As with other rankings in this book, do not discount those iconic characters at the bottom of the list. Great storytellers can give them importance by associating lower-level iconic characters with the higher-level emotional drivers we discussed earlier such as survival/safety, love and belonging, esteem, and fulfilling one's full potential.

Key Takeaway

If your entertainment idea begins with the core character archetypes that are fashioned in the guise of popular iconic characters, who then deliver either traditional or nontraditional emotional satisfaction, it is apt to have an advantage in the entertainment marketplace. That's because its foundation will have in-going appeal with audiences young and old. Give your characters extreme personas so that they stand out. Provide plenty of character opposites in order to make sparks fly.

Exhibit 22: Top Twenty Desired Iconic Characters	
Iconic Characters	Total Nationwide Sample* (Males and Females Ages 8 to 55)
1 Spy/secret agent	40.5%**
2 Vampire, werewolf, monster	34.8
3 Wizard, witch, or genie	34.3
4 Adventurer/treasure hunter/pirate	33.3
5 Mom/dad/kid	33.3
6 Warrior/soldier	31.8
7 Mythical gods (Zeus, Odin, Hercules, Thor)	27.5
8 Scientist and inventor	25.3
9 Folklore creatures (elf, dwarf, ogre, fairy)	25.0
10 Bride/groom or boyfriend/ girlfriend	24.5
11 Ghosts/spirits	24.3
12 Policemen and firemen	24.0
13 Rock star	23.5
14 Movie star	23.3
15 Dancer	22.8
16 Queen/princess/ruler	22.0
17 Teacher, principal, or student	20.8
18 Robots	19.5
19 Athlete or Olympian	18.8
20 King/prince/ruler	18.8

Sample size equals four hundred

**Percent of respondents who enjoy seeing this iconic character.* (Limited number of responses allowed. See appendix for complete list by audience segment.)*

Source: 2011 Study of Blockbuster Entertainment, conducted by C+R Research, Chicago, Illinois, exclusively for the book Creating Blockbusters!

We now have enough under our belt to have a fuller discussion about the creation of an idea. That's next.

Chapter 6

Generate Compelling Story Ideas

Creating great entertainment for films, TV series, and novels begins with a simple, succinctly stated story premise of a sentence or two. The great majority of books written about how to develop successful entertainment rarely provide insights into how, exactly, you should go about generating that story premise. They provide insights on how to shape it or turn it into a treatment or a screenplay, but rarely address the most critical issue; how in the heck do you generate a great idea to begin with?!

Write What You Can Imagine

If you're a writer, you have heard this clichéd advice many times—*write what you know*. That often leads to stories of personal experiences of hardships and joys. It may also lead you to focus on real life stories of others heralded from newspapers and cable news. Unless you are writing an autobiography or an account of a real event, ignore that advice. You heard me; don't worry about writing about what you know. It's far more important to *write what you can imagine*.

I realize that this flies in the face of one hundred years of dogma in education. But if you're a young writer starting out, chances are you haven't lived all that much, so how much can you actually *know*? And if you are one of those few writers who have had great hardships or adventures, I do apologize, but chances are your hardships are not as unique or meaningful enough to capture the hearts of millions.

I'm aware of the many exceptions to the contrary. We can point to the wonderful book made into a splendid film called *The Blind Side*. It was based upon the real life of Michael Oher, a homeless young man who became a successful football player with the help of a caring woman and her

111

family. The film made more than $300 million worldwide and won Sandra Bullock an Oscar for Best Actress.

But here's the rub; most of the money in the entertainment business does not go to accounts of true events. In fact, some of the greatest films, while based on a true event, actually inserted a story that was essentially fiction. James Cameron's *Titanic* is a great example. He created a fictional love story that he injected into the shell of a real event. It was the fictional romance placed in a tragic setting that made the register ring, resulting in just more than $1.8 billion worldwide box office. In an interview for the Academy of Achievement, Cameron said that, "Titanic was conceived as a love story. . . . I think the spectacle [Titanic and the film's visual effects] got people's attention, got them into the theaters, and then the emotional, cathartic experience of watching the film is what made the film work."

To be fair, let me add that *Star Wars*, *E.T.*, *Avatar*, and even *Titanic* can all be said to be based on *some* aspects of the screenwriters own lives that added to character or plot development. However, the thick layer of imagination that sits atop that knowledge makes these blockbusters great. George Lucas never was a Jedi Knight, but he certainly could imagine one for *Star Wars*. James Cameron never visited the planet Pandora before he wrote and shot *Avatar*. Writers may take cues from real experiences, but their imagination is what makes their work extraordinary.

As you craft a tale, certainly use all your experiences, such as people you have known and your life experiences, but unless you are writing a straight line true life account, it's your imagination that matters most. Your imagination adds the uniqueness and the magic. We all played with toys as kids and even pretended that they were alive, but making those toys actually come to life is what bridged the gap between reality and imagination and made *Toy Story* great—thanks to filmmaker John Lasseter.

Story Defined

The previous chapters were a prologue to this one. They provided the essential elements that create a solid foundation for great ideas. These include an understanding of our core emotional needs, culture and trends, and character types. This chapter brings that knowledge together and offers tools to help you imagine an infinite number of possibilities for story ideas. While I flirted with generating some ideas in previous chapters, this chapter provides more depth. The tools in this chapter will help you to explore unique combinations that give new twists to familiar, timeless narratives. No other book does this in quite this way.

First, a definition of what a story consists of. *A story is about a specific character that has a burning need to meet an important goal and must overcome a great challenge or series of challenges to reach it.*

When put into a sentence or two, the story idea is typically referred to as a logline or high concept. Having an enticing sentence that perfectly frames your idea is essential. It quickly tells the listener what the story is about and provides a sense for time, place, and mood. Having a well-articulated concept also keeps you on track to be sure that the final product aligns with your initial vision.

Inherent in the definition of a story is plot conflict. We first explored this in the previous chapter in regards to the types of villains the protagonist might thwart. Though the discussion of plot conflicts dates back to ancient Greece, it was Sir Arthur Thomas Quiller-Couch (1863-1944) who later categorized conflicts into seven basic types: man against man, man against nature, man against himself, man against God, man against society, man caught in the middle, and man and woman.

My version of plot conflicts is in Exhibit 23. It is loosely based on Quiller-Couch's conflict architecture, but I narrowed it to six categories and put more contemporary details within each. I use the "man" reference but please insert "woman" as well.

Great stories often have multiple plot conflicts embedded in the same narrative. The protagonist might have a central conflict with the supernatural, for example, but he must also resolve conflicts with his companions, his romantic desire, and his own abilities.

Exhibit 23: Plot Conflicts

Man vs. Man
Good Guys vs. Villains *(Superman)*
Family vs. Family *(Romeo & Juliet)*
Man vs. Woman *(Taming of the Shrew, What Women Want)*
Parent vs. Parent *(Cramer vs. Cramer, The Parent Trap)*
Adult vs. Child *(Home Alone)*
Child vs. Child *(Mean Girls)*
Man vs. Boss *(Nine to Five)*
Etc.

Man vs. Society
Man vs. Company *(Network, Norma Ray)*
Man vs. Organization *(Ferris Buller's Day Off, Animal House)*
Man vs. Prejudice *(The Blind Side)*
Etc.

Man vs. the Supernatural
Man vs. Demons *(Twilight, Buffy, Harry Potter)*
Man vs. Aliens *(E.T., Alien, Super 8)*
Man vs. God *(Oh God, Bruce Almighty)*
Etc.

Man vs. Nature
Man vs. the Elements *(The Perfect Storm)*
Man vs. Beast *(Jaws, Jurassic Park)*
Man vs. Disease *(I Am Legend)*
Etc.

Man vs. Machines/Technology
Man vs. Creations *(Terminator, War Games)*
Etc.

Man vs. Self
Man vs. His Flaws *(The King's Speech)*
Man vs. Mental Health *(A Beautiful Mind)*
Etc.

Taking into account the definition of a story and its inherent plot conflicts, *The Lord of the Rings* literary trilogy might be described as the story of a hobbit who must overcome intense fears and risk certain death in his quest to destroy the One Ring, defeat the Dark Lord, and save the lives of all those in Middle-earth. The film *Home Alone* is a story of a boy mistakenly left alone at home who then discovers he must find the bravery and ingenuity to defend his home from burglars! The TV series *Glee* is a story about a high-school glee club that strives to win a national championship by beating its rivals, all the while trying to rise above personal issues such as low self-esteem, relationships, and sex.

Those are great embryonic ideas.

IP Story Ideas

Some ideas when first postulated are too vague. Imagine a concept that reads as follows: *"This story is about a powerful hero who must overcome great odds to save the world from the forces of evil."* Hundreds of super hero stories fit this description.

More specific details better distinguish one super hero from the next. Superman is a great hero who comes from the planet Krypton; has great physical powers; is disguised as Clark Kent, a mild-mannered reporter; and needs to save the world from devilish villains, particularly Lex Luthor. Wonder Woman is a great hero who is an Amazon princess from Paradise Island, she has great physical powers and power-related weapons, disguises herself as Diana Prince, and must overcome great odds to save the world from the devilish villains of WWII. The original Underdog is an anthropomorphic super canine that battles evil and forever talks in rhymes. What no one knows is that the caped hero is really a humble and lovable dog named Shoeshine Boy who loves and protects Sweet Polly Purebred.

These details turn a generic idea into what I call an Intellectual Property Story Idea (IP Story Idea for short). Intellectual Property (IP) is a legal term used to refer to results of creativity that are owned by a person or company. The distinctive features that make it capable of being owned might include a unique story, characters, settings, words, phrases, symbols, designs, and so forth. This is very important when you are pitching and receiving entertainment ideas. You can't own a generic idea. You can own an expression of that idea. The expression is in the details you invent.

I was once asked to defend a large entertainment company against a writer claiming the company had ripped off his idea. My assertion to the lawyers was that while the writer's idea was generically similar, the details of his characters were significantly different, which would have led to vastly different stories, characters, and character interrelationships once the idea was developed. After I provided my written statements the lawsuit settled out of court, which is how many of these cases go. The truth is that entertainment executives are bombarded by ideas every day. They come from writers, directors, producers, actors, agents, wives, second cousins, and oddball uncles. Studios also create a lot of ideas internally. In one of many ideation sessions I have led, I helped a studio generate dozens of ideas for movies in just a couple of hours. In another session, I helped a toy company create five hundred toy ideas in one day.

My point: while many writers and creators think their ideas are special and unique, they don't realize that they are similar to dozens of others on a producer's plate, which is why I think the success of blockbusters often results in lawsuits. Many people inadvertently think a particular successful endeavor was based on some idea they pitched five years earlier when they cornered an entertainment executive at the urinal. While unscrupulous activities undoubtedly happen, most ideas simply aren't as unique as writers might think they are. Variations abound. The trick is to make your concept as unique as humanly possible by providing details that get it closer to becoming an IP Story Idea. This chapter can help.

Generating Ideas

Exhibit 24 can help you generate rudimentary ideas on their way to becoming IP Story Ideas. The columns are the key elements known to entice audiences, especially the kid in all of us. The first column lists the key character archetypes and iconic characters we all love. The second column lists the key plot conflicts and genre. The third column lists the core needs a character seeks to satisfy in the story, which the audience will experience vicariously. The fourth column lists the ways this character might transform emotionally (and perhaps physically) in order to reach some great goal or challenge. The fifth column lists some of the cultural elements and trends that might give this story a contemporary context.

Rough ideas are generated by selecting elements from various columns until your creativity makes connections. You might start by selecting a character from the first column, adding a conflict from the second column, finding an emotional need from the third column, then using a transformation for the character to experience, and finally playing with different cultural options and trends from the last column. You can actually start from any column you choose and bounce from column to column to find pieces that "fit" into a seamless narrative.

This chart can help you generate ideas you might not have considered otherwise. It can also be helpful as a way to refine ideas that you generate elsewhere.

We can find the seeds of existing story ideas in the chart. A young boy discovers he's a wizard (column 1: iconic wizard character) and is invited to enroll in wizardry school. But he soon discovers that his life is in grave danger (column 3: safety/survival) by the evil intentions of a great sorcerer who wants to kill him (column 2: conflict). Therefore, the boy must master powerful magic (column 5: on trend) to transform from not so confident to confident and from novice to master (columns 3 and 4: esteem/transformation) in order to thwart wickedness (column 2: conflict). This sounds like the humble beginnings of *Harry Potter and the Sorcerer's Stone*. This concept is a good seed. With added details like specific names and unique places, it is iron clad.

Exhibit 24: Story Idea Matrix

Archetypes and Iconic Characters	Plot Conflict and Genre	Basic Needs	Transformations	Culture and Trends
Character Archetypes Hero-Protagonist Nemeses-Antagonist Friend/Sidekick Nurturer/Protector/ Mentor Romance Character Etc.	**Man vs. Man** Heroes vs. Villains Family vs. Family Man vs. Woman Parent vs. Parent Adult vs. Child Child vs. Child Man vs. Boss	**Self-Actualization** Fulfilling Your Full Potential **Esteem** Respect, appreciation, recognition, status, fame, glory, mastery, independence, power, redemption, revenge, control, winning, rebelliousness, beauty, confidence, bravery, Etc.	**Emotional** Unconfident to Confident Shy to Bold Cowardice to Bravery Selfish to Selfless Unloved to Loved Pessimistic to Optimistic Sad to Happy Evil to Good Unpopular to Popular Alone to Companionship Boring to Exciting Life Loser to Winner Helpless to Survivor Etc.	**Entertainment** Pop Stars, Music, Concerts, Fashion World, Movies, TV Literature, Toys & Video Games, Internet, Sports, Malls, Theme Parks, Zoos, Carnivals, Travel, Jungles, Vacations, Cooking, Inventing, Pets, Parties, Nostalgia, Genealogy, Etc.
Iconic Characters Warrior/Soldier King/Prince/Ruler Queen/Princess/Ruler Adventurer/Treasure Hunter/Pirate Mythic Gods Folklore (elf, dwarf, etc) Billionaire/Rich Rock Star Movie Star Fashion Designer/ Model Dancer Famous Athlete/ Olympian Astronaut/Pilot Wizard/Witch/Genie Vampires/Zombies/ Monsters Space Aliens Doctor/Vet Historical (gladiator, etc) Racecar Driver/ Daredevil Teacher/Principal/ Student Scientist/Inventor Mom/Dad/Parent/ Kids Martial Arts Master Prize Fighter Policeman/Fireman Spy/Secret Agent Bride/Groom/Girl-Boyfriend Native Peoples Circus/Carnival Performers Etc.	**Man vs. Society** Man vs. Company Man vs. Org. Man vs. Prejudice **Man vs. Supernatutral** Man vs. Demons Man vs. Aliens Man vs. God **Man vs. Nature** Man vs. Elements Man vs. Beasts Man vs. Disease **Man vs. Machine** Man vs. Creations **Man vs. Self** Man vs. His Flaws Man vs. Mental Health **Genre** Action Adventure Comedy Drama Fantasy Horror Musical Sci Fi Romance Mystery Etc.	**Love and Belonging** Social needs for family, friendship, intimacy, romance **Safety** Personal health & well being vis-à-vis accidents, illness, financial, thwarting evil **Physiological** Human survival: air, food, water, clothing, shelter, sex, Etc.	**Physical** Weak to Strong Ugly to Pretty Rags to Riches Dumb to Smart Novice to Master Young to Older to Younger Small to Big to Small Sick to Well Mortal to Immortal Inhuman to Human to Inhuman Etc.	**Social Issues** Religion, Sex, Politics, Ethnicity, Equality, Prejudice, War & Peace, Education, Law & Order, Health, Economy, Poverty, Parenting, Marriage & Divorce, Drugs, Suicide, Peer Pressure, Etc. **Trends** Technology, Immersion Social Net. Recession Health/Obesity World Altruism, Environment, Family Shifts, Ethnicity, Spirituality Pop Star Madness Personalization Magic, Science Forever Fame, Girl Power, Terrorism Doomsday, Etc.

I seriously doubt that J. K. Rowling used anything close to this exhibit when she created the first Harry Potter story. Instead, the narrative probably developed intuitively. She instinctively knew how to fit all of the puzzle pieces seamlessly together. For the rest of us, this tool is useful to keep us on track to ensure that the key elements are present in the stories we create. It helps us avoid having a hole in our mosaic where a key element should have gone. That's critical before your idea progresses too far. It's terrible to discover a piece missing when you are already in production. This tool is also useful among experienced storytellers because it helps them see and evaluate more options faster.

I will now use Exhibit 24 to generate ideas of my own, demonstrating how you can use the exhibit to generate ideas. I tend to use slightly longer descriptions in order to make certain the emotional underpinnings are present and to provide a sense of the larger narrative. Some of these ideas might already be in the marketplace; while I know lots of existing stories, I don't know all of them. My only objective is to demonstrate how this chart is used. If you hate these ideas, then I encourage you to find better ones. In fact, I insist upon it.

Buster & Whirl Girl: This is an action comedy about a grandfather and granddaughter superhero team (column 1: archetypes, column 5: family shifts) who must unite to defeat evil (column 2: conflict). Buster is a cranky, sixty-five-year-old superhero who is forced to retire; he becomes so angry about the situation that it leads to his divorce (column 3: belonging, column 5: social issues). But an ancient evil rises and kills most of the younger superheroes (column 3: survival) so Buster reluctantly joins forces with the only remaining hero left alive, a sarcastic, know-it-all sixteen-year-old girl named Whirl Girl who wants to prove herself (column 3: esteem and self-actualization). The two do not get along until Buster discovers that she's the granddaughter he never knew he had (column 3: love and belonging, column 4: emotional transformation). His old-fashioned tactics and her new style of fighting must work together to destroy evil. [Note: There have been several family superhero ideas lately, but I think the generational conflict makes this unique. I imagine Billy Crystal as the caustic grandfather; he might save the world but he has to pee before every battle.]

Malt Shop Rock: This is a musical comedy about Susie and Ted, sixteen-year-old twins living in 1952 (column 5: nostalgia culture) who don't always get along (column 2: conflict), but they do agree on one thing—they want to be famous songwriters and performers (column 1: iconic characters, column 3: desire for fame and self-actualization). They are in the perfect time and place—Nashville in 1952, which has countless rock sensations! They work after school at their dad's malt shop called Malt Shop Rock (column 5: pop culture locale) and get to perform on the countertops with their coworkers. It's the perfect place because Malt Shop Rock is visited by soon-to-be-famous musicians like Elvis Presley (column 1: pop icons, column 5: culture). Susie and Ted need to sell just ONE song to become famous (column 4: transformation) and to save their dad's shop from going out of business (column 3: love of father, column 2: bankruptcy as villain).

Dr. Stem Cell: This is an action adventure about Willow, a young woman born with super powers who must prevent the populace from becoming mutants (column 1: iconic characters). A sinister scientist named Dr. Stem Cell (column 2: conflict) illegally created Willow in a test tube (column 5: science trend). She was whisked away before birth by a secret society living atop a fortress monastery whose aim is to protect and teach her (column 1: protector). All is well for twenty years until Dr. Stem Cell begins to turn the rest of the world into mutated beasts. Willow is the only hope, but she must find the courage to leave the safety of her monastery home and master her powers (column 4: transformations). However, Dr. Stem Cell knows how to destroy her . . . because he created her (column 3: survival).

The aim at this stage is to generate as many different ideas as you can and try not to over think the process. It is important to connect all five dots (columns) as much as possible so that the idea has the fundamental ingredients. The following are some added ideas. I'll dispense with listing the column designations because they interrupt the flow of the idea, but I'll list the key elements at the end.

N.D.E.: *Near Death Experience:* This is an action drama about a college physics student who must find his way back from the dead. David, afraid of death ever since his mother was murdered by his stepfather, has a near-death experience and is momentarily reunited with his loving mom's spirit in heaven. After being snapped back to the living, David creates a machine that he hopes will open the gates between our world and heaven so that he can continue their relationship. A miscalculation lands him in a part of the underworld ruled by his evil stepdad who recently died. He struggles to get back to the land of the living but can only succeed with help from his mom's spirit who enters the underworld to save her son and confront the man who killed her. [Elements: protagonist science student, conflict with death and evil stepdad, love/ bravery/survival emotional drivers, transformation of life/ death and David's emotional regard for it, science and spirituality trends]

3 Deadly Wishes: This is the action romance about Geniella, a beautiful genie who must prevent her master from taking over the world. An overly trusting genie, Geniella fell in love with her human master, but he tricked her, stole her powers, and left her to die on the streets of a big city. Now, she must find him to prevent him from fulfilling his three wishes, which will make him master of the world. Geniella has two hopes: the one power she has left—shape shifting—and the aid of a skeptical yet handsome police detective. [Elements: iconic genie and police detective characters, conflict with master, power/beauty/ romance/love/survival emotional drivers, transformation of powers, genie's ability to trust, and magic trend]

Spellbound: This is an action adventure about Spella, a beautiful yet evil young witch who turns good to save mankind. Spella, her mother, and her sister are witches and use magic to enslave the world. Led by Prince Mankato, humankind attempts to revolt but fails. Spella is impressed by the prince's bravery and falls in love with him, so she decides to free mankind. Chased by her evil mother and sister, Spella and Prince Mankato travel across dangerous lands to destroy the source of her family's power. Spella gradually loses her magic-made beauty and becomes more plain looking, yet naturally beautiful. This makes Mankato love her all the more. They destroy the magic source and discover that Spella is a princess who was kidnapped by the witches as a baby. [Elements: iconic witch, princess and warrior characters, family conflict, power/beauty/love/survival emotional drivers, transformations from evil to good, magic inspired beauty to natural beauty, witch to princess, and use of magic trend]

Honor among Elves: This is an action adventure about Tolari, an elf who is believed to be a coward but must now bravely save his son. Peace-loving Tolari brought shame upon his family's name for wanting to make peace with the Dwarf Kingdom. His fellow elves deemed him a coward for refusing to fight. Dwarf warriors suddenly kidnap his son, planning to sacrifice him to a dragon in three days. The fear for his son's life is greater than his desire for peace, so Tolari treks across the Dreaded Desert of Endless Fears to recover his son—no matter the cost. [Elements: iconic elf, dwarf, and dragon characters; conflict with elf society/dwarfs/dragon; power/pride/survival emotional drivers; transformation from supposed coward to bravery; war and peace cultural issues]

Astro-NUT: This is a comedy about Glenn, a twenty-year-old technical geek working for NASA who wants a chance to be a great astronaut, but his weakling body gets him rejected by NASA. To his surprise, he's selected to compete to be one of five astronauts to go to Mars! The competition and challenges he undertakes are as difficult as they are hilarious. His small-town girlfriend and family are so proud! So is Glenn, until he discovers that he was selected because he is *average,* which gives NASA a "benchmark" to judge the success of the more skilled candidates who are expected to win. Glenn must prove that even an average guy has the right stuff to reach the stars!

[Elements: iconic astronaut and every-day hero characters, conflict with NASA and competitors, pride/power emotional drivers, transformation from loser to winner, science trend]

Each of these ideas still needs work. In a later chapter, I will revisit them and critically explain their pros and cons. Importantly, I urge you to create much better ones using different configurations in the exhibit. To demonstrate the number of potential ideas on this chart alone, we can apply some basic math. I'll round the numbers to make it easy. If we have about thirty iconic character options, times six basic plot conflicts, times ten key genre, times five basic needs, times about twenty transformation possibilities, times about thirty ways to align with culture or trends, then the number of possible story ideas comes to more than five million! This number is an underestimate because there are many more twists on character types, plots, genre, detailed needs, transformations, cultural elements, and trends. You just have to pull them all out of the chart.

Notice, too, that I never added a potential actor to the actual concept but just suggested a couple afterwards. That's because an idea must be strong on its own, independent of who gets the role. Too often, studios rely heavily on a big star to open a film. That approach seems less proved these days. Great concepts stand on their own strength.

Genre Mix Up

Another fun game is to play *genre mix up*. To play, you take a story that you know in one genre and see how you can transform it into another. There are plenty of examples already in existence. The James Bond character placed in a comedy is Austin Powers, whereas if he's placed in a western it's the TV show *The Wild, Wild West*. *Star Wars* as an action adventure is *Spaceballs* as a comedy.

Extending this idea, perhaps there is potential in comedic, mainstream versions of *The Karate Kid*, the *Harry Potter Series*, and *The War of the Worlds*. Perhaps Cinderella should get her prince through science instead of magic. Perhaps

Superman should be reinvented as a western comedy. This topsy-turvy approach is just one of many methods that force your eyes to see combinations that were not yet visible.

The Moral of the Story

Whether intended or not, all story ideas when fully executed have a moral. It can be clichéd such as crime does not pay, appearances are deceptive, or honesty is the best policy. Or more nuanced such as being physically weak but morally strong can vanquish those who are physically strong but morally weak. Here are two of my favorites:

- The grass is not always greener on the other side of the road, so you might as well look for happiness in your own back yard (*The Wonderful Wizard of Oz*).
- We each have the potential to positively affect the lives of so many people in ways we do not realize (*It's a Wonderful Life*). The film can also be said to express the idea that wealth is not measured by the riches in your bank account, but by the richness you bring to the lives of your loving friends and family.

Overlaying a moral theme often happens naturally during the writing process though interpreting the theme remains the purview of the audience. Different people will interpret the moral differently because each brings his own life experience and belief system.

In many good stories, the protagonist may experience a moral dilemma. He may question what he cares about most and what is worth fighting and dying for. Such a revelation can result in a character shifting his goal. For example, his original goal may be to gain the love of a woman, but he might ultimately sacrifice himself to achieve a more important goal of saving her life (*Titanic*). Or after suffering a tragic incident as a child, a character's goal might be to attain a carefree life with no worries, until he realizes that it is not as satisfying as facing one's greater responsibilities (*The Lion King*). Pulling a character in two directions with two competing goals gives us insight into the character by the choice he makes, and in so doing, creates the story's inner moral compass.

Some executives don't care much about the moral themes that are inherently embedded in stories. They just ignore them, believing that audiences care only about tasty, nutrition-free entertainment. Other executives like the inclusion of moral themes but want them handled subtly. They fear that serving up an overt moral lesson to hungry audiences will taste like spinach instead of candy.

I think the inclusion of a strong moral point of view matters. It adds relatable depth to the storytelling by expressing issues and dilemmas that audiences face in their own lives. It inspires audiences to question their own moral compasses. Both *It's a Wonderful Life* and *The Wonderful Wizard of Oz* shout their moral lessons from their respective mountaintops. Done well, it's extraordinary.

Fearlessly Creating New

Jay Fukuto is a highly seasoned and creative executive. He is the former head of creative affairs for Disney TV Animation, the former head of the studio at Film Roman, and is an executive producer at SD Entertainment, Inc. He's always in search of the new and different. "I believe," said Jay,

> that the key creative ingredients to great kid entertainment apply to great entertainment in general. First of all, be original, and don't be afraid to put out there the most uniquely original notion, no matter what it might be. Who would have thought that a cartoon revolving around a goofy sponge in short pants would become one of the most successful kid franchises in recent history? It had the added benefit of appealing to some adult sensibilities as well. But supporting the courage to present new ideas, off the wall or otherwise, must be passion and inspiration. It requires a lot of hard work, dedication, and resilience to develop and produce a successful show, or to get any successful venture off the ground, and the necessary fuel is generally provided by a creative person's tremendous desire and vision to share a new world with an audience.

Don't shy away from ideas that are so strange that they make you uncomfortable. That's how new paths are discovered.

Hit or Miss

If an idea is off by just a bit at conception, then the final entertainment offering can easily miss your target completely. That's because the idea will have a dramatic impact on all the decisions that follow.

Exhibit 25 demonstrates this using a screenplay as an example. The initial idea will impact direction of the

Exhibit 25: Hit or Miss

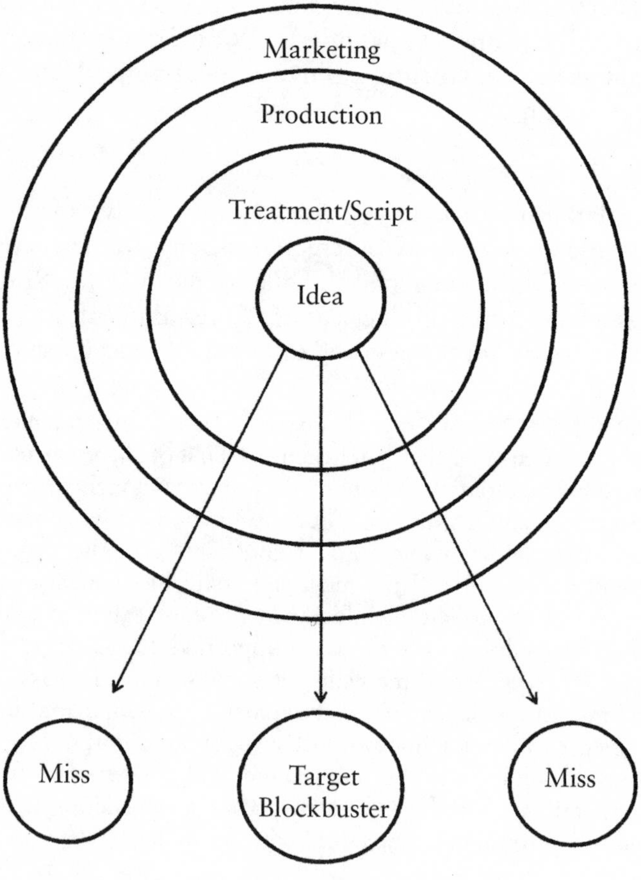

treatment and script with regard to character development, story elements, setting, era, action, and humor. Those elements, in turn, will have a dramatic impact on all the production essentials, which include casting, directing, stylization, and even editing. This will impact how it is marketed. If the idea is "off" by even a couple degrees at the beginning, all the other decisions will be impacted, which will push the entertainment further away from the ultimate goal of becoming a blockbuster.

Key Takeaway

Strong embryonic ideas stem from having the right ingredients. These ingredients include the use of critical character archetypes and iconic characters, key plot conflicts, core emotional drivers, a character's emotional (and sometimes physical) transformations, the idea's alignment to contemporary culture and trends, and even the idea's inner moral compass. That's a start, but there are other criteria that we will explore in later chapters regarding how to build components into your ideas to make them more unique, marketable, and capable of becoming franchises.

It is also very important not to fall in love with ideas too early. The best approach is to generate a lot of concepts and to refine them with unique details before you narrow them down to a more manageable few. The narrowing process should be based upon two things. First, you can use the principles throughout this book to determine which ideas appear to have the greatest potential. Second, you should obtain audience input. Since I practice what I preach, later in this book I will share the results of a research project I commissioned among four hundred consumers nationwide to ascertain if they liked any of my ideas. The results are enlightening. Stayed tuned.

For now, we turn our attention to gender and age skews. While your idea is in its embryonic state, we need to decipher who the idea is really for and, importantly, if we can broaden its appeal without losing the essence of it.

Chapter 7

Add Broad Audience Appeal

Most blockbusters capture the hearts of a broad audience. That's why I placed the chapter of human emotions early in this book. The more an idea is geared toward satisfying emotions we all share, the more likely it will attract audiences young and old, male and female.

When I'm asked to evaluate entertainment while it's still in development, a key question that often arises is whether it has potential to appeal to a broad demographic audience. The implications are dramatic. Exhibit 26 reveals the potential facing every entertainment related project. If you think of your audience as divided into four simplified quadrants—older males, younger males, older females, younger females—then each quadrant represents roughly 25 percent of your potential audience. If an idea appeals to only younger males, that segment represents only 25 percent of the potential and you have cut off the other 75 percent! This is well understood in the entertainment world where films, TV shows, and novels live and die by the four quadrants.

The quadrants create havoc. A TV show in development might have been created for adults, and then somebody along the line will ask if the storyline can accommodate elements that will appeal to the kids in the household as well. The opposite happens too. Some entertainment is developed with only children in mind, and then somebody will ask whether it can be adjusted to appeal equally to their parents—and perhaps even to single adult sensibilities.

In some cases, these questions are raised too late in the development process. When I ran the planning and research team for an advertising agency, I was sometimes asked to help craft an advertising strategy to broaden the appeal of a film

Exhibit 26: Audience Potential

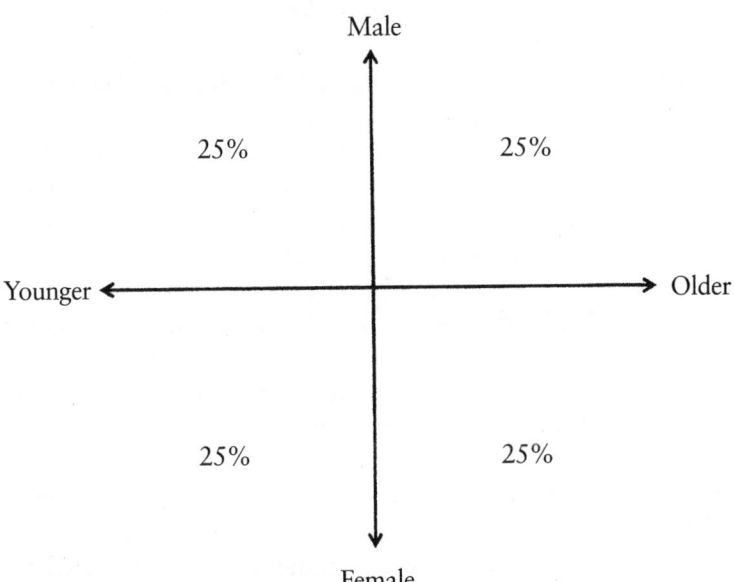

after it was completed. It's not easy. If a film is supercharged with testosterone from beginning to end, it's difficult to gain a lot of female interest. If a film is supercharged with estrogen from beginning to end, it's hard to appeal to males. If a film was crafted to appeal only to the sensibilities of preschoolers, it's hard to get a ten-year-old to care, and sometimes equally hard to get the preschooler's parent excited enough to bring the child. Typically, when marketers are asked to expand an audience once a film or TV show is complete, it means that someone is nervous that the entertainment was too narrow to begin with. As a last resort, studios may cut different trailers in a mad attempt to "market" the film to a broader audience. That's dreadfully hard when there's little in the film to attract a larger audience. If it's not on the screen, it won't be in the trailer. Oops!

If the entertainment is adjusted during the concept/

development stage, it can make a big difference. A draft screenplay that is initially geared for males, for example, might be changed to add elements like a romance angle so that the male audience will be able to entice wives or girlfriends to join them. That results in two tickets, two drinks, and a large bag of popcorn. That makes everybody happy. In the world of television, great examples of entertainment that attracted multiple quadrants include *The Simpsons, Flintstones, Roseanne, Married . . . with Children,* and *Modern Family.* In film, we can add *Beauty and the Beast, Avatar,* and *Toy Story.* In literature, we can add the *Harry Potter Series.* In the world of preschool, I'll add *Sesame Street* because of the appeal it has had among parents.

How does blockbuster entertainment appeal to multiple quadrants? What allows entertainment to cross age and gender barriers? The previous chapters have provided some answers. This chapter will provide even more.

There's an extremely important, obvious caveat—not all entertainment should be for all audiences! Thank goodness for *Casablanca, China Town, Marty, Gangs of New York, The Sopranos,* and *Mad Men.* How dreadful they would have been if the creators had tried to make them appeal to kids. Similarly, the *Vagina Monologues, Steel Magnolias,* Barbie dolls, and a plethora of romance novels should never have been anything more than what they are—for a primarily female audience. There's something to be said for selecting a key audience segment and then crafting entertainment that gains their interest without having to include superficial elements in a misguided attempt to attract a broader audience. If you try to appease every audience segment, you risk watering down the emotional fulfillment for all of them. It's hard to be all things to all segments.

This brings us to what I call the *Devil's Narrative Choice.* If you choose a story that appeals to only one quadrant, then your story idea has to be so emotionally satisfying, executed, and marketed to that 25 percent that you can justify ignoring the other 75 percent of the world. Alternatively, if you try to attract three or four quadrants representing between 75 to 100 percent of the potential audience, then you need to craft, execute, and market a story idea in a way that entices young and old, male and female, without being watered down to most. It's very difficult to be all things to all people. That's the choice. Pick your narrative devil.

If your measuring stick is box office receipts or book store sales, you must agree that by and large the most successful stories have been those that address the needs in all of us. Films, TV shows, and books that have been the most successful not only addressed several quadrants, they literally set camp in most of them. That doesn't mean a blockbuster needs to attract all four audiences equally. They often don't. Some may skew more toward males, others toward kids and so forth. The movie *Thor*, for example, had a greater proportion of males in the audience, but it had enough appeal among men, teenage boys, younger boys, and still a significant proportion of women/girls to become a blockbuster. More often than not, appealing to the kid in all of us makes this happen.

This chapter contains seven Audience Insights that will help your idea appeal to as many segments as possible without watering the idea down for each. Some of the insights are obvious, while others are more subtle and nuanced. Some of the audience insights have already been discussed in previous chapters, but I put them all here so that you have a complete list of the ways to achieve the broadest audience. Here they are.

Audience Insight #1: Satisfy an Emotion Shared by All

As stated in a previous chapter, many emotional needs are shared by all of us. These include the basic needs for safety/survival, love and belonging, esteem, and self-actualization. The more successful you are at satisfying the core emotional needs shared by all, the more likely you will capture a broad audience. A fundamental element in the film *Toy Story*, to me, has always been about friendship, a strong basis for love and belonging, which works for all audiences and on every level.

The Harry Potter universe allows us to experience the

intense, shared desires for survival, love and belonging, esteem, and self-actualization. Audiences young and old, male and female can sit side by side and feel the same, tempered only by the prism of the personal life experiences they each bring to it.

Audience Insight #2: Satisfy an Emotion Unique to Some

Even if your story is based upon satisfying a core emotional need shared by all, you still have the latitude to satisfy emotional needs unique to different audience segments. *Avatar*'s overall theme of saving indigenous peoples on the planet of Pandora is appealing to many. The film also has a strong romance element that appeals to female sensibilities (and many males, too). It also has a strong battling element that satisfies the need for power and good vanquishing evil, appealing to male sensibilities (and many females, too). It has iconic characters kids love, made edgy and realistic to appeal to the kid that lives inside adults. James Cameron, writer and director of *Avatar,* is quoted on the Web site jamescamerononline.com as saying, "I knew it was exciting, it was an adventure, it could appeal to kids but it was a dramatic, emotional story that would appeal to an adult audience as well."

In this way, the film captured all of us by satisfying our collective emotional needs, and then it captured each of us again by satisfying our different emotional needs.

Audience Insight #3: Select Broad Based Cultural Elements and Trends

The broad-based culture and trends referenced in chapter 4 can be used to create story relevance for multiple audiences. These include entertainment-based culture (e.g., music, fashion, malls, sports), social issues related culture (e.g., education, ethnicity, marriage/divorce) and various trends (e.g. technology, social networking, environmental sensitivity).

Even heavy social issues can be appreciated by adults and younger audiences if handled well. The book-inspired film *The Parent Trap* featured a divorced couple whose rambunctious children sought to reunite them. Divorce is both a trend and an unfortunate enduring part of our culture. It elicits our common fears and our common need for love and belonging. As such, men, women, and children can relate to divorce because they are either directly affected by it or they know a family that is. It permeates our society at all levels, for all audiences. Addressing the topic head-on but with a lighter touch helped to make *The Parent Trap* successful.

In a similar way, many audience segments can identify with the cultural issues that *The Simpsons* TV show has addressed. These have included race relations, religion, sex, and celebrities. Some issues are well understood and appreciated by all audience segments, and other issues are more relevant to specific audience segments. There's something for everyone, which is partly responsible for the longevity of the series.

Audience Insight #4: Create Characters That All Audiences Can Identify With

The Walt Disney Company has a long, prolific record of creating an array of highly endearing characters with unique, engaging personas we can all relate to. We discovered them in such classics as *Snow White and the Seven Dwarfs, Peter Pan, The Little Mermaid, Beauty and the Beast, The Lion King,* and so many more. Add to this the wonderful characters created by Pixar and the list expands exponentially. As the senior vice president and general manager of DisneyToon Studios, Meredith Roberts is an astute senior executive with extensive understanding of story and character development. She spearheaded the highly successful effort to bring Tinker Bell and her world of fairies to life in a series of computer-animated films. According to Ms. Roberts, "Tinker Bell is a great character because her emotions reflect our own lives. She is real, with all her foibles, and therefore she endures through time. She is an authentic character with charm that is endlessly appealing to everyone."

Audiences live vicariously through the characters they appreciate. To appeal to a broad audience, characters must be relatable and/or aspiring for all. That's a heavy burden, but blockbusters have accomplished this many times. These are a few interesting approaches.

Use an Iconic Adult Character: One approach is to select an adult, iconic character that we loved when we were children and continue to love as adults. Those were listed in chapter 5 and included warriors, kings, rock stars, aliens, adventurers, treasure hunters, and many more. Indiana Jones fits the adventurer, treasure-hunter role. Because he's an adult, male audiences can relate to him as an adult. They will also fantasize what it would be like to be him as he faces dangers, takes risks, and eventually triumphs over the forces of evil. Younger boys will also aspire to be him. The character's wit and confidence contribute to his aspiring qualities. Adult women will be attracted romantically to him and might live vicariously through his female companions. Younger girls might think the same. In this way, the Indiana Jones character has something for most segments. That's great character development and great casting.

Use a Child or Child-like Character in an Adult Role: Another successful approach is to create a child protagonist who is thrust into an adult role. Children audiences will aspire to be the character and adults will have fun watching kids with adult responsibilities. This was one of the broad appeals of *Home Alone*, the film features a boy who is inadvertently left at home while the rest of the family goes on vacation. While the initial sense of freedom is welcomed, the protagonist must soon take care of the house (an adult chore) and eventually defend it from burglars (an adult threat). The series *Harry Potter* fits this approach. The hero faces great adult-type hardships and risks. Younger audiences imagine what it might be like to be Harry and hope that, if they were in a similar circumstance, they would succeed too. Adult audiences, especially parents, are rooting for him as they would root for their own kids. The same can be said for Robert Louis Stevenson's novel *Treasure Island*. The young protagonist Jim Hawkins gets mixed up with cutthroat pirates. Children aspire. Adults relate. In a different twist, films such as *BIG, 13 Going on 30,* and *Freaky Friday* use magic to thrust children into adult bodies. Kid audiences will aspire to do the same, and adult audiences will be amused by it. Win-win.

Use Multiple Relatable Characters: A different approach is to construct multiple characters, each for a different audience segment. *The Simpsons* television series does this extremely well. Boys watch Bart Simpson and think how wonderful it would be if they could be as mischievous. Girls relate to the smart, sensible Lisa. Wives might identify with Marge, who suffers her husband's antics. Men might appreciate the stupidity of Homer, which might make them feel superior in comparison. Parent audiences can relate to the children characters. Children audiences can relate to the parent characters. All audiences can relate to the vast assortment of neighborhood characters that reflect so many people we encounter in our lives, albeit in the extreme. *That '70s Show* used a similar approach. The show depicted life in Wisconsin in the late 1970s and featured an array of characters that different audience segments would be able to identify with. Eric is the average teen who is a bit geeky and physically slight. Teens can identify. His friends represent a spectrum that we can relate to in our own lives, which is part of the show's success. Kelso is the cute dimwit. Steven is the sarcastic anti-establishment rebel. Donna is Eric's intelligent, beautiful girlfriend. Jackie is a pretty, spoiled, and selfish friend. Fez is the sweet but gullible foreign exchange student. Kitty is Eric's cheerful, nurturing mom. Red is Eric's hardnosed father with a soft interior. Laurie is the evil older sister.

Audience Insight #5: Use Nostalgia to Connect Generations

Nostalgia bridges generations. This is partly the reason for the contemporary success of older superheroes like Superman, Batman, Iron Man and Thor. Today's adults were introduced to these characters when they were kids, giving them built-in appeal among adults of today.

By using characters and stories from the past, entertainment executives can entice adults who want to experience the stories again, and they can entice kids who have yet to be introduced to the characters. This also allows parents to satisfy an emotional need to "hand down" and "share" these nostalgic characters with their children. They bond generations. As evidence by box office figures, today's parents have demonstrated their desire to hand down their childhood love of *Star Wars, Smurfs,* and *Alvin and the Chipmunks.* Tomorrow's parents will likely demonstrate a powerful need to hand down their love of *Harry Potter, Shrek,* and *Toy Story.*

Nostalgia matters. This is why *Action Comics* No. 1, which introduces Superman, cost $0.10 in 1938 but was sold for nearly $2.2 million in 2011. It's also why the Barbie doll was considered by many moms to be too sexy for their daughters more than fifty years ago when she was introduced, but she is embraced by many of today's moms because they played with her when they were young. Many see the doll as almost a rite of passage.

Walt Disney was the first to discover the power of nostalgia in a big way. He knew that childhood fairytales were a prime source of material that appealed to young and old alike. That helped inspire such Disney Classics as *Cinderella, Snow White and the Seven Dwarfs,* and *Sleeping Beauty.*

Some critics have argued that Hollywood searches for icons of the past because they are not innovative enough to invent new ones today. I don't think that's a fair criticism. I think that Hollywood simply realized that there were great stories that were underutilized.

Audience Insight #6: Address the Sensibilities of Each Audience Segment

I have conducted a lot of TV show research among different ages and genders. One of the biggest errors that writers make is when they don't address each audience's sensibility. They might have a lot of slapstick humor for young kids but not enough sarcasm and rude humor for teens. They might have sarcasm to appease teens, but not enough sophisticated wit or double entendre for adults. Or the story might have an abundance of explosions to appease a male audience but no appeals to female sensibilities. It's critical to address the sensibilities of each. While some sensibilities overlap with Audience Insight # 2 (Satisfy an Emotion Unique to Some), sensibilities go well beyond emotion alone.

Sensibilities by Gender: Exhibit 27 shows a brief list of "sensibilities" by gender based upon the study conducted exclusively for this book. We asked respondents to pick the items and/or themes they like to see in the entertainment they consume. These sensibilities do not apply all the time, but they do with enough frequency that to ignore them can be troublesome. The results by gender mimic other findings discussed in earlier chapters.

As the exhibit shows, males care more about battles, weapons/gadgets, power, being tough, winning, gross stuff, and muscles than do females. Though not included in the research, allow me to add sexual conquest (for older audiences). Guys want to rumble, and more often than not, they want to look good while in battle. Action films skew toward a male audience, as do *Transformers* action figures. Males don't mind being portrayed as soft inside, as long as they are first portrayed as tough as nails on the outside.

Females tend to gravitate toward relationships, romance, sweet/sassy personas, beauty, cuteness, glamour/fashions, playing nice, and nurturing more so than males do. Allow me to add that while beauty and glamour are important, most women will not seek them at the expense of being strong and smart. Romance novels skew toward women, as do Barbie dolls (obviously).

This does not mean that each gender stays in their respective themes. Many females care about power and being tough as shown in the exhibit. Scáthach is a figure in Irish mythology. She was a Scottish warrior and martial arts teacher who trained heroes and made kings. A strong female presence continues in contemporary narratives on TV, films, novels, and video games. Some males do care about romance and nurturing, much more than the exhibit suggests. Boys can be nurturers, for example, provided that it is done in a male-acceptable way. *E.T.: The Extra-Terrestrial* is a great example of a story in which a boy sought to protect and save/nurture an alien from outer space. Nurturing was wrapped in a suspenseful alien theme. Because of this, be careful not to ignore the items at the bottom of the list.

Exhibit 27: Gender Sensibilities of Audience

Distinguishing Male Themes	Males (199)	Females (201)
Battles	56.8%*	21.9%
Weapons/Gadgets	55.3	15.9
Power	44.2	26.9
Being tough	42.7	29.4
Winning	38.7	28.9
Gross stuff	25.6	11.4
Muscles	21.6	16.4

Distinguishing Female Themes	Males (199)	Females (201)
Relationships and friendship themes	28.1%	62.7%
Romance themes	15.1	50.7
Being sweet/Sassy	12.6	43.3
Beauty	10.6	37.8
Cuteness	11.6	34.8
Glamour/Fashions	10.1	27.4
Playing nice to make friends	15.6	25.9
Nurturing/Mothering	7.5	23.4

Percent of respondents who enjoy seeing this theme/item in stories. (Limited number of responses allowed. See appendix for complete list by audience segment.)

Source: 2011 Study of blockbuster entertainment, conducted by C+R Research, Chicago, Illinois, exclusively for the book Creating Blockbusters!

Some entertainment options have achieved a very effective balance of male and female sensibilities in ways that captured our hearts. There was probably no film with a better gender balance than Disney's *Beauty and the Beast*. Female sensibilities could appreciate the "beauty" emotional driver and related romance story. Male sensibilities could appreciate the "beast" element and its associated power and vanquishing evil themes/battles. Each gender could enjoy elements of the other, but their primary sensibility dominated.

Interestingly, when female characters are given sensibilities that are traditionally attributed to males, male audiences often respond positively. The ancient story of Hua Mulan is one of these. The Chinese legend is about a young woman who disguises herself as a man and takes the place of her aging father in the army. In Disney's film version, the heroine helps China battle a Hun invasion. Though the story features a young woman, many boys flocked to the theater. Why? Because Mulan had a personality and abilities that boys admire and wish they had. She was strong, determined, and a capable warrior. She was also beautiful, sweet, and sassy which played well with girls. *Tomb Raider* became a blockbuster video game among boys even though the protagonist archaeologist-adventurer is female. Why? Three reasons: First, Lara Croft is an iconic adventurer. The appeal of this character type crosses gender lines. Second, she possesses abilities that males admire; most notably she's smart, powerful, and has guns and knows how to use them. Third, she's drop dead gorgeous. These qualities helped the first film, based upon the game, to reach worldwide box office of roughly $275 million.

You can also use Exhibit 27 to put male and female characters at odds. This happens often in storylines. The male protagonist is crafted as more macho and mischievous, while the female protagonist is more sweet and responsible. Or switch roles completely to create a twist. One of my favorite plays is Shakespeare's *The Taming of the Shrew*. The story follows Petruchio, a gentleman of Verona, as he attempts to tame an obstinate shrew named Katherina with reverse psychology. She's a terror and violates nearly every feminine rule in Exhibit 27. In the play, Petruchio tames her. At the end of the 1967 film version, however, the writer and director allow Katherina to humiliate Petruchio by leaving a banquet without him. He gives chase, implying that she is subtly in control! With due respect to Shakespeare, I prefer the film's ending. So it is quite possible for you to create entertainment ideas that cross gender boundaries in fun ways.

Sensibilities by Age: Adding age-related sensibilities is challenging. An ever-present issue is how to add elements to entertainment that entice younger audiences without making the entertainment appear to be "childish" for older audiences. The reverse issue is how to add elements to entertainment that entice older audiences without making it too serious or sophisticated for younger audiences. The key principles cited earlier in this chapter can help, but there are added nuances worthy of discussion.

Exhibit 28 reveals the "sensibilities" by various ages. Admittedly, it's my subjective attempt, but it is based on a lot of face-to-face research with these audiences over many years, as well as insights drawn from the study conducted for this book. Before we discuss how to entice them all, we need to examine each age segment individually.

Preschoolers: These children are a very special audience, and entertainment for them is typically strictly for them. Their cognitive development is immature and needs to be safeguarded in special ways. If you're developing entertainment for preschoolers, the key emotional sensibilities include large doses of nurturing, bonding, cooperation, learning fundamentals, simple physical humor, a lot of silliness and sweet innocence, and a fantasy orientation with highly fanciful characters that take on the role of friend and nurturer. Did I hear you just say Big Bird? Yes, Big Bird will do. But there is an important adult component, too. When entertainment can truly employ all the sensibilities that preschoolers need, you make a wonderful friend in the parent—especially mom. Many years ago while working at an advertising agency, my agency

Exhibit 28: Sensibilities by Age

Category	2 to 4 (Preschool)	5 to 8 (Early Grades)	9 to 13 (Tween)	14-19 (Teen)	20+ (Adult)
Identification	Bonding with parents Nurturing	Friends, Gender ID	Peers/Cliques, Fitting in	Cliques, Sexual Attraction, Dating	Dating/Nurturing Long Term Relationships, Spouse/Parenting
Social Interaction	Cooperation (non-violent)	Competition	Competition +	Competition ++	Competition, Cooperation Balance
Mastery	Learning Fundamentals (Values, Social, Physical, Mental, Educational, Creativity, Sensory, Repetition, Etc.)	Trying to Master Basics	Exceed	Excel	Master Life Nuances, Teach/Impart
Humor	Physical Humor (simple)	Physical Humor (slapstick)	Physical Humor + Wit and Sarcasm	Wit and Sarcasm + Physical Humor, Teen Dating/Drama	Wit and Sarcasm + Physical Humor + Marriage Angst, Parenting Angst
Tone	Silliness, Sweet, Innocence	Silliness, Craziness	Sweet to Sassy to Edgy	Edginess, Rebellious, Angst (Who am I? What will I become?)	Edginess, Maturity, Juggling Responsibilities, Nostalgic, Trapped?
Fantasy vs. Reality	Fantasy ++	Fantasy +	Reality-based Fantasy	Reality-based Fantasy	Reality-based Fantasy and Escapism

colleagues and I helped to introduce a line of Mattel preschool toys using the Classic Disney characters of Mickey Mouse and friends. Using our understanding of moms, the creative part of the team came up with a wonderful tagline, "Making Friends You Can Believe In." It worked very well and spoke to both the characters and the benefits of the specific toys. Beyond the needs of the preschoolers themselves, parents are driven by benefits that include their children's happiness, development, health and safety, success, and love. Brands that deliver these in strong ways can be successful.

Early Grade-School Kids: Children ages 5 to 8 begin to identify more with friends of the same gender. Tastes and sensibilities begin to diverge along gender lines. Boys will gravitate toward battling and good vs. evil themes. Girls will begin to favor playthings and imagery related to beauty and fashion. They do have some sensibilities in common. Kids of this age begin to display a greater competitive spirit, perhaps due in part to the insertion of competitive sports. They have a better understanding of the need to master the basics, learning-wise. Physical humor and slapstick becomes very important. While silliness is still appreciated, they begin to gravitate to humor and activities that are more crazy and extreme. They are still very much in love with fantasy. This is the prime audience for a lot of animation.

Tweens ages 9 to 13: These kids sit between two worlds, the sweeter world of the child and the older, more angst-ridden world of the teen. They can be quite sweet and innocent one day and a bit sassy the next day. I've conducted several in-home research projects, called ethnographic research, with tweens. The projects entailed going into their homes, talking to their parents, and visiting their rooms. The last time I did so, it was not unusual for a tween girl to have icons of fairytales on her bed sheets and a poster of Britney Spears on her wall. They want desperately to be older, but they still find comfort in being younger. Their desire to fit in with peers rears its head. Cliques begin to form. Their competitiveness grows. They are beyond mastering some basics and are working more to exceed. Physical humor works well, but their mental abilities have evolved to appreciate more sophisticated humor like sarcasm and wit. They can be a bit sassier at this age and their tastes can be edgier. They begin to appreciate more reality-based fantasies. The book series *Goosebumps* by R. L. Stine is a perfect tween vehicle for boys and girls. It can be dark, but it isn't too dark. *The Baby-sitters Club* book series by Ann M. Martin works well for tween girls because of the strong relationship-driven stories. Videogames expand during this age for boys because they get to place themselves in the action in a way that traditional toys could not achieve. Tweens feel they need to graduate from kid stuff, so they begin to view characters and the toys they played with earlier as babyish, though they often still play with them in private.

Teens: Teens dial it up. Cliques abound, sexual attraction soars, dating is drama, and competition in many areas of their lives grows. They want to excel, especially relative to their peers. Wit and sarcasm are often more important than solely physical humor (but not always). Teen boys like greater edginess and power. Teen girls put greater emphasis on glamour and fashion. Being independent and even rebellious can be fun, within limits. Teens begin to appreciate that there are grey areas between good and evil. Reality-based stories and edgier stories are more important now. Filmmaker John Hughes owned this group with such film classics as *The Breakfast Club* and *Pretty in Pink*. If the story is based upon fantasy, it must be executed with gritty realism.

Adults: As teens dialed it up, adults begin to dial it back. Dating is still critical for younger adults along with the angst that goes with it. Films such as *The 40-Year-Old Virgin* and *The Hangover* are right on target, the latter being a story about a group of buddies who get together for a bachelor party that goes awry. Older adults transition into nurturing long-term relationships, marriage, and parenting. Competition and cooperation have a greater balance. Mastering nuances in life becomes more important. Wit, sarcasm, and physical humor stay important, and we can mix in marriage and family drama/humor. Juggling more responsibilities begins to dominate as maturity seeps in. The film, and now TV series, *Parenthood* perfectly fits this sensibility. Older adults begin to feel nostalgic for simpler times and can feel trapped by today's responsibilities. Reality is important in entertainment, as is escapism fantasy providing that it feels real.

Using Tonality and Style to Bridge Ages

Given the differences in sensibilities by age, it might appear difficult to appease all audiences at once. Not so. Adding the right tonality and stylistic execution can help attract broader age segments.

Tonality of Execution: To reach a broad audience, it is important to use a tonality that can be appreciated by young

	Exhibit 29: Top Twenty Films and MPAA Rating		
	Top Twenty Films	Domestic Box Office (Millions)	Rating
1	Avatar	$760.50	PG-13
2	Titanic	$600.70	PG-13
3	The Dark Knight	$533.30	PG-13
4	Star Wars	$460.90	PG
5	Shrek 2	$441.20	PG
6	E.T.: The Extra-Terrestrial	$435.10	PG
7	Star Wars: Episode I - The Phantom Menace	$431.00	PG
8	Pirates of the Caribbean: Dead Man's Chest	$423.30	PG-13
9	Toy Story 3	$415.00	G
10	Spider-Man	$403.70	PG-13
11	Transformers: Revenge of the Fallen	$402.10	PG-13
12	Star Wars: Episode III - Revenge of the Sith	$380.20	PG-13
13	The Lord of the Rings: The Return of the King	$377.00	PG-13
14	Spider-Man 2	$373.50	PG-13
15	The Passion of the Christ	$370.70	R
16	Jurassic Park	$357.00	PG-13
17	The Lord of the Rings: The Two Towers	$341.70	PG-13
18	Finding Nemo	$339.70	G
19	Spider-Man 3	$336.50	PG-13
20	Alice in Wonderland (2010)	$334.10	PG

As of May 2011, not adjusted for inflation.

Source: Box Office Mojo, permission granted

and old. Exhibit 29 shows the top twenty domestic grossing films of all time (as of May 2011, not adjusted for inflation). First, notice that the films predominantly include movies that connect with the kid in all of us—*Avatar, The Dark Knight,* and *Star Wars.* Of the twenty listed, only one is decidedly for adults (*The Passion of the Christ*).

The more important point is the MPAA (Motion Picture Association of America) rating given to these films. This is a good barometer of tonality. More than half of the films are rated PG-13, mostly because of the darker themes and aggressive battles. The PG-13 rating strongly cautions parents of children under age thirteen that some material may be inappropriate. The PG-13 rating was created because of the violence in the films *Indiana Jones and the Temple of Doom* and *Gremlins*. It was felt that these movies had too much adult content to be rated PG but not quite enough to be rated R.

I believe that the adoption of the PG-13 rating had a profound impact on audience participation. It allowed iconic characters that children love (e.g., Batman, Spider-Man) to be given a more aggressive treatment that adults (and kids) would appreciate. It made the playful and fanciful feel more real and gritty. Playful, iconic characters made dark and edgy works extremely well because it addresses the sensibilities of young and old simultaneously. The balanced tonality of PG-13 expanded audiences.

Exhibit 30 shows the demographics of audiences who saw PG-13 blockbuster action movies released between October 2003 and May 2011. The films attracted audiences that were young and old, male and female. The only weakness was among females under age twenty-five (17 percent), yet this is still a sizeable group.

Exhibit 30: PG-13 Action Movies

Grossing $150 Million+ Domestic Box Office (October 2003 to May 2011)

Demographic	Percentage
Males under age 25	25%
Males age 25 and up	33
Females under age 25	17
Females age 25 and up	25

N = 63 movies

Source: CinemaScore, permission granted

Still, PG- and G-rated films can capture large audiences too. The original *Star Wars* film, *Shrek 2*, and *E.T.* each captured a wide audience with a PG rating. The only two G-rated films on the list are *Toy Story 3* and *Finding Nemo*. Both are stellar examples of blockbusters because they satisfy deeply shared emotional needs.

But when in doubt, edgier PG and PG-13 ratings are more likely to help expand your audience to all four quadrants due to the tonality. Some films were rated PG, and then made trips into the PG-13 realm with sequels; this occurred with *Star Wars* as well as *Harry Potter* (not on list). Ultimately, the story will dictate the edginess of the execution, which will dictate the rating. However, as you develop your idea, keep in mind that the tonality (degree of aggressiveness/ darkness) has dramatic impact on your ability to attract multiple audiences.

While I love the musical *The Sound of Music*, I always felt that it had two separate tonalities that were never reconciled. The beginning and middle of the story have a playful quality that all audiences can appreciate. But the end is dark with Nazi youth, Nazi sympathizers, and a Nazi takeover. Playfulness drains from the story completely and never seems to come back. The story starts off like *Mary Poppins* and ends like *Casablanca*. I don't mean to diminish the true life events upon which the musical is based, but to my ear, the story's tonal quality is neither balanced nor blended. It's split. The first tone is playful and for all family members and the second is more for adult sensibilities. It's a jarring shift. I realize that the intent might have been to show the disparity in Austria before and after the Nazis took over, but I get whiplash every time I watch it. Story-wise, I think a tonal blend would have been better than a stark division. Tell me I'm wrong. Some people do.

Tonality can also apply to the type of humor. By layering your entertainment with physical slapstick loved by younger audiences and more sophisticated wit and sarcasm appreciated by older audiences, you are apt to appeal to both.

Stylistic Execution: To reach a broad audience, it's also important to use a stylistic approach that young and old can appreciate. There are various styles such as traditional animation (e.g., *Beauty and the Beast*), computer animation (e.g., *Shrek/Rango*), performance capture (e.g., *Avatar*), clay animation and stop motion (e.g., *Gumby/Chicken Run*), and live action.

Traditional, computer, and clay animation *tend* to skew toward younger audiences because of their fanciful style, unless the story also contains themes that many adults can appreciate (*Shrek*) or there are matters of life and death (*Finding Nemo*) or the material is raunchy and therefore more suited for older audiences (*South Park/Celebrity Deathmatch*).

Live action *tends* to work across the board because it suits adult sensibilities yet is relatable to kids.

Performance capture is a newer approach and has tremendous potential because it makes fanciful characters and environments look exceedingly real. The characters on the planet of Pandora in the film *Avatar* moved and expressed as real beings would. This technique bridges the divide between fantasy and reality and makes it highly relatable to all ages.

A "blended" stylistic execution is also used to entice different ages providing that the basic story appeals to the sensibilities of both. This occurs when animation, for example, is used in combination with live action. This was splendidly achieved in the 2007 hit film *Alvin and the Chipmunks*. The story is based upon an older animated series. The film uses animated chipmunks and popular live-action stars including Jason Lee. It connects stylistically with younger and older audiences because it uses both animation and live action. The added enticement for adults is that the characters are ones they knew when they were children (nostalgia). It was distributed by 20th Century Fox and made $361 million worldwide. The 2009 sequel titled *Alvin and the Chipmunks: The Squeakquel* did $443 million worldwide. This demonstrates the power of good storytelling that also blends animation and live action.

This approach was used well by the 2007 Disney film *Enchanted,* which began in traditional animation until the heroine of the story (Princess Giselle) was banished into the live-action world of New York City. It earned about $340 million worldwide. In a 2011 film titled *The Smurfs,* the computer-animated Smurfs are transported (still in computer animation) into the live-action world of Central Park. The live-action stars include popular adult actors from highly popular TV series enjoyed by a broad audience, including Neil Patrick Harris (*How I Met Your Mother*), Jayma Mays (*Glee*), Hank Azaria (*The Simpsons*), and Sofía Vergara (*Modern Family*). The Smurf characters were also very popular for kids growing up in the 1980s, which makes them nostalgic for young adults and parents. The film grossed more than $500 million worldwide.

Creating entertainment with gender and age sensibilities in mind, executed in a tonality and style that bridges audience segments, is powerful.

Audience Insight #7: Create a Happy Ending

When trying to bridge the gulf that separates kid and adult audiences, always aim for the happy ending. Adults often prefer it. Kids need it. While adult entertainment can have sad endings for dramatic effect, don't make kids cry when they leave the theater.

That advice doesn't apply for a story's beginning and middle. Beginnings and middles often need to be sad. The implied death of Bambi's mother (shot by a hunter in *Bambi*) is important for story development. The same is true for the treacherous murder of Mufasa by Scar (*The Lion King*). When asked why a favorite character in the *Harry Potter Series,* Sirius, had to die, J. K. Rowling told the Edinburgh "cub reporter" press conference that "it is more satisfying I think for the reader if the hero has to go on alone and to give him too much support makes his job too easy, sorry."

These moments are critical for story development. They provide empathy for the character, demonstrate the threat, and set the height of the ultimate challenge. As long as there's a happy ending, all audience members can enjoy it.

A Blockbuster

The previous discussion of gender and age makes it clear that while the entertainment business thinks in terms of four quadrants, there are actually more slices than that. It demonstrates the immense challenge of developing a story that appeals to most segments. Yet it is done again and again by those who know how.

Disney's *Pirates of the Caribbean* franchise is a masterpiece. A pirate is an iconic treasure hunter that appeals to audiences young and old, male and female. It's a fanciful tale that is executed in an edgy, realistic way that bridges the age divide. Men and boys can appreciate the swashbuckling battles and aspire to be Capt. Jack Sparrow. Girls and women can appreciate the love story and live vicariously through the female protagonists. Kids can appreciate the physical humor. Older audiences also appreciate the more sophisticated wit. The casting is also a perfect pitch. Many males might wish to be Johnny Depp. Many females might want to date him. Like many successful franchises, it works on every conceivable level across audience segments, enticing the kid in all of us.

Some critics don't understand the appeal of this type of entertainment. In a June 2011 article, the *Los Angeles Times* noted, "Critics love to hate the *Transformers* films, but that hasn't kept audiences away. The second movie, *Revenge of the Fallen,* was rushed into production with a ragged script due to the 2007-08 Writers Guild of America strike and earned an abysmal 20% 'fresh' rating on the Rotten Tomatoes website, yet still became the second highest grossing film in the U.S. in 2009." I trust critics more often when they review purely adult-oriented fare like *The King's Speech,* but it's trickier when they review stories that are for the kid in all of us. You need the heart of a child to appreciate great blockbusters like these. Some critics don't have it.

These same general principles apply to *Star Wars, Indiana Jones, Avatar, Toy Story, Finding Nemo, Superman, Harry Potter, The Lion King, Shrek, Back to the Future, James Bond, The Lord of the Rings,* and many more. Each is a great adventure with stories and characters that connect with the sensibilities of various ages and genders.

You can do this too. It starts with the idea and then carries all the way through execution.

A Near Miss

I watch new films and new television shows for a career. I love them. I can often readily ascertain why some are successful across a broad audience. I can also detect why some only reach a narrow audience.

One of my favorite superhero stories is *Kick-Ass*. It started life as a comic book but was soon made into a film. It is a story about a painfully ordinary teenager who is tired of being bullied by neighborhood thugs, so he creates a superhero persona, complete with outfit, and goes to the streets in a heroic attempt to confront bullies and villains. I love this idea. I imagined how cool it would be if I had the bravery to do this. The film earned about $48 million in domestic box office and another $48 million in foreign box office.

Beyond the character of Kick-Ass, the other breakout characters are a girl named Hit-Girl and her father, Big Daddy. Their goal is to grab a big-time gangster. Hit-Girl and Big Daddy are ruthless yet tremendously heroic in their quest. The intense violence and foul language garnered an R rating for the film, preventing many younger kids from seeing a movie that had extremely empowering characters. Subjectively, I think the more graphic blood and guts scenes could have been dialed down, along with the excessive foul language, in order to garner a PG-13 rating, which would have made it accessible to a broader audience without losing a great deal of teens.

I can just hear the purists and fan boys screaming at me. "Keep it violent," they will say, "because that gives it grittiness and realism that it would not have otherwise." Maybe, but lots of teens saw *The Dark Knight,* which made more than $500 million at the domestic box office with a PG-13 rating. It maintained a gritty, dark feel but was accessible to a broader audience. *Iron Man* is another example; teens were perfectly content to sit alongside younger kids and parents. I believe that *Kick-Ass* could have nearly *doubled* its box office if it had just allowed for younger sensibilities. You heard me. Doubled! There's also some evidence to support this. In a 2010 study conducted by Brigham Young University, results showed that R-rated movies make 25 percent to 35 percent *less* at the box office than a similarly themed PG-13 movie.

My point is not about grabbing as much money as you can while screwing artistic expression. My point is that box office sales represent butts in seats. Those butts are attached to real people. Higher receipts equate to more people who are able to enjoy a well-told story. Personally, I think *Kick-Ass* could have been a true blockbuster in every sense, but it's a near miss in my book. And I'm one of its biggest fans.

Key Takeaway

To capture a broad audience in ways that touch the heartstrings in all of us, follow the seven Audience Insights:

- Audience Insight #1: Satisfy an Emotion Shared by All
- Audience Insight #2: Satisfy an Emotion Unique to Some
- Audience Insight #3: Select Broad Based Cultural Elements and Trends
- Audience Insight #4: Create Characters That All Audiences Can Identify With
- Audience Insight #5: Use Nostalgia to Connect Generations
- Audience Insight #6: Address the Sensibilities of Each Audience Segment

- Audience Insight #7: Create a Happy Ending

That's all there is to it. Oh, and if you hope to turn your entertainment into a huge franchise, you need to build franchise-type elements into your idea and execution. That's next.

Chapter 8

Build in Elements That Make It a Franchise

If you want your entertainment to become a huge franchise, you need to add specific ingredients while the project is still in development. But let's first discuss what franchises are and what they are worth.

There are different types of blockbusters. Some are Single-Event Blockbusters, which are essentially one shot occurrences. They might result in one big movie or one big book or one big toy. Done and over. Then there are blockbusters that are successful and open-ended enough to extend beyond their original introduction. These are franchises. I classify franchises into two basic types—Linear-Franchise Blockbusters and Multi-Category-Franchise Blockbusters (see Exhibit 31).

Linear-Franchise Blockbusters are on-going successes in their original category but are primarily limited to that category. A successful movie may spin off several sequels but never make a real dent in consumer products, publishing, or music. A novel may be profitable enough to lead to a book series but its characters never end up in the toy aisle. A video game may be successful enough to lead to newer installments but never make the jump to film. A toy might be successful enough to warrant line extensions in the toy category but never become a movie or book series. Each of these Linear-Franchise Blockbusters might dabble in the other categories, but in my definition, they never derive significant revenue from those other categories.

Multi-Category-Franchise Blockbusters are on-going successes that are capable of jumping from business category to business category in significant ways. A blockbuster toy successfully becomes a movie with sequels, a book series, and a line of video games. Or a blockbuster film easily jumps to toys, books, and back-to-school items. Or a blockbuster television show becomes a Broadway performance, a book series, a nationwide concert tour, and an apparel line. Rather than just dabble in different categories, Multi-Category-Franchise Blockbusters have revenues from nonorigin categories that often exceed the revenue derived from its category of origin. They are the blockbusters of blockbusters.

Exhibit 31: Franchise Types

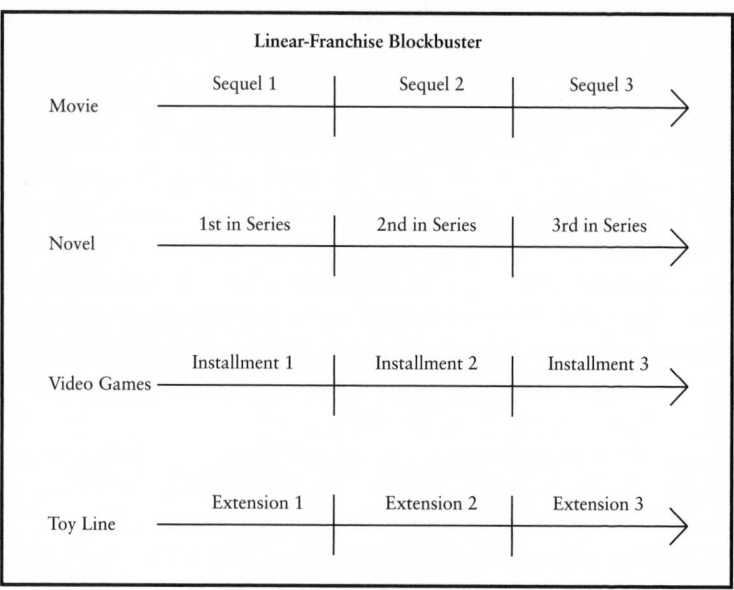

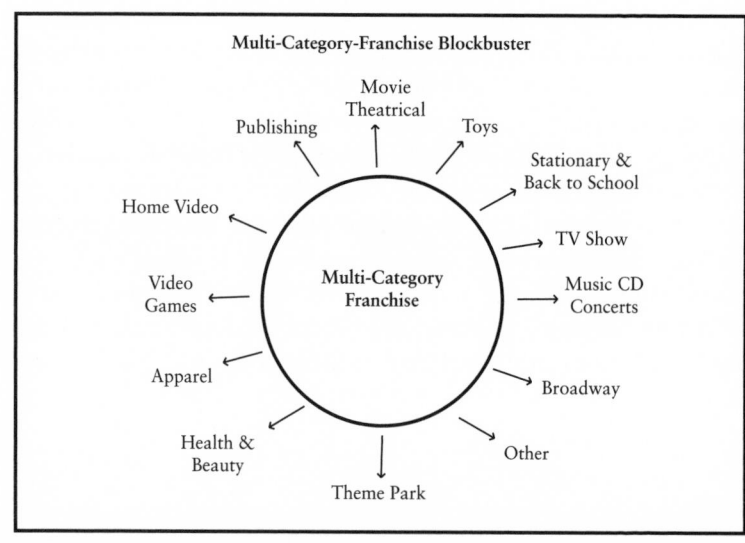

Franchise Worth

By adding elements that make your entertainment project capable of becoming a franchise, you greatly expand its worth.

The seeds of creating a modern franchise started many years ago with an unsurpassed creative genius named Walt Disney. He wore many hats over the years, including film producer, director, screenwriter, animator, voice actor, entrepreneur, and entertainer. One of his greatest creations attributed to himself and his staff was the iconic Mickey Mouse. He is one of the world's most recognizable characters and a Multi-Category-Franchise Blockbuster. Created in 1928, Mickey Mouse was introduced to the world with the release of the animated short titled *Steamboat Willie*. For audiences, it was love at first sight. The Mickey Mouse character continued on the big screen for years. As early as 1929, Walt Disney allowed the image of Mickey Mouse to be placed on writing tablets for a mere $300. With that, the idea of licensing entertainment-based properties was born. Over the years, Mickey Mouse has made his way to television, publishing, toys, apparel, theme parks, video games, and much more. The Mickey Mouse franchise is worth billions of dollars.

Despite the early success of Mickey Mouse and other Disney properties, many entertainment companies pre-1977 still did not put emphasis on creating and building franchises. There were some toys, games, apparel, and lunch boxes based upon kids TV shows and films, but financially it was often small potatoes.

The modern era of franchises began in 1977 with the introduction of *Star Wars*. Few believed that *Star Wars* would be a hit, let alone a franchise. Many studios passed on the project until 20th Century Fox picked it up. More importantly, George Lucas, the film's creator, wanted control of all rights to future sequels and ownership of all the merchandising rights. Thinking that sequel and merchandising rights were worthless, especially for a science-fiction picture, Fox agreed.

As George Lucas said in an interview for the Academy of Achievement, "I got the merchandising rights, which weren't anything at the time because there was no such thing as merchandising on movies."

Star Wars changed that. To everyone's dismay, the film sold merchandise. In 2010, Forbes reported that while *Star Wars* movies earned more than $4 billion in ticket sales worldwide, they generated an additional $20 billion in merchandise sales. That's not a typo. The merchandise sales from *Star Wars* toys, video games, apparel, books, and so forth reportedly generated about five times more sales than did the films, though this does not take into account revenue from the videos/DVDs.

Star Wars demonstrated that great stories were portable. Consumers wanted to wear it, play it, eat it, drink it, and even belong to it. Wearing a picture of Luke Skywalker on a T-shirt suddenly meant you were a part of something. It communicated a consumer's interest in a story and a character. It became a badge.

Advancing technology and the ability of stories to cross business categories has accelerated the growth of Multi-Category-Franchise Blockbusters. According to Elie Dekel, president of Saban Brands,

> We are living through a time of hyperkinetic change in terms of entertainment and the nature of how we spend our leisure time. Audiences are changing behaviors faster than ever before. Now, it's about instant access, wireless, on-demand, sharing, posting, blogging and choice, all in the hands of the consumer. It's an entirely new paradigm that will never devolve to its former state. Looking forward, content creators and marketers need to think and act in a transmedia universe. Stories and mythologies must flow seamlessly from one platform to another. Storytelling is no longer linear, but rather it becomes immersive and experiential to its audience. For content creators, the challenges are greater than ever, the bar has been raised and re-shaped.

In a 2011 speech to Disney investors, the chief financial officer of the Walt Disney Company, Jay Rasulo, demonstrated the difference between what the company considers a franchise versus one that is not. The very successful 2010 *Alice in Wonderland* film drove about $1.6 billion in ultimate retail sales, with most of that coming from the film. That's quite impressive. However, the 2010 film *Toy Story 3* not only drove worldwide box office to about the same degree as *Alice in Wonderland*, but it resulted in far greater retail sales derived from merchandise across various business categories. Disney expects ultimate retail sales for *Toy Story 3* to be nearly $10 billion through the traditional film channels and ancillary markets. That gives *Toy Story 3* about six times the retail success of the extremely successful *Alice in Wonderland*. That's the power and potential of a Multi-Category-Franchise Blockbuster.

Exhibit 32 shows the top ten most successful movie franchises as of August 21, 2011, using worldwide box office receipts as the barometer (not adjusted for inflation). *Harry Potter* is at the top with eight films and worldwide box office of $7.54 billion. *James Bond* is second, followed by *Star Wars*, *Pirates of the Caribbean*, and *Shrek*. While the dollar figures shown are only for box office receipts, each of these is also a Multi-Category-Franchise Blockbuster that has impressive sales across multiple industries.

Interestingly, most of these did not start as films. *Harry Potter*, *James Bond*, *The Lord of the Rings*, and *Jurassic Park* started as literary successes. *Batman* and *Spider-Man* started as comic book successes. *Pirates of the Caribbean* started as a successful theme park ride at Disneyland. *Transformers* began life as a toy line. Only two of the top ten began as movie successes; *Star Wars* and *Shrek*. If we looked deeper into the list we would find *Star Trek* and *Mission Impossible*, both of which are based upon TV shows.

The point of this is that where you start doesn't matter. Where you have the potential to go does.

Exhibit 32: Biggest Movie Franchises (As of August 21, 2011)

Film Franchise	Number of Films	Worldwide Gross Box Office (rounded in billions)
Harry Potter	8	$7.54
James Bond	23	$5.07
Star Wars	8	$4.41
Pirates of the Caribbean	4	$3.72
Shrek	4	$2.95
The Lord of the Rings (Peter Jackson)	3	$2.91
Batman	8	$2.64
Transformers	3	$2.59
Spider-Man	3	$2.50
Jurassic Park	3	$2.07

Source: Nash Information Services, LLC, permission granted

As of August 21, 2011, some films above are in theaters and accumulating receipts.

(Note: The numbers are not adjusted for inflation)

Exhibit 33 shows the retail value of entertainment/character-based merchandise in 2010. The total is a staggering $10.63 billion. Top categories include traditional toys/games, video games and software, accessories, apparel, and then publishing. It demonstrates the potential for those franchises that are able to jump (be licensed) across categories. It also identifies the key business categories to consider as you are creating and developing your entertainment idea.

Baby Steps and Risk

Often, no one knows for sure if a new novel, film, TV show, or toy/video game will be a franchise until after it is first introduced. So they take baby steps. If the entertainment is successful in the category in which it is born, then executives gauge consumer

Exhibit 33: Retail Sales of Entertainment/Character-Based Merchandise, By Product Category, U.S. & Canada, 2010

Category	2010 Retail Sales (in billions)	2010 Share of Market
Toys/Games	$2.99	28.10%
Video Games/Software	$1.24	11.70%
Accessories	$0.92	8.70%
Apparel	$0.85	8.00%
Publishing	$0.80	7.50%
Stationery/Paper	$0.56	5.30%
HBA	$0.45	4.20%
Gifts/Novelties	$0.39	3.60%
Food/Beverage	$0.37	3.50%
Infant Products	$0.37	3.50%
Consumer Electronics	$0.33	3.10%
Footwear	$0.31	2.90%
Furniture/Home Furnishings	$0.29	2.70%
Domestics	$0.27	2.50%
Housewares	$0.22	2.10%
Sporting Goods	$0.20	1.90%
Other	$0.09	0.80%
Total	$10.63	100.00%

Source: The Licensing Letter, permission granted.

interest in a second offering in that same category (Linear Franchise). If they dipped their toe in other business categories like consumer products and that was successful too, then more will be considered (Multi-Category Franchise). If the second round looks promising, then the licensing machine really cranks up. Of course, filmmakers look for promotional partners as a way to defray costs for even the initial efforts, but partners are harder to come by without in-market proof of success.

The *Diary of a Wimpy Kid* franchise took baby steps. It was first published as a Web comic online, which eventually led to a book series. When that proved successful, a movie was produced which also did well. But was the film capable of a sequel? As the general sales manager for 20th Century Fox, Bert Livingston told the *Los Angeles Times* in March of 2011, "When you make a sequel, you don't know if it's going to be a franchise. But when the sequel opens bigger than the first film, and you gross in the first three days more than it cost you to make the movie, you've created a franchise."

There are cases, however, when a new film might get the Multi-Category-Franchise Blockbuster treatment the first time around. That is often related to the strength of the idea and the track record of the studio backing it. Even in these situations, tie-in partners are very cautious to give full support. Big promotional partners often require a movie's release date to be guaranteed, but release dates often shift, which leads to concern. This is particularly true since many partners have a long lead time to produce goods prior to a film opening. Toys and video games, for example, often need to begin development before the movie is even shot. This is one reason why toys and video games stemming from blockbuster films have an uneven record. They must be innately appealing in their own right, independent of the film they stem from.

To reduce risk, many entertainment executives want a "readymade audience." A studio might prefer to make a movie based upon a best-selling novel than to create a wholly new story of its own. It's less risky, though even successful books are typically read by only 10 percent or so of movie-going audiences. The strength of the concept matters more.

Risk also comes with exorbitant expectations. Merchandise sales for *Star Wars: Episode I—The Phantom Menace* were reported to be one-third of what was hoped for. Yet it still achieved $1 billion in merchandise sales, a great success by any measure other than grandiose expectations.

A franchise stops being a franchise when consumer interest falls. Once again, we see that the consumer is at the center of it all. Then what, exactly, do audiences want? We come full circle again. They want a deeply emotional experience that touches the kid in all of them. Without a deeply emotional experience, they won't read the next novel, see the next film, buy the next toy, or play the next video game. Hence, they won't turn your entertainment into a franchise.

Six Key Ingredients for Blockbuster Franchise Success

In total, there are Six Key Ingredients that executives can build into an entertainment project that will help it attain franchise status. These Six Key Ingredients probably account for 95 percent of all Multi-Category-Franchise Blockbusters. Key Ingredient #1 is required of all successful blockbusters. The remaining ingredients will turn a single blockbuster hit into a blockbuster franchise.

- Key Ingredient #1: Craft Entertainment That Satisfies Audiences' Deep Emotional Needs
- Key Ingredient #2: Include a Theme or Story That Is at Least Minimally Open-Ended
- Key Ingredient #3: Create Characters Worth Emulating
- Key Ingredient #4: Make It Vastly Playable
- Key Ingredient #5: Create Fanciful, Exciting Environments
- Key Ingredient #6: Include Unique Iconography

Each category of business (film, TV, toys, video games, publishing, apparel, etc.) has different dynamics and will therefore use these ingredients differently. Each industry is also a fortress onto itself. It's very difficult for a novel to bust through the fortress walls of a studio to become a movie. It's hard for a toy or a TV show to burst into the fashion industry to become a line of apparel. But it can be done.

Ann Andrade is a seasoned expert when it comes to translating films into merchandise, as she has done for some of the world's biggest franchises. According to Ann, "Entertainment properties are like shiny, sparkly objects that attract your immediate attention. One key to success, once consumer interest is piqued, is to create the need to bring a piece of the experience home. This can be accomplished by incorporating moments or elements from the entertainment property itself into the merchandise to drive purchase intent."

These Six Key Ingredients can help. They will allow a novel to take over the movie industry or a film to dominate the toy aisle or a TV character to infiltrate the apparel category.

Key Ingredient #1: Craft Entertainment That Satisfies Audiences' Deep Emotional Needs

This has been the topic of this book from the start. Unless the entertainment makes a strong emotional connection with the intended audience, it will fail and never be successful enough to become a blockbuster, let alone a Linear Franchise or a Multi-Category Franchise. That's why I have repeated these elements across chapters. They are that important. In summary, the basic needs we all need to satisfy include safety/ survival, love and belonging, esteem, and self-actualization. Satisfying these basic needs provide a sense of fulfillment, discovery, and excitement. When you add the variations contained within these along with compelling characters audiences care about, it's easy to see why franchises are so successful. Batman allows audiences to feel the triumph of conquering evil. Indiana Jones allows us to be adventurers. Barbie allows girls to fancifully fulfill their dreams to be models, doctors, and pilots. Bart Simpson makes us feel mischievous.

Importantly, deep emotional drivers have the power to travel between categories. If your movie makes your audience feel as if they triumph over evil, that emotional reaction will often transfer into a book series, video games, and a toy line. If your TV show makes women feel beautiful, that can transfer into fashion and beauty aisles of a department store. Emotions move with the consumers who posses them. They walk around with them down every aisle of every line of business. Your entertainment can go with them, in multiple forms, provided you satisfy deep needs in the category of origin. The more apt the entertainment is at satisfying emotions we all share, the broader the franchise can ultimately become.

Key Ingredient #2: Include a Theme or Story That Is at Least Minimally Open-Ended

The original theme or story needs to be open-ended enough to allow for at least a couple more versions within the same category, such as when a movie has a sequel. This helps Single-Event Blockbusters become Linear-Franchise Blockbusters, which are capable of adding sequels within their category.

Story-wise, that often means keeping the characters alive at the end of the first tale. It's an obvious point but worth pointing out. It is harder (but not impossible) to make *Romeo and Juliet* or *West Side Story* into a sequel since the characters we loved in those stories died. Think hard before you kill off your protagonist!

There are several ways to take advantage of open-ended stories. The Shrek series created a "life cycle." In the first film, Shrek and Fiona meet, fall in love, and get married. In the second film, evil Prince Charming tries to break up their marriage. It doesn't work. By the fourth film, Shrek and Fiona are raising triplets until Rumpelstiltskin alters reality and Shrek finds himself without a family; he gets his loved ones back in the end. In this way, the sequels allow you to progress through the "open-ended" lives of the characters you enjoy.

Another way to take advantage of open-ended stories is to use the Bigger Bad formula. This is often reserved for action and horror films. The belief is that the next villain needs to be more evil than the last one to gain interest. Or at a minimum, the new villain needs to be more interesting. This accounts for the vast array of villains in the comic book universe. Horror movies take advantage of this approach. The level of terror and body count often increases with each sequel. This works for teen audiences. Horror films are ripe for the creation of strong Linear Franchises. They are also relatively less expensive when compared to many other blockbusters, thus increasing their profit margins.

The Greater Riches formula keeps audiences interested. This is used in adventure stories like *National Treasure*, *Pirates of the Caribbean*, and *Indiana Jones*. Upping the ante on the size of the booty/reward can get audiences' attention. As long as there are greater treasures to be found and more daring events to recover them, the overall story remains open-ended.

Another way to take advantage of open-ended stories is use of the Saga. This is a story that arcs over several sequels or books. *The Lord of the Rings* and *Harry Potter* are prime examples. You need to read the whole book series or see all the films to discover how the bigger story ends. These work best when each segment has its own beginning, middle, and end within the larger story so that the audiences feel they have at least reached a milestone with the latest installment. This is risky because if an installment doesn't do well enough for the series to stay financially viable, the series is dead in the water. I call it "storious-interruptus." This happened when NBC cancelled the series *Heroes* after four seasons. The show was about normal people who discovered they had extraordinary powers. When the series ended, the story arc wasn't complete. It left the audience hanging. Rats!

Prequels are rather new, but they can work very well. George Lucas went forward with several sequels to *Star Wars* and then threw the arc in reverse. The prequels allow us to see how it all began. A prequel only works if the original story is a success and if there's a fascinating back story (mythology) created that is worth telling.

Creating an entire universe of characters and stories will make the franchise more open-ended and immensely more valuable. The Avengers is a team of superheroes in the Marvel Comics universe. The team originally consisted of Iron Man, Thor, Ant-Man, Wasp, and Hulk. Captain America and others came soon thereafter. By creating a universe of characters and associations, it allows for an endless number of stories. For the movie venture, the studio first released individual films for key Avenger characters (Hulk, Iron Man, Thor, and Captain America) to familiarize audiences with them. They plan to merge the characters together in *The Avengers*, scheduled for a 2012 theatrical release. More characters with more individual stories and merged narratives lead to a massive franchise. In fact, they lead to a franchise brand hierarchy; individual heroes like Thor support the hierarchy from below, leading to the grouping of *The Avengers* on the next tier alongside other groupings like *X-Men*, leading to the global Marvel franchise/brand at the top. Each enhances the image of the other.

The 2011 film *Puss in Boots* is a character spinoff from *Shrek*. Character spinoffs are a successful way to take advantage of an open-ended universe. The packaged goods industry calls these line/brand extensions. In the entertainment world, they are very powerful franchise extensions. They come from being open-ended.

There are other ways to create open-endedness. If it's a toy, for example, the open-ended nature of the fantasy will allow children to imprint just about anything upon it. The Bratz doll can be a fashion model one moment and a rock star the next. It's simply a matter of the new story being told. Toys that make the leap to the big screen need storylines that are not only open-ended, but also big enough to fill the screen with enough excitement and adventure to capture a broad audience. *Transformers* comes to mind.

Because film-based franchises introduce sequels a year or two apart, the revenue derived from them is cyclical, having peaks and valleys with each movie's rise and fall. This is different from other franchises, such as Mickey Mouse, that have a large, even flow of revenue year-round. Each type of franchise is valuable when managed properly. Keeping them *Ever-Cool* will be the topic of a later chapter.

One caution: while keeping a story open-ended can help set up a sequel, it is important to avoid doing it in a way that damages the current project. Christopher Nolan, the writer/director of *The Dark Knight*, stated in an interview with IGN, "I said a lot about *Batman Begins* and it was genuinely the truth, is I don't think in terms of sequels. I think in terms of making this film the best film it can be and the most complete film it can be." Along those lines, the original Romeo and Juliet characters in the classic tale needed to die at the end of the story. It was meant to be a tragedy. Had they not died, I doubt we would remember the tale. Tony needed to die at the end of *West Side Story*. Jack needed to die at the end of James Cameron's *Titanic*. They just had to. That was right for each narrative. Tear jerking.

But if achieving an open-ended tale can make both the current project successful while setting up the sequel and perhaps even a larger universe, do it.

Key Ingredient #3: Create Characters Worth Emulating

Most blockbusters are derived from characters that audiences care enough about to want to emulate. Examples include Superman, Harry Potter, and Luke Skywalker. As I mentioned in chapter 5, we live vicariously through these characters. Audiences feel triumph when characters triumph. We can relate to their personal stories. Audiences often fantasize about walking in a character's shoes, both figuratively and literally, for several reasons.

Audiences sometimes admire a character's attitude and personality. This might include coolness (James Bond), sweetness and innocence (Cinderella), mischievousness (Han Solo), empowerment (Mulan), and even grumpiness (Shrek). Audiences want to reflect those same personalities on their T-shirts, lunch boxes, posters, video games, and toys. In this way, great character attitudes and personas travel from business category to business category.

Audiences sometimes admire a character's possessions. Have you ever wanted Luke Skywalker's light saber or Cinderella's glass slipper or Harry Potter's wand? Role-play toys are important because they allow children (and adults) to emulate the heroes they aspire to be. Key character possessions are not just important for merchandise, but first and foremost, they are often integral to story and character development. Their importance in the story allows character possessions to travel across business categories.

Audiences sometimes admire a character's distinctive look or design. Fashion lines have been themed to the design/look of various TV series including *Sex and the City*, *Gossip Girl*, and *Lizzie McGuire*. Real life celebrity-inspired fashions are plentiful, including those from Jessica Simpson, Elizabeth Hurley, and Mary-Kate and Ashley Olsen. Reports are that Lady Gaga may be thinking of starting her own clothing line.

In some cases, audiences don't want to emulate the look as much as they just love the design. These are design-driven franchises as opposed to media-driven franchises. Strawberry Shortcake started as one of these. Owned by American Greetings, Strawberry Shortcake was originally used in greeting cards. Her ultra-cute appearance then helped the character jump to posters, a toy line, apparel, video games, and onto television. Hello Kitty is another prime example of a design-driven franchise. Great character looks/designs travel from fashion category to fashion category with surprising ease.

There is a dramatic difference in potential between entertainment that has enticing characters and entertainment that does not. While the Etch A Sketch, Hula Hoop, and Frisbee are blockbuster toys, they cannot easily jump into other business categories because they have no character persona, possessions, or look that audiences relate to. Their potential to expand is diminished.

As these examples attest, the desire for audiences to emulate the characters they love is powerful. No matter what category of entertainment business you start in, you must give serious attention to whether your idea can be supported with a story and characters. If you don't, you are limiting the potential of your idea. I am often invited to toy colleges so that students can "pitch" their toy ideas to me. My number one comment is typically: "It could be a great toy, but you need to add a story with aspiring characters that can turn it into a great franchise."

Some products just don't fit the character/story mold. That's okay. Some shouldn't. Yet I'm surprised at the number that could have, but didn't.

Key Ingredient #4: Make It Vastly Playable

Multi-Category-Franchise Blockbusters contain elements that are highly *playable*. By *playable,* I mean they inspire the development of toys and games to *play,* music to *play,* and even books to *play/read.* When developing stories, writers need to give attention to how their narrative can be adjusted so that it provides a foundation for *play.* This gives entertainment the depth and breadth it needs to explore tangents leading to multiple categories of business.

In the toy and game category, this is not just about emulating a character as mentioned in Key Ingredient #3. This is about *playing* the *narrative.* While it might look to adults that kids are playing with *Star Wars* toys, they are really playing with *Star Wars* stories! Action figures, for example, allow kids to both reenact the good vs. evil story embedded in the films as well as to create their own personalized narratives. Millions of *Star Wars* toys have been sold as a result. Kids are playing *Star Wars* far more than they are watching *Star Wars.*

The most prominent toy and game play pattern is good vs. evil, which probably accounts for the bulk of toys/games sold within franchises. Stories that connect with a girl's desire for mothering/nurturing or beauty/glamour have a large potential as well. Other key play patterns include speed/racing, mastery, creating, and sports.

Toys aren't just for kids. The *James Bond* franchise has sold plenty of cars. The *Star Wars* franchise has sold lots of upscale light sabers to teens and adults. In April of 2011, the *Los Angeles Times* ran a headline that read, "Quidditch still sweeping U.S. college scene." Quidditch started as a fictional sport in the *Harry Potter Series* played by wizards and witches while flying on broomsticks at Hogwarts. These young adults grew up on the Harry Potter story, and they are continuing to "play" Harry Potter even as they age.

Play can also enter the food category. The *Harry Potter* franchise sold lots of Bertie Bott's Every Flavour Beans, sweets with every flavor imaginable.

Great music is great storytelling. When done well, audiences will *play* the music to reexperience the emotional narrative. It's difficult to think of James Cameron's *Titanic* without thinking of the song *My Heart Will Go On* performed by Celine Dion. The lyrics are haunting and speak directly to the tragedy of the narrative. ("Near, far, wherever you are. I believe that the heart does go on.") The story and song blend into a powerful emotional experience. The song triggers thoughts of the movie. Thinking of the movie triggers thoughts of the song. They are part of the same whole. Brilliant!

Music has driven the narrative in a wide variety of works from films starring Elvis Presley and the Beatles to more contemporary works like *Beauty and the Beast, Toy Story,* and *High School Musical.* The most recent success cited in earlier chapters is the TV show *Glee.* The characters do not sing songs at random. The songs are specifically selected to emphasize an emotion or event that is relevant to the characters' lives. The music-based themes allow franchises to jump to CDs and concerts.

Reading is *play* for those who love it. If the original entertainment is enticing enough, audiences will want to read more. That may include reading more stories, reading narratives in different styles (e.g., storybook, comic book, graphic novels, and standard novels), reading about happenings behind the scenes, and reading more about the cast. Many consumers have spent more time reading *Star Wars* than they have watching *Star Wars.*

If the story is crafted in a way that leads to play patterns, an emotional music treatment, and/or added narratives, audiences will come to play. It will lead to a Multi-Category-Franchise Blockbuster.

Key Ingredient #5: Create Fanciful, Exciting Environments

The environment you choose for your story is critical to franchise potential. Unique, fanciful, and exciting environments lend themselves to toy environments, theme park rides, parades, books, etc. *Star Wars, Harry Potter,* and *Pirates of the Caribbean* all have enticing environments that added to the excitement of the story and translated well into merchandise.

My wife and I were just at Disneyland in California (yes, we go even without our kids). The rides are story-based because Disney is story-based. In the Indiana Jones Adventure ride, we journeyed through the legendary Temple of the Forbidden Eye in search of "unimaginable" rewards. And we got them; they included the thrills of being put in the role of treasure hunters as we experienced the dangerous environments that existed in the film. We emerged unscathed thanks to a last-minute save by Indiana Jones himself.

The unique world of Harry Potter set the stage for the introduction of the Wizarding World of Harry Potter theme park. Audiences who come to the theme park can have a pint of Butterbeer at the Three Broomsticks tavern, buy a wand at Ollivanders, or ride the Dragon Challenge, which is a high-speed roller coaster. That's total story immersion. At Star Wars Miniland at Legoland in California kids of all ages can experience a 1:20 scale version of the *Star Wars* world, complete with war machines and cityscapes.

Uniqueness of the environment is very important, because if you are lucky enough to create a franchise, competitive generic product will invade your turf. They will make their playthings as close as possible to yours without violating copyright. The more unique you can make your environments in the story, the better it will thwart competitive offerings on the toy aisle.

More importantly, compelling environments are not just about selling toy play sets. Primarily, they are about allowing audiences to escape to a different world. As Jerry Bruckheimer, producer of the *Pirates of the Caribbean* films, said in an article appearing on latinoreview.com, "I think people want to get out of their daily lives and they want to go to another place. Life can be pretty rough sometimes, so you want to be entertained and fantasy is a great way to forget about it all and live in another world."

Storytellers who create unique worlds help audiences to

escape. To relive the experience, audiences will revisit those worlds when they are re-created at theme parks, in play sets, on cruises, on Broadway, in video games, and on lunch boxes. Worlds build franchises.

Key Ingredient #6: Include Unique Iconography

Some blockbusters contain iconography that lends itself to merchandising. When that happens, audiences want to adopt the iconography for themselves. It makes them feel more connected to the story and characters.

Iconography refers to story- and character-inspired logos, character designs, environment designs, and so forth. You might recall the black and red T-Rex design from *Jurassic Park* or the skull and crossbones design from *Pirates of the Caribbean*. These elements are often displayed on clothing, stationery, posters, school items, and packaged goods. They are a way for audience members to say "Look at me . . . I love this story!"

The best iconography typically comes from the heart of the franchise. This might be a key figure in an action pose, a critical storyline moment, a memorable phrase, or a key emblem. Great icons remind you of what you loved about the entertainment. These are "triggers" that connect audiences to the greater whole. It's helpful when storytellers insert unique iconography. The inclusion of these items helps build franchises.

Six Key Ingredients for Blockbuster Franchise Success in Action

Intellectual property rights for Batman began in 1939 with the character's introduction in *Detective Comics* #27 (then called the Bat-Man). For the first several decades, this character (known at times as the Caped Crusader and the Dark Knight) appeared on early radio shows of the 1940s, in a 1943 film, in a live-action TV show in 1966, in an animated TV show in the 1990s, and in video games starting in 1986. Still, the Batman franchise was only simmering across these categories. It wasn't yet hot. It finally came to a quick boil as a Multi-Category-Franchise Blockbuster with the 1989 film titled simply *Batman*, directed by Tim Burton and starring Michael Keaton in the title role and Jack Nicholson as the Joker. It was served up in a realistic fashion and with a gritty tone. This made it relatable to adults (not childish) while providing a fanciful element of aspiration for kids (I could be Batman!).

The film's fundamental story pulled emotional heartstrings. Check. It had characters worth emulating. Check. The story was open-ended to allow for sequels. Check. The elements were vastly *playable* in other categories, including action figures and a soundtrack that included songs by Prince. Check. It had fanciful and exciting environments. Check. It had lots of unique iconography. Double-check.

The 1989 film raked in more than $400 million worldwide. The merchandise sold was estimated to be between $500 million to $750 million. That's a Multi-Category-Franchise Blockbuster. Some of the sequels slowed it down a bit. However, the tide changed with the 2008 film titled *The Dark Knight*. It earned more than $1 billion worldwide. The movie barreled through theaters like a runaway train through Gotham City. Explosive! Audiences wanted to see it, play it, drink it, eat it, and wear it. And they did, in massive numbers.

Pitch the Franchise, Not Just the Story

If you are a new screenwriter, toymaker, novelist, or video game developer, realize that the ideas you present to industry executives are among many dozens that they are considering at any one time. One of the criteria in the back of their minds is can this be a franchise? If they think so, they might then wonder if it could be a Linear- or Multi-Category-Franchise Blockbuster. Unfortunately, there are still some creators who pitch their ideas with little consideration of this. They don't often develop ideas with a franchise in mind. They give little attention to how their idea might be able to cross into different product categories, into different industry fortresses. That gives their project a competitive disadvantage. Entertainment companies want franchises. Multi-Category-Franchise Blockbusters are ideal because they maximize profits, build companies, boost careers, and increase salaries.

When entertainment companies hire me to evaluate ideas, I always address whether the idea has potential to become more than it appears. If I think the idea has merit to begin with, I attempt to find ways to refine the idea so that it can become the launch pad for a franchise. Can a storyline be added to the toy line so that it can easily become a book series? Can the lead character in a TV show be given a distinct fashion sense to lead to an apparel line? Can a musical component be central to the story idea so that it might launch music CDs and concerts? Is the idea just a movie or can it become a woman's lifestyle brand that will include apparel, fragrances, jewelry, and so forth. If you don't ask yourself if your idea can be a franchise at an early stage, somebody like me will do so later on. Guaranteed. So you might as well address it yourself. I once tested a TV show and one particular actress was extremely appealing to the audience. I turned to the executive producer and asked if she could sing. He smiled, as the idea had already entered his mind. "We're on it," he said. She's now a major pop star.

For Critics

Some consumers and consumer advocates complain about the over-commercialization of entertainment. The complaint sometimes focuses upon Multi-Category-Franchise Blockbusters. They cite that there is too much stuff being sold across too many categories. Crass commercialism!

I don't understand that argument. If you create a character in a novel that children love, why should we deprive them of the plush version of the character that they can hold at bedtime? If teens love a film, why should we deprive them of T-shirts that display their affection? If women love the fashions inspired by a TV show, why should we bar them from buying those fashions?

Audiences vote with their dollars. They pick a few winners and condemn lots of losers. They decide to what extent they wish to participate in the winners. Many times they do resist, and that's good because it sends a message to executives about the extent of their interest. The fact that audiences are willing to participate across categories is proof that the story is emotionally satisfying across categories and that it has value. We shouldn't apologize for that. We should celebrate it because most entertainment dies.

When to Say No

There is a time when executives must say "no" to requests for more merchandise. Once your blockbuster has established itself, companies will be coming from all directions to participate in its success. They will offer you cash to align your blockbuster with everything from laundry detergent and mouthwash to preschool toys and diapers. It's very easy to get caught up in it. This is especially true when a giant retailer (you know who) comes to you and says that if you slap your blockbuster's logo on a line of baby items he can move a million units and pay your company a fat fee. It can be very hard to turn down the short-term cash, but you want a blockbuster for the long term.

If the product isn't a natural fit with your brand's core idea, don't do it. There should be a natural link or it will dilute the meaning of your franchise.

If by catering to one audience you alienate another audience, don't do it. For example, if by adding your entertainment's logo on preschool toys and apparel you risk tarnishing the blockbuster's cool image among older tweens and teens, beware.

If you risk saturating the market with too much of your franchise, don't do it. Audiences burn out quickly. Some believe that in the television world, the show *Who Wants to be a Millionaire* is an example. It had very high ratings so the network decided to run it multiple times a week. Ratings fell. Other successful shows have taken a less aggressive route to prevent overexposure. It reduces wear out and keeps the ratings high.

Keeping a blockbuster's image strong for the long term may mean turning down easy cash today. The story is more important than the fast deal. As vice president and publisher of *Kidscreen* magazine, Jocelyn Christie has a front row seat to the immense licensing and merchandising world. Billion-dollar bets are placed each year in hopes that dollars are chasing potential blockbusters. Jocelyn very astutely states that with opportunity comes caution. "Too many times, producers get caught up on the licensing and merchandising and market potential of a project and forget that at the heart of the most successful entertainment franchises, there have always been great stories, well told. Great stories market themselves and naturally find ways to resonate with their audiences beyond the screen. So as the backbone of all hit properties, they warrant serious investment of passion, expertise and care during the creative process."

One Last Big CAVEAT

It's hard to create a franchise, and most films, novels, toys, and video games will never become one because they were not meant to be. If you have a great idea for a film and jamming more content into it to create a toy line destroys its integrity, then don't do it! Keep it pristine. I understand and respect that. More non-franchise entertainment gets produced than franchise entertainment. My intent is to help you create, not destroy. To my knowledge, *Home Alone* didn't sell a vast array of different merchandise nor did the film *The Breakfast Club*. Yet each provided endless hours of audience enjoyment. We need those.

Key Takeaway

As you craft and develop your entertainment idea, keep in mind the Six Key Ingredients that can turn it into a blockbuster franchise.

- Key Ingredient #1: Craft Entertainment That Satisfies Audiences' Deep Emotional Needs
- Key Ingredient #2: Include a Theme or Story That Is At Least Minimally Open-Ended
- Key Ingredient #3: Create Characters Worth Emulating
- Key Ingredient #4: Make It Vastly Playable

- Key Ingredient #5: Create Fanciful, Exciting Environments
- Key Ingredient #6: Include Unique Iconography

Next up, as you continue to develop your idea, you need to resolve common problems of execution.

Chapter 9

Fix Common Execution Problems

We have come a long way in this book. We have discussed how to craft ideas for entertainment that satisfy audiences' emotional needs, how to align those ideas with culture and trends, how to add relatable and aspiring characters, how to mix in sensibilities to widen the age and gender appeal, and how to plant the seeds of a franchise. But before you finish the screenplay or novel, there are a couple more things to discuss.

One of these is how to avoid common problems of execution. Like other knowledge I provided thus far, my insights regarding elements of execution come from the point of view of the audience. When discussing the execution of entertainment, the opinions of thousands of consumers over the years are in my head. They have told me what they like and what they don't like. Sometimes they are turned off by the story's premise. When that happens, they often don't arrive at the theater at all or they don't turn to the new TV show. If the premise excites them enough to participate, sometimes they are disappointed with the way the entertainment was crafted.

All writers struggle with these issues. I certainly did while writing my two young adult novels. The first novel was lucky enough to receive a starred review in 2004 from *Booklist,* the publication of the American Library Association. The sequel received the Young Adult Choices Award by the International Reading Association in 2008. The effort needed to hatch an idea for the novels and then to pound them out in several hundred pages each was daunting. I had to stay on track with my story arc at all times. I needed to create characters that were relatable and aspiring while slowly evolving the central protagonists so that they could transform emotionally and physically in dramatic ways to meet their ultimate challenges. I had to be sure that each character's persona was different enough from others to create sparks that fed the larger story. I had to make the threat of evil believable. I needed to insert key plot points that pushed characters in directions that readers would not expect. I had to keep challenges for the characters coming so that readers would continue to turn pages. Finally, I needed a hugely satisfying emotional ending. That was a lot of "I's," because writing a novel is a solitary process. It takes a lot of work. A couple readers said that they cried at the end of my books. I hope that was a positive thing.

I've also researched and consulted on many TV shows, films, toy lines, and video games. Many did quite well. Some became blockbusters. I know that the task before the creators is no less daunting than writing a novel. Sure novels are longer and require more pages. But while screenplays require fewer words, each scene in the script has a much larger load to carry. I could develop the characters in my novels over many chapters. The screenwriter often has to do it in one or two scenes. I envy the screenwriters for the fewer pages they write, but I don't envy them for the enormity of the task.

Despite all the work writers put into their projects to get the story, characters, and elements of execution right, it's impossible to make them perfect. Painfully for writers, audiences tend to catch the imperfections.

In a study conducted specifically for this book, we asked four hundred people across the nation what, if anything, they do not like about the movies, TV shows, and books they have seen or read. Audiences picked five key criticisms as shown in Exhibit 34: lack of relevance, lack of action/excitement, lack of humor, complexity (confusing), and lack of uniqueness. Most failure is a direct result of these five horsemen of the narrative apocalypse. Other items on the list like "It was just stupid" and "it was too long" are often a result of one or more of the aforementioned issues. The upside is that "lack of uniqueness" is one of the least of audience's complaints, suggesting that while audiences find most entertainment to be different enough, they don't always think they have enough relevancy, action, humor, and/or simplicity. This chapter will tackle each criticism and how to avoid it.

Exhibit 34: Audience Entertainment Dislikes	
Dislikes	**Total Nationwide Sample (Males and Females Ages 8 to 55)***
Relevancy Issues	
Didn't interest me from the start	44.5%**
Characters not relatable or aspiring enough	22.8
It's more for someone else	22.0
Action/Excitement Issues	
The story was boring	59.3%
It was too slow	46.8
Not enough suspense	33.8
Not enough action	32.8
Humor Issues	
Not funny enough	38.5%
Complexity Issues	
Too confusing	33.3%
Uniqueness Issues	
Not different enough	16.8%
Characters not different enough	14.0
Other Issues	
It was just stupid	50.3%
It was too long	31.5
Characters didn't conflict enough	13.3
Not extreme enough	10.3
None of the above	7.0

*Sample size equals four hundred

**Percent of respondents who have this complaint about stories they have seen/read. (Limited number of responses allowed. See appendix for complete list by audience segment)

Source: 2011 Study of blockbuster entertainment, conducted by C+R Research, Chicago, Illinois, exclusively for the book Creating Blockbusters!

Criticism #1 (Lack of Relevancy): *"It really didn't interest me. It was more for someone else."*

This seemingly gentle rebuke kills entertainment. This complaint is shared across genders and ages (see appendix). This stems from audiences not buying into the premise and/ or not finding a relatable or aspiring character they could identify with. This statement is often followed by *"It's more for kids"* or *"It's a chick flick"* or *"My boyfriend might like it"*—death for any entertainment project that was hoping for a broader audience.

This criticism speaks directly to the insights provided in the last couple of chapters. Rather than repeat everything we learned, here's the summary. In order for the fundamental concept to be relatable and aspiring to as broad an audience as possible

- Emotionally, go big or go home (chapter 3)
- Theme the story with relatable, broad-based cultural elements and trends that impact us all (chapter 4)
- Develop characters in ways that give different audience members entry points for them to relate to and/or aspire toward (chapter 5)
- Add sensibilities that appeal to both genders and across ages (chapter 7)

Sometimes the concept is broad and appealing, but the execution is disappointing. When this is the case, I hear, *"I thought it was going to be good* [from the advertising], *but I was disappointed."* This means that either marketing threw audiences a curve ball by promising something the story did not deliver or that the execution did not fulfill the story's premise. Chapter 10 will discuss marketing. Assuring good execution will be addressed throughout the rest of this chapter.

Criticism #2 (Lack of Action/Excitement): *"The story was boring . . . too slow . . . not enough action."*

When audiences state that a story is boring, it could easily be due to a concept that is not able to support an exciting execution. So while this complaint could be related to the first criticism regarding a lack of relevancy, I classified it as a lack of action/excitement because it is sometimes difficult to differentiate concept from action when applied to boredom. Regardless, it's obvious to state that stories need action, yet I have conducted research on entertainment that didn't have any, at least in the opinion of the audience. When that happens, I'll hear comments like

"Boring!"
"Nothing happened."
"I got up and left."

This complaint is heard loud and clear across all audience groups (see appendix). Action keeps audiences at the edge of their seats. We've all walked out of movies, turned channels, and left novels half read when we've lost interest. It's only getting worse because audiences are getting pickier, particularly when it comes to action. They have seen so much amped up action sequences in recent years that the bar is set high. It's hard to surprise these days. Yet the kid in all of us demands it.

If there were awards given for surprising, innovative action sequences, I would give it to the *James Bond* franchise. Every movie begins with a bang, a sequence that always seems to elicit the response, *"Wow, I never saw that before."* My favorite scene is in the film *GoldenEye* when Bond narrowly escapes from villains by riding a motorcycle off a cliff to reach a pilotless plane that is in a nosedive. He freefalls and catches up to the plane, reaches the controls, and then pulls it up. As a research guy, I think to myself, "Gee, I wish I had tested that film. I would have loved to hear the audience cheer." As a novelist I think, "Gee, I wish I could have come up with something as unique for my books, darn!"

Many types of action excite audiences. The elements you use will depend on the story you are telling, but it's not unusual for multiple devices to be utilized in one narrative. Across all of these devices, the audience must perceive the character's goal to be important, and the risks to himself and others must be great. Here are the action-oriented themes that audiences respond well to.

A Ticking Clock: Audiences loves stories in which time is running out and our heroes must rise to the occasion to save the girl or the city or the world before it all ends. Fleeting time adds pressure for the protagonist. This was inherent in the blockbuster television show *24*, a series in which the hero had twenty-four hours to save the world. Each episode represented one hour in the twenty-four-hour period. You could hear the clock ticking, literally. Tick-tock. You could feel the sands of time spill to the bottom of the hourglass as a terrorist planted his bomb. Tick-tock. Every moment mattered because the prospect of bad things happening was always close. Tick-tock. Heroes had to run to save time. Tick-tock.

When there's no time pressure, characters tend to meander and suspense falls precipitously. I am surprised at the number of stories I've read that could have had a ticking clock but did not. They wandered.

An Engaging Battle: This is what we usually think of when we think of action. Guns, bombs, sword fights, light saber battles, racing cars, bows and arrows, knives, rocks, blowguns, pea shooters, whatever. This type of action tends to be more preferred by a male audience, but that's minor compared to other related issues.

Importantly, the battle is not an end in itself. It's not enough to add a grenade to make audiences cheer. What makes audiences applaud is the ultimate triumph of a hero that they love and feel intense empathy for. The intensity of the battle is important only insofar that it signifies the enormity of the risk to the hero. The fighting, like all elements of execution, should not overpower the story. Rob Marshall, director of *Pirates of the Caribbean: On Stranger Tides,* told the *Los Angeles Times,* "The idea was absolutely to distill what is best about the franchise and concentrate on that. The effects should work in service of the story too, not the other way around."

In most cases, audiences don't appreciate far away battles as much as they prefer those that are close up and personal. A bomb dropped from afar is not as satisfying, story-wise, as is hand-to-hand combat in close quarters. Male audiences want to feel that they are a part of the battle. They want to see their enemy's eyes. It makes the story feel more real. This was very much achieved in the film *Saving Private Ryan,* so much so, that it was rated R. The concept is still viable for all audiences when executed in less bloody fashion, such as in *The Karate Kid.*

Belief That the Hero Could Die: What often keeps audience at the edge of their seats in action films is the belief that the hero (or his loved ones) could die! They must believe that the storyteller is crazy enough to kill him. If the audience thinks to themselves, "Don't worry, he can't die," then it lessens the emotional satisfaction. Yes, we want a happy ending to attract the kid in all of us but don't let the audience know that. If the hero's challenges are light, if the risk is not great, or if there's no doubt that the hero will live, then big explosions don't matter.

A brilliant scene in *Star Wars* is the moment when Obi-Wan Kenobi is apparently killed by Darth Vader. That moment did two critical things. It transferred the mantel of responsibility to young Luke Skywalker so that he was now tasked with carrying the burden. It made us wonder if he was up to it. Importantly, that scene also indicated that the creator/writer George Lucas was willing to kill one of his great heroes. Crap! If he could write the obituary for Obi-Wan, then even Luke Skywalker wasn't safe. He could kill him off too and turn the responsibility over to Princess Leia. Killing off Obi-Wan Kenobi gave us doubt. The doubt told us that no character was safe, which heightened the risk and raised the suspense. It made us worry for young Skywalker. Obi-Wan Kenobi is brought back spiritually later on, but we didn't know that at the moment of his demise.

In my first novel for young adults, *The Pearl of Anton,* I had demons kill off a couple school boys in the first few chapters. They were acquaintances of my hero. An editor was initially concerned about the intensity of the scene. I explained that I wanted the reader to know that the threat was real, and what better way to demonstrate that threat than to show my hero's school chums being skillfully slaughtered. The scene stayed in. Near the end of the tale, I took another page from George Lucas and had my hero's mentors get killed in a massive battle right before he had to face the Big Bad. Ultimately, they connected again spiritually to create the happy ending the readers deserved. I learned from the greats.

Related to the last point, the villain, whether he's a demon from hell or a category 5 hurricane, must at first be far more powerful than the hero. The audience must think to themselves, "Our hero is toast!" The film *Finding Nemo* would not have been as fulfilling if the threats were not greater than the protagonist. Tragedy creates sympathy. Evils that are bigger than the hero make for risk and empathy. That's the fun of watching the protagonist increase his or her abilities just in time to meet the final challenge. In the video game world, the biggest bad is always left for the final level. If not, why bother?

The realism of the life and death struggles doesn't apply to those films that are primarily comedic. Audiences know that Austin Power's life is not really in dramatic jeopardy, but they should have doubt for whether Agent K in the first *Men in Black* film (played by Tommy Lee Jones) will make it out of the alien's belly after he's swallowed. They should wonder if Nemo will really make it back home before being eaten (*Finding Nemo*). That's great storytelling.

Great Character Relationship Friction: For many stories, you don't need bombs or life and death moments. Characters and their interpersonal conflicts are action. *The Taming of the Shrew* is action, derived from fast wit and a battle of wills between a man and a woman. *The Social Network* is action, stemming from a legal clash between intensely intelligent schoolmates that speak at light speed, which in turn makes the audience try to catch up. The TV show *Gilmore Girls* accomplished this as did *The West Wing*. Their fast, relationship-driven dialogue was mental gymnastics for audiences. When done well, relationship-derived action is no less impactful than physical battle. *When Harry Met Sally* is a romance comedy and not an action film, but the growing, fun intensity of the characters' relationship gives it action nonetheless.

A couple years ago, my wife and I were strolling down the streets of Rome, Italy. We heard a car screech to a stop. We turned and saw a beautiful Italian woman dash from the passenger's door, race around the car, and then drag a man out of the driver's seat so that they were face to face in the middle of the road. She began to loudly assault him in Italian. People on the sidewalk froze, their mouths gapping open. Traffic backed up. Car horns blared. My wife and I did not understand the language, but we knew this guy really screwed up somehow, and she was telling him exactly how. We were sure that it had nothing to do with his driving skills. For what seemed like five minutes, she screamed and beat him senseless with her voice. The poor bastard slumped at least five inches, eventually making him far shorter than she. Her eyes suddenly flashed with victory. Triumphant for reasons I'll never know, she disappeared back into the passenger's side where she had emerged. The battered man slithered into the driver's seat and they drove away. They left a dozen tourists glancing at each other, smiling and bewildered. Traffic resumed. That was action, and she never laid a hand on him. My point: you don't need a car to explode to get attention, but you do need a crash. That was a doozy!

The one caveat I will mention relates to kid audiences. Children under age thirteen get more out of physical action than verbal action. I have tested a lot of shows meant for kids, and if dialogue stretches for more than a minute without action to accompany it, it can be death. This is especially true among boys. I have watched them in focus groups begin to fidget after thirty seconds of dialogue. After a minute, they might be under the table. If they had been at home in their natural habitat, they would have left the TV completely and started playing video games. However, dialogue shouldn't be short-changed. It advances the story, reveals important information about our characters, ignites character clashes, and adds wit and sarcasm that older kids and adults appreciate. But too much dialogue in films slows storytelling and puts younger audiences to sleep and a lot of older ones too.

Suspense and Surprises to Keep Them Guessing: The action elements cited above are part of the ingredients that make for suspense and surprise. The writer's objective is to make the audience wonder: Will the clock run out? Is the hero really in danger? Will my beloved heroine die? Is he up to the challenge? Will the relationship explode? The more you keep audiences guessing, the more you add surprises, the more the audience likes it. "I am your father!" said Darth Vader to Luke Skywalker in the epic *Star Wars*. That was a showstopper. Audiences want to *guess* where a story is headed, but they don't want it to be so obvious that they *know*. I have seen trailers at the theater where I could tell the beginning, middle, and end of the story. I didn't waste the money to actually see the whole film.

Criticism #3 (Lack of Humor): *"It Wasn't Funny. It Was Stupid."*

If there's one criticism I have heard often for comedies that disappoint, it was that they were not funny enough. Audiences want a belly laugh. I'm not talking about a muted chuckle. I'm talking about a roar. This is most true among younger audiences (see appendix). I've not only witnessed the difference in theaters for years as you have, but I've observed audiences from behind one-way mirrors as they watched new films and TV shows in a research setting. Most blockbusters give them a belly laugh. In an earlier chapter, we discussed adding the type of humor that works for various ages and genders, but we will delve deeper into this now.

Audiences will often describe the level of humor in various degrees,

- *"It was hilarious. I couldn't stop laughing."* This is the gold standard.
- *"It was sorta funny."* This is a polite way of saying they wanted more.
- *"It didn't have any funny parts."* This means that there

was either no humor at all (perhaps it wasn't intended as a comedy) or that humor was intended but wasn't recognized. I hear this a lot when writers for children's shows insert mainly adult wit that goes right over kids' heads.

- *"It tried to be funny but it wasn't. It was just dumb."* Ouch! The writer got caught. The audience could identify the scenes that were supposed to be funny, but they didn't think they were.

The negative responses often mean that the humor didn't meet the sensibilities by age or gender. Perhaps it didn't have enough physical humor for all audiences or enough sophisticated humor for older audiences or enough testosterone comedy that males appreciate or enough relationship-driven humor that connects with female sensibilities.

Other times the humor is just too common (been there, done that). Writers need to remember that by the time a child is about ten years old, they have seen ALL standard gags. ALL! There is no audience more accustomed to comedies than kids. This is because they receive a steady diet of it from the time they are preschoolers watching *Sesame Street*. The last two decades have also witnessed an explosion of highly popular comedies for tweens, especially on Disney Channel and Nickelodeon. Comedy Central and MTV have followed with their own brand of extreme comedies (and dramedies) for teens and young adults.

By the time audiences reach adulthood, they have been thoroughly saturated, making it difficult for writers to get them to crack a smile. Still, it happens. There's a special class of comedies that gets high praises for the way the humor is executed. When this happens, I often hear, *"It was hilarious; some parts were so dumb that it was funny."*

Several R-rated films have accomplished this, including *The Hangover, The Hangover: Part II,* and *Bridesmaids.* Young males put the TV show/movie *Jackass* in this category. Earlier films such as *Dumb and Dumber* did well and were available to a wider audience due to a PG-13 rating.

Getting a belly laugh often requires including extremely stupid or evil characters that do extremely stupid things, or extremely horrible things happening to extremely nice people. Sometimes those things, like in the case of *Jackass*, are dangerous. It's like watching a comedic train wreck. You know these idiots are going to crash, and it's going to hurt, and you shouldn't be encouraging them by watching, but you just can't look away.

The choice of reaching a young male audience like that achieved by *Jackass* or a broader adult audience such as *The Hangover* goes back to the earlier discussion about the devil's choice. As applied to humor, it reads as follows: If you choose the type of humor that appeals mainly to one segment (say male teens), then your humor has to be so emotionally satisfying to them that you can justify ignoring the other 75 percent of the planet. Alternatively, if you try to be funny to three or four quadrants representing 75 percent to 100 percent of the potential audience, then you need to craft the humor that is well layered to entice young and old, male and female, without being watered down to most. That's the choice. Pick your comedic devil.

But capturing a broad audience with humor is very doable. Senior marketing strategist Monika Salazar sees this as a benefit of astutely crafted humor. "Laughter! This is an oldie but goodie. Laughter is still the best multi-generational medicine and presents family co-viewing opportunities."

Here are some suggestions when executing humor. Whether you are trying to be funny to one segment or many, the same hints often apply.

Go Extreme: A lot of humor I research tends to be too cutesy and mild. It gets brief smiles instead of laughs. It needs to be pushed to extremes. A writer-producer took me out to lunch to get free advice (I often provide ideas in exchange for a burger and fries). He asked me how he could improve his show for a male audience. Among other things, I suggested that the humor needed to be extended into the realm of crazy. I mentioned that in another show I just saw, two guys took a turn too fast and tumbled off their motorbikes, rolling to a stop on the pavement. The intent of the scene was to make the audience laugh but it failed. Audiences have seen that before, so it's not all that funny. I said that the scene should have been extended into the absurd. The guys should have been tossed over a railing, down an embankment, and tumbled head first into a massive, stinking, fly-infested pile of cow dung. That's funny, but I'm not done yet which brings me to the next item.

Go Mega Gross: For a male audience, gross works. I could extend the above scene further. When the guys raised their heads in unison from the dung, the cow should have peed in their faces. For a male audience, that's a belly laugh moment. Still too common? Perhaps one of the guys, say the stupid one, licks the pee from his lips and proclaims, "It's yellow, but it doesn't taste like lemonade!" You might think that this would turn off female sensibilities. Maybe not. The blockbuster film *Bridesmaids* (rated R) included a scene in which the bride to be, unable to control an oncoming bout of diarrhea, suddenly squats in the middle of a busy street in her bridal dress and poops. As this is happening, one of her bridesmaids throws up on the head of another bridesmaid. The female crowd around my wife and I roared.

Go Mega Embarrassing: It's funny when the world witnesses the character's misfortunes. Still using the scene I created, once the guy gets peed on, he should look over and realize that the woman of his dreams was watching all along with ten of her friends. The guy should make a half-hearted wave in an ill-fated attempt to save the situation, but the cow then steps on his head and pushes it deep down into the dung. End of scene. This isn't just funny. The embarrassment builds empathy for our protagonist, making his eventual triumph all the more satisfying. The diarrhea scene from *Bridesmaids* would not have been as funny if the bride to be had squatted in the restroom instead of the busy city street where all could see.

Go Gender Combatant: The battle between genders is timelessly funny. For a reason I won't bother to explain, many women find it hilarious when mischievous, egotistical males "get what's coming to them." This accounts for the success of many family comedies where the slightly mischievous husband's plans are foiled, leaving the wiser and more responsible wife to gloat. I know it's formulaic, but years of TV ratings tell us that the formula works. The trick for future entertainment is to find unique approaches. The formula was best achieved by the 1950s television sitcom *The Honeymooners*. It featured the long-suffering, responsible wife Alice Kramden and her more irresponsible, always-with-a-scheme husband Ralph Kramden. Their clash of opposite personas is hilarious. Interestingly, men loved it too. They can feel superior to the Ralphs of the world in the same way they can feel superior to Homer Simpson of today.

So back to the earlier example I came up with; it's even funnier if the guy who is face down in the cow dung had earlier insulted the woman he was trying to impress. In that case, female audiences will think that the guy "had it coming."

Go Painful: We like to see characters get hurt. Comedy is pain inflicted upon others. As long as it is not us, it is funny. This is especially true when the pain is extended, such as when an extremely stupid, clumsy character falls down a mile-long flight of stairs and into the street. "I'm fine" he yells to his friends as he staggers to his feet and brushes himself off, smiling. Then a bus plows into him and tosses him out of view. It's been done, but it still surprises. Funny.

Don't Just Beat Rivals, Humiliate Them: It's satisfying when a rival gets what's coming. If you can humiliate that rival in the process, it's hilarious. This entails publically stripping the villain of his or her dignity or anything that he or she holds dear, including respect, recognition, status, fame, glory, riches, power, control, masculinity, femininity—oh—and clothes. Naked is funny.

Yank That Fish Out of Water: Funny happens when characters are put into environments they are unfamiliar with. Examples include a mom who switches bodies with her daughter (*Freaky Friday*), a boy who becomes big and goes to work for a toy company (*BIG*), or a man who dresses up like a woman (*Tootsie*). In each case, these characters were yanked into a different world. Unfortunately, in many fish-out-of-water stories, the change is too subtle and so the distinction isn't as hilarious. To get the most out of the situation, the switch has to be great.

Make Sure Your Characters Have True Opposites: As mentioned in chapter 5, a lot of humor can be mined when opposite personas clash. These include the intensely smart character who must suffer the insanely dumb one, the overly responsible person who must suffer the overly irresponsible one, and the eternal pessimist who must suffer the eternal optimist. When humor isn't working in the entertainment I am testing, it is sometimes due to a lack of opposite personas.

Don't Shoot Too High: Sometimes writers are way too clever. Their scripts are filled with lots of sophisticated wit, sarcasm, and subtle satires but little else. While many adults will appreciate that type of humor, it doesn't create belly laughs, nor does it connect with younger audiences. None of us is too high and mighty that we can't laugh at extreme physical humor like when a bride poops in the middle of a busy street. As mentioned so many times throughout this book, your entertainment needs to have a good dose of both physical humor and sophisticated humor. Many classic cartoon characters have a wonderful balance. Bugs Bunny engages in lots of physical humor. All audiences love that. However, Bugs Bunny also spouts lots of wit and sarcasm that older audiences can appreciate. This is known as the two-fer. One character that uses two types of humor to capture two audiences.

Don't Take Your Story Too Seriously, Even if the Core of It Is: Audiences sometimes tell me that while a particular action adventure film is great, it could have used some humor. It is human to want moments of laugher even during the rough patches of our lives. The same philosophy applies to entertainment that audiences will love, if for no other reason than it lightens the mood. One of the most memorable scenes in *Raiders of the Lost Ark* occurs when a crowd parts and

Indiana Jones, whip in hand, finds himself facing a huge, sword-swinging warrior. You might expect a sword/whip fight. Instead, a battle weary Jones nonchalantly pulls his revolver and casually plugs him. It was witty and physical all at once. Hilarious. It also gave insight into the character; he doesn't always feel the need to "play fair." Disney films often use characters for comic relief in those movies that carry more serious storylines. We get to laugh at the antics of Timon and Pumbaa in *The Lion King*, while our main protagonist, Simba, can attend to more serious matters of growing into manhood, accepting responsibilities, and reclaiming his rightful place in the circle of life.

Funny matters. Audiences are disappointed when the story lacks the kind of humor that they appreciate. Using the right blend can capture them all.

Criticism #4 (Complexity): *"It was too confusing. I couldn't follow it . . . too complex."*

Some stories are just too complex. They have too many twists and turns. This complaint is more often cited by younger audiences, but it is still voiced by older audiences as well (see appendix). Sorry to say this, but most people don't want to think when they go to the movies, watch television, or read novels. They want to escape. There are exceptions, such as murder mysteries or entertainment with storyline puzzles (e.g., the film *Inception*). Other than that, too many breadcrumbs leading in too many directions is just painful for many audiences. This happens in television shows when the storylines become too complex and people get *Lost*. The double meaning was intended. *Lost,* the television series, was a phenomenal success because of the premise and mystery. It also won numerous awards. Nevertheless, complexity of storyline may have resulted in a drop in interest. The first season of *Lost* averaged a reported 15.69 million U.S. viewers per episode, whereas the final season had an average of about 11 million U.S. viewers per episode. Despite the drop, the ratings were impressive to the end. However, the ratings still dropped. When storylines become too complex, some viewers just give up. New viewers may be hesitant to join in because there is too much backstory to catch up on. The key is to add just enough complexity to draw audience interest, but not so much that audiences turn away.

Criticism #5 (Lack of Uniqueness): *"It wasn't different enough. The characters weren't different."*

This criticism is the least of audience's complaints. That's good news. This indicates that storytellers are doing a wonderful job overall of creating differentiated stories and characters. Creating differentiation may appear to be difficult since there are a limited number of plots, character archetypes, and genre to use. But as I demonstrated in chapter 6, there are millions of combinations of these elements that can bring fresh perspectives to familiar narratives. If you are looking to create greater differentiation from earlier works, here are some popular ways to do it. Some of which were referenced in earlier chapters.

Change the Protagonist's Demographics: Lara Croft is a female archeologist/adventurer much in the mold of Indiana Jones. The gender difference between the two leads to vastly different associations. The same gender-switching approach created differentiated stories for amateur detectives, Nancy Drew vs. the Hardy Boys. Differentiating characters by age creates immensely different storylines for Superman vs. Superboy.

Change the Protagonist's Psychographics: The soft-spoken character of Colombo in the 1970s TV detective series of the same name is much like the soft-spoken detective Monk in the 2000s TV series *Monk*, except that Monk is racked with endless phobias (Achilles' heel). That difference leads to vastly different storylines and personal associations. The alien in *E.T.: The Extra-Terrestrial* was sweet and gentle, yet the alien in the movie *Super 8* was vicious and deadly (until we discovered that he was just a misunderstood protagonist).

Change the Antagonist (Plot Conflict): The narrative in

both *Jaws* and *The Perfect Storm* includes men being tested at sea. The difference in antagonists (shark vs. storm), among other things, leads each story down a very different path.

Change Era and Locale: Disney's *Pocahontas* and James Cameron's *Avatar* both used a love story amidst a backdrop of native peoples being encroached upon by a more advanced society, but the stories are separated by eras and locales. When combined with other differences, this leads to a vastly different feel. Eras and locales also create differentiation via the cultural components they feature.

Change Genre: As mentioned in chapter 6, *James Bond* as an action adventure is *Austin Powers* as a comedy. *James Bond* as an action adventure is the TV show *The Wild, Wild West* as a western. The change in genre propels the narratives down different paths.

Change Exceptional Style/Tone: The 1960s series *Batman* was a light, tongue-and-cheek version of the *Batman* franchise. The later films encompassed a more realistic, darker, and edgier style/tone. Among other things, the Duke Nukem game added humorous sarcasm, which helped it to stand out among the other strictly serious games.

Change Character Needs: The movie turned TV series *Kung Fu* was about a Shaolin monk who is a martial arts expert striving for enlightenment while coming to the American Old West to seek his half-brother. The film *The Karate Kid* is about a boy who needs to learn karate to prevent being beat up, though he learns a bit about enlightenment along the way.

There are other ways to create more uniquely differentiated entertainment options, but those cited above are the most common. Importantly, you might have noticed that each of the above examples changed several elements, not just one, to help aid differentiation. The more factors you adjust, the more different your story and characters will become.

The Action/Comedy Combo Plate

The amount of action and comedy that any given story possesses will be dependent upon the genre and aim of the narrative, so trying to ascertain the "best" balance doesn't make much sense here. Many times your story will be primarily action with some humorous beats, or it will be a comedy with some action or dramatic beats.

There is great benefit in trying to attain the combo platter; these are stories that have a splendid balance of action and comedy. The original 1997 film *Men in Black* is one of these. This is the story of two agents who monitor aliens in New York City while trying to prevent them from blowing up Earth. It was a blockbuster hit with a wonderful balance of action and comedy. Another combo blockbuster was the 1984 film *Ghostbusters*. This film is about New York City parapsychologists who discover a way to trap ghosts, and they do so to save the world from a coming apocalypse. Both films had action and adventure via battles, a ticking clock, heroes at risk, a world in jeopardy, and lots of different types of comedy that appealed to younger and older sensibilities.

Action and comedy are two powerful elements that, when seamlessly combined, are bigger than the sum of their individual parts. Many blockbusters have been born from them.

Game Play Execution

If your career is in the video game world, the advice throughout this book is the same but different. It's the same in that the story idea, the characters, emotional needs, and motivations all apply. So do the trends and cultural issues discussed in earlier chapters. Those insights can provide a wealth of knowledge to help you create and develop video games.

The video game industry is different because it provides something to audiences that other storytellers cannot—the ability to give its audience ultimate control! In many games, audiences "live" the story by becoming the characters. They are the warriors, princesses, elves, and trolls. They can customize their character's appearance. They make decisions that impact consequences that change the course of their *personal* story. No other medium has been able to approach this. It's pure story empowerment.

Developing a video game is also different from other story mediums because the narrative needs to be seamlessly integrated with game play. This includes not just story elements like heroes and villains, but all of their powers, weapons, enchantments, and environments. Cinematics and cut-scenes are integrated into the game to set up the storyline and push it along, but not so much that it takes from game play. Dialogue is used to move the story as well. Too little dialogue and the player won't have enough information. Too much dialogue and the player will get antsy to get back to playing the game. It takes a lot of skill and aspirin to get right.

Keeping the gamer engaged is more difficult than in other mediums. The storyteller needs to create a larger set of challenges, plus add rewards, punishments, and minor villains (level bosses) leading to the biggest villain (end boss). It's the same mounting suspense and excitement found in novels and films, but it's far trickier because these elements need to be integrated. If the game play is too easy, audiences get bored. If it's too hard, they get mad. It's like writing a novel while trying to balance the character's weapons on the tip of your nose.

Where is all this heading? For those of you who are fans of the TV franchise *Star Trek: The Next Generation,* you are familiar with the ship's holodeck. It's a virtual-reality room where a fantasy world engulfs you. You can eat, drink, battle villains, and save damsels in distress within the confines of a room that simulates your fantasies. You can pull your simulated sword, smell the dragon's breath upon your cheeks, and be burned by the heat of his intense fire. You can run and never touch the sides of the room because of a virtual treadmill. The total emersion makes it feel real. Maybe it is. Maybe that's where you are right now. Spooky.

Structure

Story "structure" provides the roadmap for the tale you are telling. When done well, the structure is critical as a means to grab the audiences' attention and to keep them engaged through the story's set up, the protagonist's challenges and conflicts, and finally the resolution. Though this chapter was not about story structure, I do want to provide some great resources for you to consider:

- If you are a screenwriter, I highly recommend *Essentials of Screenwriting* by Richard Walter of UCLA. It not only includes the nuts and bolts of effective screenwriting, but it provides keen insights into the entertainment business in general. You should also read Syd Field's *Screenplay: The Foundations of Screenwriting*. I also like the "beat sheet" approach to structure from screenwriter Blake Snyder in his book *Save the Cat! The Last Book on Screenwriting That You'll Ever Need*.
- If you are a novelist, I like *How to Write a Damn Good Novel* by James N. Frey.
- For fiction writers of children's books, I recommend *Writing Fiction for Children* by Judy K. Morris.
- For help in creating and structuring all types of drama, I really like *The Dramatic Writer's Companion* by Will Dunne. It has a lot of great advice and exercises.
- If you're looking to make audiences laugh, I suggest reading *What Are You Laughing At?* by Brad Schreiber. It not only provides a framework for creating comedy, the book itself is funny.
- If video game storytelling is your thing, I recommend *The Ultimate Guide to Video Game Writing and Design* by Flint Dille and John Zuur Platten. You'll appreciate the talent needed to integrate story and game play.

Despite all of the advice given in this book and others, challenges still creep into storytelling, especially in those venues that require film. These challenges include problems with financing, nuances of screenwriting, casting, acting, direction, cinematography, sound/music, and editing. It's a wonder that any piece of entertainment achieves blockbuster status. Though these topics are beyond the scope of this book, I thought it worthwhile to add a quote from someone who knows the challenges well. While discussing one of his latest films, Steven Spielberg told the

Hollywood Reporter, "The thing about filming is, [almost] everything goes wrong. It's using the parts that go right in the finished film that counts."

Key Takeaway

Generating a great idea is one hurdle but bringing it to life is even more daunting. There are so many ways to blow it. Here are some hints to combat audience complaints.

Criticism #1 (Lack of Relevancy): *"It really didn't interest me. It was more for someone else."*

Solution: Emotionally, go big or go home. You should theme the story with relatable, broad-based cultural elements and trends that impact us all. Develop characters in ways that give different audience members entry points for them to relate to and/or aspire toward. Add sensibilities that appeal to both genders and across ages.

Criticism #2 (Lack of Action/Excitement): *"The story was boring . . . too slow . . . not enough action."*

Solution: Add a ticking clock. Make the physical battle engaging, close up, and personal. Make audiences believe that the hero could actually die. Create intense character relationship friction. Add suspense and surprises to keep audiences guessing.

Criticism #3 (Lack of Humor): *"It Wasn't Funny. It Was Stupid."*

Solution: Be surprising. Go extreme. Go mega gross. Go painful. Go gender combatant. Go mega embarrassing. Don't just beat rivals, humiliate them. Yank that fish out of water. Make sure your characters are pit against true persona opposites. Don't shoot too high by being too clever. Don't take your story too seriously, even if the core of it is.

Criticism #4 (Complexity): *"It was too confusing. I couldn't follow it . . . too complex."*

Solution: Untie some knots and reduce the number of twists and turns. Focus on the big ones.

Criticism #5 (Lack of Uniqueness): *"It wasn't different enough. The characters weren't different."*

Solution: Alter the protagonist's demographics,

protagonist's psychographics, nature of antagonist, the era and locale, the genre, the style/tone, and/or the needs of the character (protagonist or antagonist).

Consider the action/comedy combo plate, which gives audiences a taste of both. They find it yummy because they don't have to sacrifice action for humor or vice versa.

Now that you have beaten the bugs out of your entertainment, there are some final elements you can add to make it more *marketable*. When done well, you will have created *marketable artistry*. That's next.

Chapter 10

Create Marketable Artistry

The entertainment that you create is your artistry, be that a novel, a movie, a TV series, a toy, or a video game. Extremely successful artistry is created in ways that makes it marketable to a broad audience. It's what I call *marketable artistry*. This helps people who eventually have to *sell* your artistry do their job well.

Richard Walter, professor and screenwriting chairman at UCLA's famed film school, put it this way, "Throughout the millennia audiences have demonstrated an uncanny knack for finding the worthy stuff. This is not to suggest that all popular movies are good and unpopular ones bad. I'm simply saying that in order to last, movies need to succeed both artistically and commercially."

Marketable artistry leads to effective marketing that breaks through clutter and communicates an enticing message that motivates audiences to take action. That action might entail buying, watching, listening, joining, or playing. Effective marketing succeeds by shining a sparkling light upon the central premise of the entertainment, the execution that brings it to life, and the emotional satisfaction that audiences will gain if they participate.

When entertainment bombs in the marketplace, it's not uncommon for creators and executives to blame marketing. Others blame the entertainment. Depending on the circumstances, one or both might be right. More often than not, in-market failure is often a result of a suboptimal product that wasn't marketable enough.

First, Get the Product Right

Many years ago when I was working at an advertising agency, the team was summoned to a meeting with a client's marketing director. He flew into the room, sat, and told the assemblage of marketing and advertising professionals that his new product did not research well among the target audience. He then said we had to figure out a way to sell it anyway. The team members glanced at each other with a knowing look. Sure, we can try to put lipstick on a pig, but in the end it's still a pig. We wasted too many resources trying to save it. It didn't work. It should have been killed, but sometimes politics get in the way of good business decisions.

In a different joint project with my client partners, we once conducted an analytical study to ascertain what factors led to in-market success. Many years of data were tossed into a computer to see which factor had the greatest impact. The most important factor was innate product/conceptual appeal. That factor was more important than advertising campaigns and media weight. That makes sense, since the advertising and media weight are simply means to communicate the product itself. It's very difficult for poor and mediocre products to be saved by great marketing. I'm sure there are cases, but it's rare. Unfortunately, millions of dollars are often wasted in an ill-fated attempt to save a movie, TV show, or toy that is conceptually doomed anyway. On the flipside, the best media professional in the entertainment business, Cherie Crane, tells me that "while great product sells itself, it's the tough ones where we are supposed to earn our keep." And she has.

Blockbuster entertainment is created in ways that makes it marketable. We will discuss how you can create *marketable artistry* momentarily, but first, to put this discussion into a broader context, let's discuss the marketing tools.

The Marketing Framework

Exhibit 35 is an extremely simplified framework of the key marketing tools and the role each plays in generating awareness, interest, involvement, purchase, recommendations, and repurchase. Though the four tools (publicity, advertising, consumer promotions, and viral marketing) can play any role throughout the process, I marked in black those roles they are most noted for each, in grey those roles that tend to be secondary, and left it blank for those roles that tend to be tertiary at best.

I worked in an advertising agency for seventeen years, so I realize that each marketing tactic can play all of these roles depending upon the circumstances. I also realize that there are tools not listed. I did this for brevity. The important point is that there are communication needs and marketing tools to satisfy them. It's also important that those who create entertainment keep these in mind during the creation process; that way the entertainment itself can be built with marketing in mind.

Publicity: The objective of publicity is to get beneficial editorial coverage and third-party endorsements, which gets people talking. This is often used to generate some early awareness and interest for the entertainment (create "buzz"). It can also lead to some involvement (audience active participation). I think it is less effective as a converter to actual purchase, generating recommendations from friends, or generating repeat purchases. It can do these latter things, but other tools often play more important roles. Publicity is also used for damage control when negative press is circulating.

Publicity does this by assembling intriguing facts and insights that will get attention from news media outlets and

Exhibit 35: Integrated Marketing Model						
	Pre-Sale			Sale & Post-Sale		
Tool	Awareness	Interest	Involvement	Purchase	Recommendation	Repurchase
Publicity	black	black	grey			
Advertising	black	black		black		grey
Consumer Promotions	grey	black	black		grey	
Viral Marketing	black	black	black	black	black	grey

eventually potential audiences. This includes developing press kits that hype the story, the cast, and interesting production elements. It also includes inviting journalists to visit the production sets, pitching behind-the-scenes events, setting up early screenings and celebrity interviews on key talk shows, and hosting parties for opinion leaders.

Publicity costs less than most other marketing disciplines but it is harder to manage once the news is "out there." At that point, professional critics, influential bloggers, and friends take over.

Advertising: Advertising is most often used to generate a lot of awareness, interest, and purchase. In that capacity, its role is to position the entertainment in the minds of the audience. Depending upon the message, advertising can stimulate active audience involvement. It is often used to stimulate added repurchases such to motivate audiences to see a film again (it happens), to buy the DVD, to buy deeper into a line (e.g., toys), or to keep participating in the series (e.g., novels, TV series). It is less well suited to inspire recommendations from friends.

Depending upon the business category of the entertainment, paid advertising venues include television (broadcast/cable), newspapers and magazines, radio, out-of-home tactics like billboards, in-theater signage and trailers, paid Internet advertising, and direct-response vehicles. TV advertising and in-theater trailers are particularly effective because the audio/visual abilities allow the medium to communicate the essence of a product/film in a way that radio and print cannot.

Paid advertising is often the five-hundred-pound gorilla in the room because it allows executives to reach a broad and targeted audience many times (reach and frequency). It, therefore, carries much of the burden for communicating the overall positioning and key messages. Advertising is also controllable, which is a big plus, and highly flexible, which allows marketers to change messages, media, and even target audience in response to market conditions. Because of these benefits, advertising remains the number one venue for audiences to hear about new products across most industries.

Consumer Promotions: Consumer promotional tactics include contests, sweepstakes, prizes, loyalty programs, tell-a-friend efforts, product placement, retail deals (two for one), and promotional tie-in partnerships. They are often carried via advertising vehicles and their role is very similar. Consumer promotions are ideally suited to increase interest, active involvement, and motivate purchase, but they can generate early awareness if the promotion is motivating enough.

Promotional tie-ins with other manufacturers are particularly important because they provide entry into other business categories. A studio may work with a restaurant chain to offer playthings for a kid's meal or with a retailer to provide cross promotions or with a packaged-goods manufacturer that will license a character for use on a box of cereal. Such alliances can easily triple or more the total size of the marketing budget because multiple companies are pitching in to sell the entertainment. The better the fit with the brand, the more the message extends.

Viral Marketing: This refers to a wide range of efforts to spread positive word of mouth via social networks, such as friends, clubs, and influencers, often by way of the Internet. This entails having a Web site that audiences can frequent, using rich display ads, sending e-mail blasts to enthusiasts, and providing items that friends can pass along such as trailers, images, and games. This type of marketing is complements of a digital explosion, which allows content and messages of all types to flow freely across the Internet. Viral marketing also includes sending cell-phone messages, buying up search words, and giving inside information to opinion leaders (e.g., popular bloggers) in hopes that they become evangelists that inspire the masses. The aim is to motivate a handful of people who will in turn motivate millions. That's social networking. Facebook, Twitter, and YouTube are prominent sites used to influence the spread of opinion.

This effort, like publicity, often begins long before paid advertising starts. Done well, viral marketing can lead to early awareness, interest, active audience involvement, purchase, recommendations to friends, and to some extent repurchase. Because social networking efforts can have many roles in the purchase process, it is becoming more critical. It's also cheaper than paid advertising, which adds to its allure. The downside to social networking is that it is uncontrollable and unpredictable; at some point, audience and opinion leaders take over the message, making it harder for marketing to hide a stinker.

I intentionally did not call these Internet-related tactics "new media," as it is often referred to. I hate that term. While the tools used to create social networks are new, the discipline is ancient. It's about getting friends to influence friends with positive word of mouth (now with clicks). "New media" implies something that is cool and sexy as opposed to old media (advertising, publicity), which conjures up images of aging horses being sent to glue factories. That image doesn't reflect the actual importance of more traditional media.

The role that each of these tools plays will differ by category, by the media habits of each campaign's target audience, and by specific market conditions, so please regard Exhibit 35 as a rough model. Ideally, all of these tools should be integrated to work together to achieve synergistic efforts. A TV commercial might communicate the key brand message and then send your audience to a Web site. The site might inform them of a consumer promotion and allow them to see the commercial that ran nationally. A consumer promotion might be a contest that requires the audience to find hidden messages in your commercials.

Marketing Insights

The brief review of the marketing tools provided a foundation for the real purpose of this chapter—creating marketable entertainment. After all, I assume that most of the people reading this book are interested in creating a Blockbuster Franchise that will march across the world much like Genghis Khan conquered Eurasia.

Think of the creator and marketer of entertainment as two teammates in a relay race. The creator of the artistry (e.g., movie, TV series, novel, etc.) begins the race and dashes around the track, his sights on the next runner (marketer). The marketer watches the creator's progress as he nears. Upon the creator's approach, the marketer begins to dash forward but not so much that the creator can't reach him. With ease, the creator hands the baton to the marketer who then sprints toward the finish line. In many ways, you should not be able to tell when one ended and one began. It should be a fluid process. The creator of the artistry should anticipate the marketing of the entertainment and build components into the entertainment that help sell it. This creates marketable artistry. The marketer should be aware of the elements early on and begin creating ideas to promote the marketable artistry.

Many times, prominent filmmakers have a very heavy hand in the creation of the marketing campaigns. The creator and the marketer are the same. Other times they are not. Battles between creators and marketers are legendary.

What follows are ten key marketing insights. They apply across all entertainment categories. The more aligned your entertainment is with these insights, the more likely it will become a blockbuster. These were constructed to help creators invent something that is marketable, as well as to guide marketers when selling entertainment to audiences. The first insight is the guiding principle.

Marketing Insight #1: Create Marketable Artistry

Great filmmakers, TV show developers, and toy designers intuitively create marketable artistry. They add elements to their creations that they know will be enticing and newsworthy. After all, who wants to create a piece of entertainment that only a couple thousand people will enjoy when you could create a piece of entertainment that millions across the globe will cherish.

But it's a balancing act. Entertainment needs to be "marketable" first and foremost for the story it is telling. Adding bits and pieces of other elements to make it more marketable can help but within limits so that the "artistry" is not weakened.

When I was with Ogilvy & Mather advertising, I worked with a very smart senior executive named Freddy Bee who managed the worldwide Mattel account. Freddy created a presentation he titled "Creating an Advertisable Toy." He did so because many times inventors would create complex storylines or features for toys that could not be communicated in a thirty-second television commercial. Freddy and I presented that document for years in an effort to help inventors think like marketers. We discussed building toys that satisfied core emotional needs and only adding those features and play patterns that supported them. It worked. Toys were better when they were more focused on big emotional drivers, with fewer superfluous bells and whistles. The eventual marketing efforts were streamlined and the benefits of the toys were more easily communicated. The toys were marketable artistry—a principle that works for all entertainment venues.

Creating marketable artistry is central and provides the basis for all the other insights that follow.

Marketing Insight #2: Create Artistry with an Audience in Mind

Anne Parducci is a stellar entertainment executive. She was a senior marketer at Mattel before becoming the executive vice president and general manager of family entertainment at Lionsgate. To her, great marketing is driven by powerful yet simple principles. Says Anne,

> I find that the most successful films and easiest to market are those where one can easily answer the following questions; Who is the film for . . . the consumer target . . . and does it deliver against that audience in terms of the genre, the story, the emotional experience, the casting, etc.? While that seems so elementary, I am always amazed by the number of films where the answer to these questions is not clear. Since the entertainment industry can often be deal driven versus consumer driven, we are often subjected to films where you scratch your head and wonder how they got financed and made. Create a positioning statement for the film, just like in traditional brand marketing. Ensure each element supports

that positioning and what appeals to the target demographic via their emotional needs. While that may not guarantee huge audiences, it will certainly allow the marketing team to create the best plan, impactful creative materials, and be most efficient with precious marketing dollars.

Great entertainment has a strategy. That strategy details who your audience is and what specific, emotional thrill ride you are going to take them on. This will not only help your entertainment become marketable artistry, it will provide a basis for subsequent marketing plans. A strategy should also include a well-articulated IP Story Idea if it is a film (chapter 6) that will detail the protagonist's challenges, his or her emotional journey, and the ultimate noble goal. The strategy might also include subplots that might be used to gain the attention of a broader audience.

Some companies define audiences by demographics alone: men, women, girls, or boys of a certain age. Then they will add genre. It might look like this; men ages eighteen to thirty-four who like action films. That's what led to the quadrant analysis in the earlier chapter. While the demographic/genre approach might be useful for films that are targeted to very specific segments, it is not the best approach for most blockbusters. The biggest blockbusters often transcend demos. They touch many of us emotionally. Because of this, it's often useful to define an "emotional target audience" as separate from a "media target audience." The emotional target audience is used to create the messages for advertising. The media target is used to select the vehicles to reach the demos that are expected to be interested. As an example, if a story is about a downtrodden character that has a chance to rise to greatness, the emotional target might be defined as *for all underdogs who need to feel empowered.* With that emotional target in mind, marketers will build empowering messages into the entertainment's positioning and ultimate advertising to make it marketable to that audience mindset. Hence, the way the audience is defined (by emotional needs) is aligned with the way the entertainment is positioned (by emotional benefit). That's likely to grab a greater audience than if the advertising team is thinking that their audience is men ages eighteen to thirty-four who like action films. The media team, however, can use the age/genre target to select vehicles for the audiences that might be enticed with the empowerment message. The emotional target vs. media target is not just a nuance. If the advertising team thinks of their target as primarily men in the eighteen to thirty-four age range who like action films, they may inadvertently insert too many male cues into the ads that would turn other audiences away.

Developing a well-articulated strategy (audience and message) will help you create concise, untangled entertainment. This will lead to concise, untangled marketing. Whether you are introducing a movie at the theater or a toy on the shelf, the effective principles of creating a focused, motivating message that positions your offering in the minds of your audience remain the same. How many times have you watched a trailer for an upcoming movie and didn't have the slightest idea what the film was about? Or you saw advertising for a toy with so many bells and whistles that you are not sure what the overall emotional benefit is? It happens a lot. Confused marketing is often a result of confused entertainment.

Marketing Insight #3: Select a Name/Title That Communicates
Your marketing message starts with the name/title. Good names tell you what your story or product is about. It's a critical part of your marketable artistry. Great names also start the process of making an emotional connection. *The War of the Worlds* is a great title. It immediately tells us that a battle of universal proportions is at hand and that our entire civilization is in grave jeopardy. *Raiders of the Lost Ark* is a great title. It tells us that we are going to be in the midst of a great adventure. It's also aspiring because many of us would like to be a raider. *Finding Nemo* is a great title. It not only sets up the adventure, it generates immediate concern for the protagonist. Who is poor little Nemo? Where did he go? Why

is he lost? How can we find him? Instant empathy.

Some titles are simply character names or descriptions. They can work quite well if they communicate something intriguing. I'd put *E.T.: The Extra-Terrestrial* and *The Karate Kid* into this category.

When there's a success worthy of sequels, each new installment gets its own twist. I prefer those titles that tell us something specific and unique about the next great adventure. For example, *Raiders of the Lost Ark, Indiana Jones and the Temple of Doom, Indiana Jones and the Last Crusade,* and *Indiana Jones and the Kingdom of the Crystal Skull.*

I think the Indiana Jones approach for sequel titles is more effective than the approach taken for *Shrek: Shrek, Shrek 2, Shrek the Third,* and *Shrek Forever After.*

The descriptive Indiana Jones titles are more likely to paint a picture in audiences' minds of what the new story is about. The Shrek titles require further explanation. Anytime something requires further explanation, it's a missed opportunity. Titles of sequels that are too vague also lead to confusion afterwards. Have you ever thought back to a film series and tried to remember what each sequel was about? It's hard if the title doesn't help. This might not sound important on the surface, but if you are a parent trying to pick the right DVD for a child, being able to correctly identify the one he loves most is important.

Because the Indiana Jones titles communicate a "place" or an "activity" of each story, they help create interest in the icons associated with it. Teens might want a T-shirt embossed with a Crystal Skull. Kids may be encouraged to desire a Temple of Doom playset.

Titles also need to address the sensibilities of the various audiences. Imagine if *Beauty and the Beast* had been titled *Beauty*. It might have cut off half its audience in one fatal blow. Girls would have showed up, but boys would have stayed home. It was a masterful stroke when Disney changed the title of *Rapunzel* to *Tangled* and included a prominent male character into the mix. The *Rapunzel* name would have signaled that the film was for a primarily female audience, but *Tangled* was gender neutral and could be interpreted in several fun ways. As Ed Catmull, president of Pixar and Disney Animation Studios, told the *Los Angeles Times*, "We did not want to be put in a box. Some people might assume it's a fairy tale for girls when it's not. We make movies to be appreciated and loved by everybody."

The classic *Cinderella* is an interesting case. The title and the story so perfectly connect with female sensibilities that it can successfully gain a sizeable female audience. However, I humbly submit that a twist of the storyline and a title change to *Cinderella and the Warrior Prince* would have been even better! Call me crazy, but I think girls would have still gone to see the movie and boys' interest would have increased. Critics are apt to hate me for that comment because classics are sacrosanct.

Titles matter. They start the marketing communication process. They are part of the marketable artistry. They should rise out of the soul of the idea, start the process of making an emotional connection with audiences, sequel in ways that are descriptive, lend themselves to vivid imagery that can work on key art and merchandise, and address the sensibilities of genders/ages if need be.

Marketing Insight #4: Include Highly Marketable Scenes

The moment after audiences see a movie they love or complete a novel they cherish, they can recite much of it. Then they begin to forget. After a week or a month, they might remember the overall story idea and about ten key scenes if you are lucky. A couple months later, they might be able to recall only three key scenes before they begin to stall. Think for a moment. What are the key scenes you remember from any of the films in the following series: *The Lord of the Rings, Harry Potter, Batman, Shrek*.

Unless you are a big movie buff, you probably remembered about three scenes right away, and then started searching until you came up with others. When you think about all the work that goes into building a story, that fact can be rather depressing. But here's the good news; for most stories, audiences can't remember any scenes at all. They often can't remember a film they saw last week. So if they can remember a couple scenes from your story after a year, that's great.

I once conducted an awareness study for a Mexican restaurant chain in San Diego and Minneapolis. At the time (and perhaps still today), San Diego had a ton of Mexican restaurants and Minneapolis had only a handful. Despite the difference, the average number of Mexican restaurants anyone could easily recall in either city was three. That's just the way our minds work.

As you craft a blockbuster or are developing a marketing plan for one, think about the scenes that epitomize the story. Which show the emotional need that your story will satisfy? Which scenes are so startling that they are apt to be remembered long after? Which shows the character at a turning point or relatable crisis? Which is the moment when time stops and everything hangs in the balance? Which scene will have the audience rolling with laughter? Importantly, can you push these scenes even further into the extreme so that they will make it into long-term memory? The highest scoring scenes as found in subsequent research will be used in marketing, providing that they help tell the story and position the film appropriately. Too much entertainment has too many subtle, forgettable moments. Great entertainment has long-lasting marketable moments.

When I say *When Harry Met Sally*, I know which scene most people will think of. If you have seen the film, you know it too. It was a showstopper, a unique scene pushed to the extreme.

The blockbuster film *Alien* is about an extraterrestrial that tracks and kills the crew of a spaceship. It was executed in a highly realistic fashion that mixed advanced science fiction with shear horror. It was *Jaws* in space and it scared the crap out of many viewers. Which scene are you thinking of right now? I bet it is the one in which an alien bursts from a crew member's chest. Right? Had I asked you which scene you remember from Alfred Hitchcock's *Psycho*, I bet I would have gotten that one right also. Unforgettable. Scenes pushed to the extreme are marketable artistry.

Marketing Insight #5: Create Relevant, Marketable Dialogue
As you construct a story, think about a line of dialogue that is the linchpin of the narrative. That line of dialogue might become the cornerstone of the story's marketing and ultimate franchise. Who can forget "May the Force be with you," "One Ring to rule them all," "Rosebud," "Houston, we have a problem," or "To boldly go where no man has gone before."

I realize it seems obvious to include marketable dialogue, but sometimes the obvious isn't obvious until after the entertainment is complete and there's no dialogue to help marketing messages. Some action films have little dialogue, which creates marketing angst. It's also true that we don't know what pieces of dialogue audiences will adopt until after they experience the entertainment. It's hit or miss. Yet it helps if we try.

Great, pithy dialogue with a sharp attitude is often adopted by audiences. It also sells a lot of merchandise because audiences want to wear the attitude. Do you recall the various sources of these quotes? "Don't have a cow, man!" "Eh . . . What's up, Doc?" "I'm not bad. I'm just drawn that way." "Do or do not. There is no try." "Hasta la vista, baby."

Elements of great dialogue stay with the audience long after they put down the novel, turn off the TV, or leave the theater. I seem to be blending story development and marketing again. Right! I am! That's because story development *is* marketing.

Marketing Insight #6: Devise Marketing that Makes Audiences *Feel*
Great marketing should communicate the story's idea in a way that makes the audience *feel*. Trailers for *Pirates of the Caribbean: On Stranger Tides* were exhilarating. One trailer began with a line that defined Jack Sparrow's new adventure, "Death lies before us as we sail to the fountain of youth!" The

pounding music swelled as audiences saw all of the elements they love about the franchise, but now made fresh with the introduction of Blackbeard, mermaids, zombies, and Angelica played by Penélope Cruz. That trailer, along with one or two others, provided just enough detail to build anticipation, but not so much that the audience would feel that the trailer told the whole story, leaving nothing else to be discovered. It was a wonderful balance. That's marketable artistry.

I would say that of all the advertising I see for films, less than 20 percent do a great job moving me emotionally, and I'm at the theater nearly every week. Effective taglines should help communicate a sense of story while providing an emotional hook. I have listed some of my favorites:

- "In space, no one can hear you scream." *Alien*
- "The truth is out there." *The X-Files*
- "Just when you thought it was safe to go back in the water." *Jaws 2*
- "They're back." *Poltergeist II*

These taglines show up in surveys as some of the most popular (some are incorporated into the entertainment itself). They galvanize a *feeling*, not just a concept. They are independent of demographics and connect with an emotion we all share. When each tagline is added to a crisp, single, arresting visual, the combination becomes compelling key art. I'm willing to bet that you still recall the single image selected for several of the taglines referenced above. My personal favorites are the visuals used for *Jaws/Jaws 2* and *Alien*. Do you remember? That's great advertising!

Identify the emotional foundation of your entertainment and allow it to spread throughout the advertising, publicity, consumer promotions, and viral marketing. Making an emotional connection applies to marketing directed at the kid in all of us as well as to marketing directed to kids alone. Ken Kauffmann understands the soul of the child. Having created toy advertising for Mattel for many years, and now doing the same as vice president of advertising for MGA Entertainment, Ken knows far more about kids than most. Says Ken,

Kids are oppressed; their lives are ruled by parents, teachers and adults. Fantasy play affords kids a healthy escape from this oppressive reality to a world they create and exercise complete control over. With toys we offer kids absolute power over a world of their own making. Fantasy is independent and rebellious and our toy advertising should celebrate that if we are to appeal to kids.

Emotion is everything.

Marketing Insight #7: Allow Audiences to Live the Story

When 20th Century Fox launched *The Simpsons Movie*, they allowed consumers to experience the world of *The Simpsons*. The studio had 7-Eleven stores transformed into Kwik-E-Marts, which are featured on the show. Real cities with the name Springfield competed to host the premiere of the film. Audiences created their own Simpsons-like avatars online and had a chance to star in an upcoming episode. These types of efforts allow audiences to *live* the film/story experience.

James Bond films are known for featuring cool cars. The BMW Z3 roadster was in the film *GoldenEye* and was loaded with spy features such as stinger missiles. Because of the film, nondestructive versions of the car were sold to drivers who wanted to feel like James Bond. It was deemed to be one of the most successful product placements in 1995. Consumers could, in small ways, "live" the life of Bond, James Bond.

For many years in the children's arena, *Power Rangers* characters went on promotion tours to neighborhoods throughout the country. The tour allowed kids to meet their heroes and have a *Power Rangers* experience in their hometown. Allowing audiences to *live* the franchise, not just view it, allows for an active, engaging experience.

The creator of the entertainment should think ahead and ask himself am I creating characters and environments worth emulating? How can I craft my entertainment so that audiences can *live* my story? That not only helps create franchises, as we discussed in a previous chapter, but it becomes the foundation of marketable artistry.

Marketing Insight #8: Create News You Can Use

We have already discussed using news as a way to invent entertainment. When done well, it creates marketable artistry.

News is created when the entertainment piggybacks on other prominent news, such as when James Cameron explored and photographed the real *Titanic* in preparation for his film.

News is created when the entertainment's technology is advanced. When James Cameron advanced the performance capture technique for the movie *Avatar,* news outlets turned their cameras toward him and the project.

News is created out of controversy. Duke Nukem, a first-person shooter game, includes strippers in the game play. It's not appropriate (or rated) for all audiences, but it did create lots of controversy when it was first introduced.

News can be created by promoting fictional events as real. *The Blair Witch Project* is a 1994 film about the events surrounding the disappearance of three student filmmakers in the woods in Maryland while shooting a documentary. As the story goes, the footage was found but the bodies were not. They were supposedly killed by the Blair witch who you never see. The shaky, handheld footage gave the film a sense of realism. The film was marketed as though the event was real, the student filmmakers were dead, and a real witch lived in the deep woods of Maryland. The Internet buzzed as people visited the film's Web site to find out more. Friends began telling friends about this "real" witch story far in advance of the film's release. The movie earned about $248 million worldwide on a production budget of about $60,000.

News can be created by what you don't show. In the trailer for the film *Cloverfield,* audiences did not see the actual alien. That approach makes audiences wonder what it looks like. Audience imagination is often scarier than reality.

News is also created when influential bloggers and critics are invited to early screenings/events and (hopefully) love what they see. For the introduction of the Wizarding World of Harry Potter theme park, executives made the announcement to only seven popular Harry Potter bloggers during a secret Webcast.

Excited by what they heard, the bloggers sent the message to thousands of followers. The message was picked up by news outlets and word was out to 350 million people around the world in just days. Seven people started an avalanche that engulfed 350 million—for free. It demonstrated that for established franchises, the opinion leaders are the evangelists of your marketing efforts. If you are lucky enough to find the right handful of enthusiasts, they will do the rest.

News can be created by allowing audiences to sample the entertainment. Pixar released a ten-minute clip of the film *Ratatouille* online. It was hosted by writer/director Brad Bird. More than a trailer, less than a complete story, the clip allowed potential audiences to sample the film. It was a great tactic since the title of the film requires a bit of an explanation.

News can be created by selecting a marquee-quality producer, director, and cast. All of which can lend credibility to the strength of the story, especially if the cast creates news, such as when Tom Cruise performed his own jaw-dropping stunts atop the world's tallest building in the 2011 film *Mission: Impossible—Ghost Protocol.*

Finally, news is created when your entertainment is in short supply. Young men will line up at midnight to be the first to buy a new video game that's rumored to be scarce. Parents line up when there are reports that a popular toy is about to sell out right before Christmas. I would never endorse creating the *impression* of scarcity to create demand. However, if demand is *actually* outstripping supply, it's worth mentioning.

Marketing Insight #9: Target the Kid in All of Us

Blockbusters typically engage us all, old and young, male and female. All audiences will find emotional satisfaction in the final product, though not necessarily in the same way. All audiences should also find emotional enticement from the marketing efforts, though not necessarily in the same way.

Many years ago I received a brochure for the Disney Cruise. The pamphlet showed what a marvelous time the entire family could have. My teenage son could hang out at the teen lounge with other teens and play video games. My younger daughter could be swept away to a play group each day, freeing up my wife and I to enjoy the ship activities that were intended for adults. It looked intriguing. The brochure came with an invitation to attend a seminar at our local auto club to find out more. We all attended, listened to the pitch, and watched a brief film about the ship and its ports of call. We all felt it would be a magical experience, though we each defined that magical experience in a different way. We signed up, and to date, it is the best family trip we've ever taken. Here's my point; it is very possible to pull one heartstring, defined in different ways for the child-like soul in each of us.

The Disney Cruise is marketable artistry. It sold itself.

Marketing Insight #10: Optimize Spending

Great entertainment needs an adequate budget to gain sufficient awareness, interest, and purchase. Without it, even the best entertainment can't achieve the velocity it needs to reach orbit. Many tools are often necessary including paid advertising, publicity, consumer promotions, and viral marketing, but they can be expensive.

Many years ago, I spearheaded a study to ascertain the optimal level of ad spending that would maximize sales for a new product launch in a particular entertainment category. The results indicated that the level was higher than the company had been spending. It was also higher than the industry average, but it worked. The sales generated by the increased spending paid for advertising and more. We also discovered that if spending was beneath a certain threshold, then we might as well not spend anything. That's because it takes a certain degree of shout to be heard. If the competitors are shouting louder, you are drowned out completely.

Each industry is different and has its own thresholds, but my point is that there is an optimal amount of marketing spending. Chances are you are not spending it. There is also a minimum threshold, and if you are not at least spending that, then what you are spending is wasted. You need to find your optimum and minimum thresholds.

It is also very easy to spread your marketing dollars too broadly on too many efforts, each supported too thinly. I believe it is often best to pick a handful of efforts and do them really well than to pick two dozen efforts and do a mediocre job on each. When budgets are tight, this might entail narrowing your audience or your geography so that you are reaching more critical targets more often.

A Comment about Teaser Campaigns

Beware of teaser campaigns. These early marketing efforts communicate a minimal amount of supposedly intriguing information in hopes of piquing audience interest. The classic example is the film *Ghostbusters,* which teased audiences with posters depicting a white ghost contained by a crossed-out sign (red-colored circle with a line through it). Teasers also signal your release date to other studios, sort of like marking your territory.

I'm not a fan of teaser campaigns. Their success tends to be more antidotal than measured. In most cases, I think they waste resources that would be best spent on the full marketing campaign.

The trailers I saw for *Super 8* were emotionally suspenseful, and I am willing to bet they put most audiences at the edge of their seats. However, I suspect they did not communicate enough about the film's plot. What was the basic storyline? What was the protagonist's goal? The title, *Super 8,* didn't help explain it and probably added confusion. To me, it felt like the marketing effort stayed in teaser mode. It just needed to tell slightly more about the story to aid communication while keeping the emotional intensity that the trailer captured so well. I don't know if that mattered at the box office. The film itself was brilliant! But if even 10 percent of the people who saw some form of marketing for the movie were confused enough to pass it by, that was money left on the table.

Never pass up the opportunity to communicate what your

story is about and how it will emotionally move the audience. Don't give too much of the story away, either, particularly any hints of the ending. Tell and sell but don't over tell. This is the best approach to marketing your artistry.

Bringing it All Together—Synergy

Marketing, like building a franchise, requires synergy to be the most effective. All the marketing elements and partnerships need to work seamlessly. If you are fortunate enough to work with a large entertainment company with a vast array of divisions, then all of the elements are available in-house. The preview for the company's new movie might run on the company-owned cable channel, the consumer promotions for the film might include winning a day at the company-owned theme park, and the actors from the movie might do interviews on the company-owned radio station. This helps create a clear, cohesive marketing effort as long as all marketing venues are communicating the same central positioning of the entertainment.

The introduction of *Avatar* was a successful marketing effort. It was an event. On August 21, 2009 (deemed Avatar Day), a sixteen-minute preview of the movie was shown in one hundred IMAX 3-D theaters worldwide. It unveiled the basic story and the technology that brought it to life. It accompanied the disclosure of a toy line and a trailer for the video game, in addition to the media interviews James Cameron did to discuss "news" of the performance capture technique he used for the film. The Twitter effort required audiences to send a tweet in order to hear music from the film, inspiring friends to pass along messages. The Internet buzz began. Conversations on Facebook topped one million. Videos on YouTube had millions of views. Along with advertising and promotions, awareness and interest soared. *Avatar* did roughly $2.78 billion worldwide. While its marketing budget was large, reported to be $150 million, much of the awareness and interest was generated by news and audiences themselves. They spread the message willingly, happily.

To achieve even a fraction of that hard-earned success, creators need to ask themselves how they can mold their entertainment into marketable artistry, worthy of news. Marketing executives need to ask themselves how they can craft marketing plans that are as emotionally newsworthy as the entertainment itself.

Key Takeaway
Blockbuster entertainment deserves blockbuster marketing. The key insights:

- Marketing Insight #1: Create Marketable Artistry
- Marketing Insight #2: Create Artistry with an Audience in Mind
- Marketing Insight #3: Select a Name/Title That Communicates
- Marketing Insight #4: Include Highly Marketable Scenes
- Marketing Insight #5: Create Relevant, Marketable Dialogue
- Marketing Insight #6: Devise Marketing that Makes Audiences Feel
- Marketing Insight #7: Allow Audiences to Live the Story
- Marketing Insight #8: Create News You Can Use
- Marketing Insight #9: Target the Kid in All of Us
- Marketing Insight #10: Optimize Spending

If you are lucky enough to have created a blockbuster, I bet you want to include elements that will help it to live forever! That's next.

Chapter 11

Apply the *Ever-Cool* Formula

Let's say that you have created a blockbuster. It started with an idea that you astutely developed, marketed, and sold. Perhaps it even has the seeds of a franchise. You wake up one morning and realize that as difficult (and lucky) as this accomplishment was, you would like your blockbuster to stay popular for a while, maybe forever!

Industry people talk about creating "evergreen" properties in reference to brands that last. I never liked that term. It tells you what the result is (a perpetual brand), but it doesn't tell you how to make it happen. So many years ago, I coined the term *ever-cool* to reference properties that last forever because they have a talent for staying popular with audiences. It became the foundation of my first youth marketing book, *Creating Ever-Cool: A Marketer's Guide to a Kid's Heart.* The book did quite well in youth marketing and entertainment circles. Since then, I've noticed that the core principles of the *Ever-Cool Formula* apply to virtually all consumer and entertainment businesses.

The Ever-Cool Formula adapted to entertainment is: *To become and stay successful, your entertainment must satisfy your audiences' timeless emotional needs, but routinely dress itself up in contemporary clothing, particularly in popular culture and trends.* Exhibit 36 shows this graphical relationship.

This formula is a combination of the timeless emotional needs and culture/trends we discussed in earlier chapters that can be used to invent entertainment. I'll now show you how they can be used to keep franchises perpetually cool, extending them indefinitely.

Simple yet powerful, the formula forces executives to always consider two central issues. First, it reminds them that their offering must continue to satisfy emotional needs first and foremost—this never goes out of style. Straying too far from what your brand delivers, emotionally, is often disastrous. Second, the Ever-Cool Formula reminds them that while satisfying emotional needs is critical, their brand will become stale overtime if it is not continuously updated (dressed up) to reflect the new culture, trends, and fads of today. If your brand delivers emotional satisfaction exactly the same way every time, it's like experiencing the tenth rotation on a Ferris wheel. Let me off already!

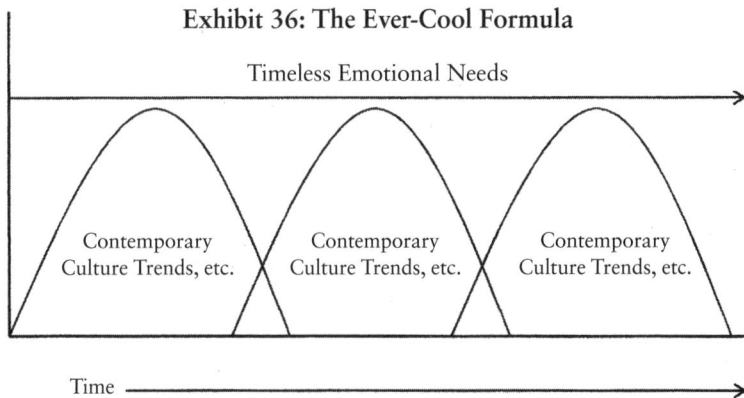

Exhibit 36: The Ever-Cool Formula

Ever-Cool in Practice

Madonna is ever-cool. Her edgy, rebellious attitude has stayed nearly constant and provides emotional satisfaction to many. Nevertheless, she alters her approach to stay fresh. She went from punk to boy toy to material girl to erotica to Kabbalah with several other stops in between. Madonna doesn't just reflect fads, she makes them. Lady Gaga follows this same playbook.

Many brands across many industries have applied the Ever-Cool Formula with great success, though they have not always called it that. Unlike Madonna, most companies don't invent the pop culture they use; they more often use pop culture created by others.

McDonald's Happy Meal was launched in the Kansas City market in October 1977. It was immensely successful. The Happy Meal satisfies timeless needs by providing delicious meals for kids that are convenient and economical for mom. The Happy Meal stays contemporary by associating itself with changing pop culture. If a certain Disney movie is expected to be popular, McDonald's inserts a Disney plaything into a Happy Meal. If kids suddenly desire Shrek, add that plaything next. Playthings in Happy Meals have been themed to characters from *The Lion King, Alvin and the Chipmunks, Barbie, Batman, The Flintstones, Spy Kids, Star Trek, Transformers,* and more. By dressing itself up in trends and fads, the Happy Meal not only stays contemporary, but it adds additional emotional satisfaction via the nature of the playthings it offers. When issues were raised regarding the meal's healthiness, McDonald's provided more nutritious options to meet parents' concerns. It's timeless and timely. The appeal of the Happy Meal seems obvious now, but it wasn't so obvious before it was introduced. Youth marketing had changed forever.

Toy companies have applied the Ever-Cool Formula. The Barbie doll fulfills girls' dreams of what they might become, providing a timeless, emotional satisfaction. The doll stayed cool by being updated to fit girls' broadening aspirations. When girls desired to be fashion models, so was Barbie. When little girls wanted to be nurses and stewardesses, so was Barbie. When little girls' aspirations soared, Barbie broke through the glass ceiling and became a pilot and a doctor. I was working for Mattel's advertising agency when we introduced many of these dolls. Over just a decade, Barbie sales grew from roughly $300 million to roughly $2 billion. But was her kingdom impenetrable? Nope. Many years later, I consulted for MGA Entertainment just after they introduced the Bratz doll. For a good while, Bratz took significant share from Barbie using edgier dolls (a different emotional driver) themed to a more contemporary culture. It demonstrated the power that even upstart brands can have against giants if they know how to shrewdly employ the Ever-Cool Formula.

Creating Ever-Cool Entertainment

Many nonentertainment companies use a continuous stream of new movies and TV shows to make their products stay cool. If you are a storyteller, you might ask, "Gee, these other guys are using my entertainment to make their brands look cool, but how do I make my franchise stay cool across movie sequels or multiple television seasons?"

Answer: the Ever-Cool Formula applies. In April 2011, the *Los Angeles Times* reporter John Horn wrote that studios draw distinctions between previous films in a franchise and new ones. "*Cars 2* isn't an animated movie but a spy thriller," he summarized, and "*Puss in Boots* is more than a Shrek spinoff: It's a Sergio Leone western that happens to star a talking cat." These distinctions are important. Studios have to prove that the next sequel has the connective tissue that audiences loved of earlier versions, but with new twists to make them feel new and cool.

While the need to extend the life of entertainment is top of mind once it's a success, writers/creators should consider how their entertainment could stay fresh even as they are constructing version 1.0. Why? Executives who buy ideas often want to know if the ideas have longevity, which is a criterion they will use when comparing multiple ideas. If it's clear that, all things being equal, one idea has greater potential for sequels than another, that idea may have an edge. So it makes sense to give this serious thought. Senior marketing strategist Monika Salazar stresses the importance of planning for longevity from the beginning. "The lifecycle and demographic of the brand needs to be strategically and carefully planned from the beginning. Technology and design trends should grow with the brand over time but the crucial identifiers of the brand should not change. Storylines that are well developed will be able to take the story through to the next generation. Updating old archetypes in stories is one way to always stay relevant."

There are ten ways to keep entertainment ever-cool as shown in Exhibit 37. Some blockbusters use a couple of these while others use them all. Which you employ depends upon the circumstances. Some of these techniques were referenced earlier as ways to invent franchises or create marketable artistry, but I included them here because they also help keep entertainment ever-cool. This is your comprehensive go-to list for ideas to help your franchise stay fresh and contemporary forever.

Ever-Cool Technique #1: Keep Stories Open-Ended

As discussed in the franchise chapter, the original theme or story needs to be open-ended enough to allow for at least a couple more versions/sequels. Without that, the chances of achieving ever-cool are diminished. It's harder for Shakespeare's original *Romeo and Juliet* to have a sequel than it was for Disney's *High School Musical,* which has a Romeo and Juliet type plot. In Shakespeare's version, the characters died at the end of the story. Not so with *High School Musical;* so Disney was able to introduce two more successful films.

Once the story is open-ended, there are several ways to take advantage of it to keep the franchise feeling fresh and cool, including increasing the risks for the protagonist (Bigger Bad formula), enhancing the protagonist's potential rewards/riches (Greater Riches formula), spinning off a popular character from the larger franchise (e.g., Shrek's Puss in Boots), and creating the saga, which splits a story over many sequels. Yet another option is creating the prequel, which sends the story back in time. An innovative prequel approach was used in the 2009 film *Star Trek.* The movie not only sent the story back in time, but also changed events in the past. This put the science-fiction series on a new, different timeline, allowing future films within the franchise to deviate from the constraints of previously used storylines. This is a brilliant way to allow for a fresh approach.

Recently, some movies have included final scenes that foreshadow the next, continuing story. This builds anticipation

Exhibit 37: Apply the Ever-Cool Formula

1: Keep Stories Open-Ended
endings, bigger bads, greater rewards/
riches, sagas, foreshadowing

2: Use Re-Imaginings
style, narrative

3: Use Current Culture
Entertainment-Based
pop stars, music, concerts, fashion world,
movies, TV, literature, toys and video
games, Internet, sports, etc.

Social Issues-Based
religion, sex, politics, ethnicity, equal-
ity, prejudice, war and peace, education, law and order, health, economy,
poverty, etc.

4: Use Current Trends
technology, social networking,
recession, obesity, environment,
family shifts, ethnicity, spirituality,
personalization, sensory explosions,
magic/mysticism, soaring science,
terrorism, doomsday, etc.

5: Use Different Needs
Self-Actualization
your full potential

Esteem
respect, recognition, status, fame, glory,
mastery, power, independence, redemption, control, rebelliousness, beauty,
confidence, bravery, etc.

Love and Belonging
social needs for family, friendship, inti-
macy, romance, etc.

Safety
personal health, financial, thwart evil, etc.

Physiological
human survival: air, food, water, clothing, shelter, sex, etc.

6: Use Fads
music and music artists, films/TV
and their celebs, literature, fashion,
playthings, dance, self-help, etc.

7: Use New Characters/Cast
warrior/soldier, king/prince/ruler
queen/princess/ruler, adventurer/
treasure hunter/pirate, mythic gods,
folklore (elf, dwarf, etc.), billionaire,
rock star, movie star, model, fashion
designer, dancer, athlete, astronaut/pilot,
wizard/witch/genie, vampires/zombies/
monsters, space aliens, etc.

8: Use New Transformations
Emotional
shy to bold
cowardice to bravery
selfish to selfless
unloved to loved
evil to good
loser to winner, etc.

Physical
weak to strong, ugly to pretty, rags to riches, dumb to smart, novice to master, etc.

9: Intro to New Generations

10: Create News
piggy back on news, advance technology, new footage, etc.

in ways that keep the overall franchise feeling cool. At the end of the third *Pirates of the Caribbean,* Capt. Jack Sparrow begins a new journey to find the Fountain of Youth, which sets up the fourth film. Near the end of the fourth film, Jack Sparrow heads off to find a way to return his ship, the *Black Pearl,* back to its original size (it had been shrunk). After the end credits of the fourth film, Angelica, who Jack Sparrow marooned on an island, finds a voodoo doll of Jack. These final scenes may set up a fifth film.

After the end credits of the 2010 film *Iron Man 2,* a scene shows a government agent arriving at a large crater in the desert. What created the massive crater? The Hammer of Thor! It was the perfect way to foreshadow the 2011 film *Thor.* These superheroes, among others, will eventually unite in the film *The Avengers,* which is planned for 2012. As the anticipation builds, so does the coolness of the franchise.

Creating the feeling of an open-ended adventure can even be delivered via theme park rides. The revamped *Star Tours* motion-simulator ride at Disneyland and Walt Disney World now has more than fifty different adventures chosen randomly, each featuring different *Star Wars* characters and locales. The different options motivate guests to come back to experience them all, making the ride feel fresh each time. Keeping a story open-ended, in consumer-speak, means that the adventure continues!

Ever-Cool Technique #2: Refresh with Re-Imaginings
Some properties stay cool by being re-imagined. Lewis Carroll's 1865 novel *Alice's Adventures in Wonderland* was re-imagined by Disney in its 1951 animated classic *Alice in Wonderland,* which also included some elements of Carroll's second novel *Through the Looking-Glass, and What Alice Found There.* Disney re-imagined it again in 2010. Directed by Tim Burton and starring Johnny Depp as the Mad Hatter, this highly successful film used a combination of computer animation and live action to achieve a uniquely fanciful realism (those two words don't always go hand in hand, but it works this time). Because of this success, studios are

reportedly re-imagining other classics such as *Snow White,* *Hansel and Gretel,* and *Sleeping Beauty.*

Sometimes the re-imagined work is more about stylistic changes than narrative adjustments. Sometimes the narrative is drastically altered, so much so that it's a different story altogether. A brilliant example is the musical production of *Wicked,* based upon a novel by Gregory Maguire. The premise is that the Wicked Witch of the West in the classic *The Wonderful Wizard of Oz* is actually the hero and not the villain of the story. The story of Dorothy that we thought we knew turns out, according to *Wicked,* to be a slanted perception of a bigger narrative. It's an amazing twist.

Ever-Cool Technique #3: Refresh with Current Culture

We discussed tapping into cultural elements earlier as a means to generate new blockbusters, but it is also a great way to refresh existing ones. Examples:

Entertainment-Based Culture: Blockbusters keep themselves looking fresh and cool by tapping into entertainment-based culture. Some use a flow of contemporary pop stars and music (e.g., *Glee*) and elements of the contemporary fashion world (e.g., *Project Runway*). The blockbuster TV series *The Amazing Race* uses ever-changing exotic destinations to help stay fresh. The *CSI* television series has created line extensions using city-based culture. It began with the Las Vegas-based *CSI: Crime Scene Investigation. CSI: Miami* and *CSI: NY* followed. After many years of running about at the Tipton Hotel, Zack and Cody of *The Suite Life of Zack and Cody* took their antics to sea in *The Suite Life on Deck.* Cruises are a big part of our culture. The show stayed true to its premise but changed locales to keep it fresh.

Social Issues Based Culture: Changing social issues provide a platform for keeping entertainment contemporary. As mentioned in an earlier chapter, *The Simpsons* keeps fresh with storylines that feature current issues—religion, politics, sex, and pop culture celebrities. This is noteworthy because many of the other elements never change, including the central characters, basic premise, setting, and the period. The television series *South Park* uses a similar formula, keeping the fundamental elements the same while delving into changing culture to stay fresh. This is how many family comedies and dramas stay timeless yet contemporary.

Ever-Cool Technique #4: Refresh with Trends
Your story can be refreshed by associating it with current trends. A fuller explanation of each of these trends was in chapter 4. Here are just a few examples to spark your thinking.

Environment: Sequels for films have been themed to environmental concerns in order to provide a contemporary storyline twist. The storyline in the 1986 film *Star Trek IV: The Voyage Home* was based upon the future extinction of humpback whales on Earth. It did more than $100 million at the domestic box office.

Terrorism: This topic will continue to be front and center despite the demise of Osama bin Laden. The hugely successful *24* TV series milked this for eight seasons by depicting Counter Terrorist Unit agent Jack Bauer dispatching one terrorist after another. Refreshed terrorists led to refreshed plots.

Technology and Science: Trends in technology and science are at your disposal to help your property stay cool. Cloning, DNA manipulation, and stem cell advances will be fodder for film sequels, updated video game installments, and novel series. This can give older entertainment a fresh coat of paint while delving into contemporary moral issues such as the appropriateness of man acting as God.

Any one of the remaining trends in Exhibit 37 can be used to create a compelling sequel, including themes related to the Internet, recession, obesity, family shifts, ethnicity, spirituality, personalization, magic/mysticism, and doomsday concerns. The full list can be found in chapter 4.

Ever-Cool Technique #5: Refresh with Different Basic Needs
Entertainment can also be refreshed by satisfying more emotional needs in the context of the updated story. The

Indiana Jones franchise allows audiences to feel as adventurous as the lead character. For sequels, the storytellers layered in other emotional drivers. One story was about gaining *freedom* for enslaved kids (*Indiana Jones and the Temple of Doom*), whereas another story included subtext regarding the strained yet *loving relationship* between a father and son (*Indiana Jones and the Last Crusade*). In this way, adding new ways to achieve emotional satisfaction helped the franchise stay contemporary.

John Lasseter, the chief creative officer at Pixar and Walt Disney Animation Studios, said in an interview appearing on cinefantastiqueonline.com that

> The secret to these films [*Toy Story*] is that each movie is not trying to repeat the same emotion or the same story. . . . We're able to tap into completely different set of emotions. . . . In the first film, Woody is concerned about being replaced by a new toy. . . . In *Toy Story 2* the toys deal with being torn, broken and not being played with. . . . In the third film, we really deal with that point in time that the toys are most concerned about . . . being outgrown.

Different needs are often derived from using different plot conflicts as described in chapter 6. In one story, the plot might pit your protagonist against technology, but in the sequel, it pits your protagonist against some aspect of society.

Years ago while working for an advertising agency on a studio's business, I recall that when one particular film did well, the head of the studio said something like "The movie did great. For the sequel, we're gonna give our hero a gun and a girl." It was a funny way to put it, but his meaning wasn't lost. He wanted to raise the risk level for the protagonist and add romance. Both were used to dig deeper into emotional drivers so that audiences would come back for the sequel.

One caveat: while you can add new emotional drivers to stay fresh, in most cases, you should not stray far from the core emotional reasons that brought audiences to the franchise to begin with. When I think of Indiana Jones, I fantasize that I'm every bit as daring and as adventurous as he is. When I read the Harry Potter novels and see the films, I feel as though I can gain enough courage and power to defeat Lord Voldemort, thus saving the wizarding world and all those clueless, naïve Muggles. A caveat to the caveat: on *very* rare occasions, it pays to shift to stronger emotional needs. The Nerf brand was introduced in 1970 as a ball for use indoors. Because of the soft foam material, its benefit was that it wouldn't damage things in the house. It was *fun* on the *inside*. The company sold millions, but the emotional need was limiting. Line extensions were then crafted to hit more emotional chords. These included Nerf Bow 'n' Arrow, Nerf Blasters, and Nerf Rocket Air Launcher to name a new. This branching out connected the brand to wider, stronger emotional needs for power, mastery, and even good vanquishing evil. The brand was not only refreshed, but it found stronger emotional benefits that it could satisfy over time.

Ever-Cool Technique #6: Refresh with Fads

Fads can help refresh entertainment. The key places to look are as follows:

Music and Music Artists: Music, musicians, and pop stars can be used to create fresh installments for blockbusters. This is certainly the case with the hit series *Glee,* as cited earlier, which relies on a string of popular music artists to create a contemporary aura. It's also an element behind the success of the video game series Guitar Hero and Rock Band.

Film/TV and Their Celebrities: Popular films, TV series, and the celebrities they create can be used to create fresh installments for your entertainment. In an earlier chapter, I referenced how the 2011 film *The Smurfs* was relying on popular celebrities like Neil Patrick Harris (*How I Met Your Mother*) to increase interest among adults. The actor's popularity can rub off on the movies' characters, helping them appear cool again.

Fashion and Style: New fashions and styles help refresh entertainment. A Japanese art style known as anime swept the planet and created a contemporary look for characters in comic books and cartoon animation.

The other key areas to search for fads include literature, playthings, dance, and self-help. While fads can be used to give your property a fresh take, be cautious of them. They are catnip. They taste great but result in temporary euphoria. Then they are gone.

As a storyteller and creator, keep in mind that your job is not to ride the coattails of a fad. Your job is to create the fad that others will follow. With luck, your fad can be extended throughout a TV season and across novels and movie sequels for many years, thus taking itself from fad to a more enduring part of culture and trends.

Ever-Cool Technique #7: Refresh with New Characters and Cast

This is the most common technique. Entertainment is often recharged by associating it with different characters and new cast members. It's probably one of the easiest solutions, but there are downsides. Some celebrity actors have gotten so expensive that they erode the ability for a film or television show to make a profit. It is also the case that big stars no longer guarantee big opening weekends, so some studios have cut back on using mega stars as a way to create or refresh franchises.

Many franchises have successfully used a continuous stream of iconic characters as a way to stay fresh. The TV series *Supernatural* has featured iconic characters from folklore, Pagan mythology, and Christianity. Episodes have included demons, werewolves, vampires, the devil, angels, shape-shifters, hellhounds, ghosts, the Grim Reaper, and fate. Disney Channel has tapped into an array of iconic characters with shows based upon rock stars, wizards, and dancers. Entertainment such as this stays fresh with the introduction of each new iconic character.

Pirates of the Caribbean: On Stranger Tides, the fourth film in the series, introduced iconic mermaids, added an iconic pirate character (Blackbeard), and an iconic location (the Fountain of Youth). The creators seamlessly integrated these three icons, refreshing a familiar story.

Ever-Cool Technique #8: Refresh with New Transformations
Your entertainment can be refreshed by associating it with new character transformations. In one installment, your protagonist might transform from strong to weak (e.g., Superman loses his powers). In another installment, he might transform from smart to dumb (e.g., a villain injects Superman with a drug that reduces his mental abilities to that of a two-year-old). And in another, he might transform from good to evil (e.g., Superman turns sinister).

If you are working on a family comedy, episodes might be about a child's misguided efforts to transform from being dumb to smart, ugly to pretty, or rags to riches, along with all of the inherent morals that the child might learn (e.g., how we should define smart, pretty, and rich). New twists on character transformations keep franchises fresh.

Ever-Cool Technique #9: Introduce to New Generations
Keep in mind that your audience is not static. A five-year-old today is a twenty-year-old in fifteen years. In those fifteen years, a completely new crop of consumers has been born and a different crop of consumers has aged out of your target. Entertainment executives are presenting their narratives to a parade that passes by.

Many kids have not seen films we mistakenly think that everyone knows like *Snow White and the Seven Dwarfs*, *Raiders of the Lost Ark*, *Home Alone*, *Jaws*, or *E.T.: The Extra-Terrestrial*.

A brilliant strategy that accounts for generation gaps stows films away for a time and then introduces them to a new generation. This is the strategy behind the Disney Vault. The Disney Vault recognizes that audiences are a parade of people in various life stages. It gives newer audiences the opportunity to participate in classics that, frankly, are not "classics" in the strict sense because they are "new" to younger audiences who have not seen them. The Disney Vault rereleases the classics for a limited time, which motivates audiences to buy soon, because you never know how long it will be before the vault opens again. It also entices collectors who are always on the prowl for unique introductions of older films. The recognition that audiences are a parade and not a standing army is invaluable. It keeps franchises fresh.

Ever-Cool Technique #10: Refresh with News

Creating *news* cannot only be used to invent and market your entertainment as discussed previously, but it can also be used to keep your entertainment contemporary and fresh.

Fresh news is created by landing a popular celebrity for a film's sequel.

Fresh news is created by advancing technology (e.g., the performance-capture technique used in *Avatar* or converting an older film to Blu-ray or 3-D format).

Fresh news is created when brands piggyback on broader news stories (e.g., Barbie themed as a presidential candidate during an election year).

Fresh news is created by providing new elements of the entertainment (e.g., DVD release has never-before-seen footage of the director's cut).

Key Takeaway

Creating a blockbuster is incredibly hard. Keeping it on top is even harder, but it can be done by applying the Ever-Cool Formula: *To become and stay successful, your entertainment must satisfy your audiences' timeless emotional needs, but routinely dress itself up in contemporary clothing, particularly in popular culture and trends.*

The ten techniques to keep franchises ever-cool are:

- Ever-Cool Technique #1: Keep Stories Open-Ended
- Ever-Cool Technique #2: Refresh with Re-Imaginings
- Ever-Cool Technique #3: Refresh with Current Culture
- Ever-Cool Technique #4: Refresh with Trends
- Ever-Cool Technique #5: Refresh with Different Basic Needs

- Ever-Cool Technique #6: Refresh with Fads
- Ever-Cool Technique #7: Refresh with New Characters and Cast
- Ever-Cool Technique #8: Refresh with New Transformations
- Ever-Cool Technique #9: Introduce to New Generations
- Ever-Cool Technique #10: Refresh with News

We have covered a lot. By now you realize that inventing and building blockbusters requires hundreds of decisions. Unless you include the voice of your potential audience in those decisions, you're just asking for trouble. Research is vital at every step in the process. That's next.

Chapter 12

Use Research to Optimize Decisions

Danny Kaye is the executive vice president of research and technology strategy at 20th Century Fox. He is one of the finest researchers and strategists I know. According to Danny, "Research isn't just a *project*, it's a *process*. It provides a flow of just-in-time information, turned into insights, that help movie makers make critical decisions. Research can't always replace your gut, but it is invaluable when used in conjunction with intuition and experience to deliver the best outcomes." You can't argue with contnuous successes like *Star Wars* and *X-Men*.

This chapter outlines the key research steps that can help create blockbuster entertainment for the kid in all of us. Though I am a novelist and story consultant, my background is in market research. After receiving a BA in economics and an MBA with emphasis in marketing and research, I was hired by General Mills, where I conducted a wide array of research projects that included concept tests, positioning tests, product taste tests, packaging tests, advertising tests, volumetric studies, test marketing, attitude and usage surveys, and sales tracking. I was there for only about two years, but it was research boot camp. I learned good, basic research practices that I applied to the rest of my career.

I then went to Ogilvy & Mather advertising in Los Angeles as a research project director and eventually rose to become senior vice president, director of planning and research. Our clients included Paramount Pictures, Mattel toys, Microsoft, and a host of other businesses. My department's task was to be a conduit to their consumers. That's a chore because consumer tastes change rapidly, particularly in the entertainment category. Audiences are

237

always on the prowl for something new and exciting so it can be difficult to catch up. But we must catch up to audience desires if we want to optimize offerings. That's been my aim since starting my own consulting business more than a dozen years ago.

Some critics mistakenly think that entertainment companies are like Pied Pipers, playing mesmerizing tunes that entice kids and adults to march toward their music. If you are in research, you know this is not true. Consumers are in the driver's seat. Kids might drive in one direction. Parents either agree or grab the wheel and turn the car around. Young adults might go elsewhere if given the keys. Researchers are in the backseat as they scribble notes in an attempt to remember the course.

The Research Process

When handled properly, the research process optimizes end results. The insights research provides can help you invent new ideas, refine them, and test them for potential. It helps executives make important decisions regarding what products to pursue and how to market them. The process gives you the confidence you may need to kill bad ideas and elevate good ones. But at its best, research is just one factor among many that executives use to make decisions. There are times when research should be ignored. I'll get to that, but first let's discuss the process.

The basic research steps are shown in Exhibit 38. If you work in a large entertainment company, this process should look familiar. You probably have a large research team with substantial resources to test and retest your entertainment and its marketing. If you are an independent writer or inventor, you need to know the process. Your entertainment may be accepted or rejected because of research that you didn't even know was conducted.

What follows are the key research steps along with an insight or two that you need to keep in mind along the way.

Exhibit 38: Research Plan

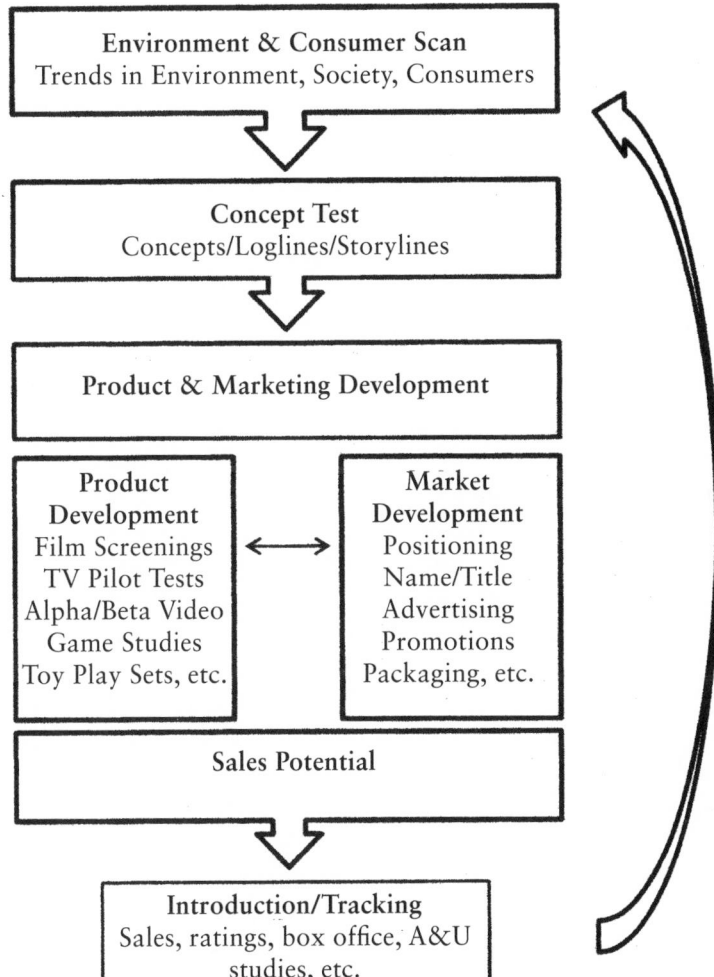

Environment and Consumer Scan

This is where initial insights are derived. The objective of this research is to gather and synthesize information on the entertainment environment. Key places to examine include

- Trends in entertainment—popular films, TV shows,

plays, books, video games, toys, music, fashions, and celebrities
- Trends in society—culture, social, economic, political, and geo-political landscape
- Trends in consumers—segments, demographics, lifestyles, attitudes, perceptions, usage, and behaviors

The inflow of this information should be constant so that new observations can immediately impact decisions. It will paint an ever-changing mosaic of the world in which entertainment options exist.

Many large entertainment companies spend hundreds of thousands of dollars a year to either acquire this information from third parties or conduct the studies themselves. Many times it is a combination of both. While the money spent on this type of research is often put to good use, executives need not wait for researchers to deliver insights in nice binders.

All executives need to be researchers at heart! After spending thirty years both buying research from trend gurus and conducting research myself, I must say that most of what is presented on the environment can be found online and in old school, big city newspapers. Visit a half-dozen Web sites and blogs that cover news, entertainment, trends, and fads and you just about have it nailed. Read newspaper headlines for a couple of weeks, and you can identify most of the political, cultural, social, and demographic trends. Add publications such as *American Demographics, Time, Seventeen,* and *People*. List the trends you see and add to the ones I've started in this book. It's neither hard nor as magical as outside trend consultants will make you believe. If you are working on an idea that takes place in a carnival, camp out at a carnival. Talk to the people who work there. Better yet, work there. Get a sense for the people, the jobs, the environment and its iconography, the joys and woes, the successes and failures, and consumer experience. See it from your audiences' point of view. I am sometimes paid to do this for writers, but writers can do this for themselves.

If you are a writer or inventor, there's another reason

why I want you to be your own researcher. It will provide an unfiltered experience. It will also help you to generate ideas that are "on trend." Then when you pitch the idea, your presentation can include tidbits from the real world to demonstrate to entertainment executives that your idea has merit. This also gives the executive ammunition as he or she begins to pitch your idea up the chain of command.

Filmmaker Ron Howard entered into a partnership with Canon to launch a photo contest in which eight winning entries will be the basis of a short film that will unify the photos into a single story. Call it what you will, this is research. The contest draws information from different people's lives in order to create a mosaic linked together by a human thread. Ron Howard is intensely creative, but somewhere deep within is a researcher who sees, learns, applies, and repeats.

Though I urge you to be your own researcher, don't think you don't need researchers. Good ones will uncover diamonds that could not be readily uncovered from observation alone. So learn from the information and insights that researchers provide, but scan the environment yourself.

Concept Testing

All entertainment executives have hundreds of ideas for movies, novels, TV shows, and toys just spurting out their ears at any one time. They can get them from a number of sources, including internal brainstorming sessions, writers/ producers/directors, and their great-aunt Betsy. I have run many brainstorming sessions to generate ideas across these categories, and each time, the sessions have resulted in hundreds of ideas.

The problem is figuring out which ideas to chase. A few, rather famous people in the entertainment industry have great gut instinct and probably don't need research to help guide them. Unfortunately, everyone in the entertainment business thinks they have great gut instinct, whether they do or don't! This explains why most entertainment projects have a poor return on investment. Most of us need research to help guide wayward guts. Smart executives know that they don't know everything. They are open to learning, especially from their future audience.

Concept testing can be used to discover which ideas have the most potential. It can detail the strengths and weaknesses of each concept to help you to refine those deemed successful enough to move forward. It can also tell you which heartstrings are being pulled among which audience segments. Concept testing can save you fortunes by helping you avoid bad, soul-sucking ideas.

When I was working for a packaged goods manufacturer, one of my responsibilities was to test rough food concepts with consumers. I would receive about twenty product concepts each month from the marketing team. My task was to write a concise statement for each that described the key features of the concept and the emotional and rational needs it would satisfy. I would then hire an artist to draw an illustration for each. The concepts would be tested among a couple hundred consumers across the country. When the results came back, they included the consumers' responses to a five-point interest scale for each concept: definitely would buy, probably would buy, might or might not buy, probably would not buy, and definitely would not buy. I'd write a report and send it around. If the top box purchase interest was above the norm for past successful concepts, I would recommend that the product development team spend resources to create an actual product, which would have its own subsequent research hurdles.

Some entertainment industries have similar types of concept research. Toy companies test pictures/descriptions of new toy ideas. Some will also shoot videos of toy concepts or create very rough mock-ups in an attempt to show features, moving parts, and play patterns.

Concept testing is not standard in Hollywood. Instead, movies are more often green-lighted based on criteria other than direct audience input. Executives might bet that a best-selling novel or comic book series is capable of becoming a blockbuster film. To gain or keep an association with high-profile talent, the studio executive will also green-light their pet projects. The studio executive himself might have a project he's been hoping to make for years, and then an opportunity arises. The problem with this approach is that best-selling novels and comic books don't always translate into film, and even high-profile talent can get it wrong. After the studio green-lights a project, concept testing seems moot. To test an idea or concept for a film in development is like going backwards when the horses are bucking to charge forward.

Because of the fickle nature of the business, studios need concept testing the most, but they often use it the least. I believe that's one critical reason why the failure rate is so high. Virtually any other industry would call this approach haphazard. Many studios call it standard operating procedure.

The rational case against concept testing for films is that the embryonic idea, when expressed in only a paragraph or two, isn't sufficient to express the vision of the film and so research results will be misleading. I see that as a challenge. I have obtained very insightful input from audiences when I have presented them with written story concepts that communicated the *essence* of the idea and its *emotional* foundation. In one study, I asked the studio to provide a ten-minute video of two different films using storyboard-type drawings. Each had a brief beginning, middle, and end and used a dramatic voiceover to push the story along and provide an emotional hook. We obtained great audience feedback, and the research accurately predicated which film would do best. In another study, a video game developer provided a concept board that clearly stated the overall theme and challenge of the game, and then several other boards, one for each of the game's levels, that illustrated each level's key objective, game play, challenge, and villain. It worked extremely well. I have also tested hundreds of loglines in focus groups for TV shows and films. In each case, I made sure that emotional underpinnings were present in the statements. We received great audience input that enlightened the creative teams in ways that made the final product better.

I believe that the reason concept testing is not standard practice in the film industry is because of emotional resistance. Many of those who generate, sell, or buy ideas are leery of consumer input for fear the consumer will disagree with their assessment. So instead, they wait until millions of dollars have been spent on production to find out if they guessed right. Concept testing isn't perfect, but when added to your judgment it's better than a 50/50 coin toss.

When concepts (and even prototypes) are not suitable for testing, it's typically because emotional content wasn't adequately captured in the concept. This leads me to a story.

Once upon a time, a handsome inventor invented a debatably not-so-handsome doll. It had a bit of early success, so a rival toy company took notice and decided to test this doll to ascertain if it was a threat. The research came back, and they decreed it was nothing but a so-so doll. The intergalactic toy company decided not to bother with this doll or its handsome inventor. It was expected to disappear. But it did not disappear. It grew and grew and grew. "How could this be?" thought the gods of toys. "Not-so-handsome dolls cannot succeed in a world that covets extreme beauty."

The intergalactic toy company had researched the wrong thing. They researched the physical appearance. However, that wasn't the *concept*. The concept was the emotion beneath the appearance. The doll line was Cabbage Patch Kids.

Alan Fine is a superb entertainment marketer and researcher who spent many years working on some of the world's largest entertainment brands. He is familiar with the reasons why the toy company's research missed the emotional benefits inherent in Cabbage Patch Kids. According to Fine,

> The toy company produced a straightforward video for about five large dolls. One video was for Cabbage Patch Kids and four were for competitive dolls. They were then shown to about 200 girls. When asked which doll they preferred, most girls selected the other dolls. That was because the Cabbage Patch Kids video limited communication of the emotional appeal of Cabbage Patch Kids. It paid too much attention to the physical attributes of the dolls and

not enough to the emotional connection, for example, that the dolls needed a mommy. While the video included the adoption papers, it did not stress that each doll was different with a distinct look and name so that girls could select a one-of-a-kind baby. By comparison, the other dolls in the test had the usual pretty faces, blond silky hair, and appealing as well as easily demonstrable attributes such as the ability to walk, magically apply makeup, or other attractive play feature. The toy company that eventually did manufacturer the doll created excellent marketing and promotion that communicated the emotional appeal. The original commercial included a girl raising her hand pledging to be a good mommy. Following this, there was a severe shortage of dolls for at least the first six to nine months after launch. Parents that acquired a Cabbage Patch Kids for their girls were heroes and the dolls became status symbols among owners.

Many years ago I had the privilege of presenting to the Cabbage Patch Kids inventor, Xavier Roberts, when the advertising agency I worked for was helping a toy company gain the license for the line. He was a nice guy with a keen vision. He cared for these dolls as though they were real, and he wanted to create that feeling among little girls too. All the elements he created, from the adoption papers to a place of birth to the outstretched arms, were an attempt to create the impression that these were real babies in search of real parents. The baby with debatable cuteness seemed to scream "Pick me up, adopt me, love me, because I need a good parent and a good home!"

The intergalactic toy company had tested the doll, but they missed the emotional concept. That's a problem with all research, especially when testing something that does not convey the emotional vision. But if you know that, the research can be adjusted to accommodate. Like all research, concept testing doesn't replace intuition and experience, it adds to it.

Product Development

Congratulations. If your idea made it this far, it means that a toy company or studio thought enough about your idea to begin development. Your toy idea gets a 3-D model, your film idea gets a draft screenplay or perhaps has been shot, or your TV show idea is turned into a pilot. It's real.

At this stage, research is used to establish if the idea, when developed further, still has potential. Toy companies will allow kids to play with working samples to determine the level of appeal, the extent of play patterns, and if there are any unforeseen product issues. Studios will conduct test screenings to ascertain appeal of the near final movie by audience segment, the movie's potential marketability, to clear up elements of confusion in the narrative, and/or to change unsatisfying endings (if possible). Video game companies will conduct tests to determine the appeal of the game, the extent of bugs, and game playability.

During this part of the research process, understanding the emotional underpinnings of the product continues. Is the movie still about survival, or when executed, do audiences now think it is more about an ill-fated romance? If the product is an action figure, is the core of it really about power, or is it really more about mastery?

Knowing these subtle emotional differences at this critical stage help the creator understand the perception of the project from the perspective of the audience. The emotional heartstrings that we think we are pulling aren't always the ones being pulled. If there is a discrepancy, research will tell us if the new direction is beneficial or lacks the stronger promise inherent in the original concept. Compounding this issue is that different audiences will read something different into each project. One man's action adventure might be a woman's romance. That could be a good thing.

As with the earlier concept research, this stage will help you to identify the audience with the greatest interest (primary audience) and secondary audiences that may warrant subsequent marketing efforts as well. It will also help you to ascertain if the story and execution can be tweaked in order to expand the audience. This is particularly important when you are trying to target a *feeling* that connects to the kid in all of us, instead of just a demographic.

Like concept research, product development research can be misleading, too. When I do research with grade-school girls, they often want the evil characters to be "nicer." I have heard this response for thirty years, and I have never listened to that advice. Why? Because making evil characters "nicer" weakens the story by weakening the villain and the ensuing conflict. Girls want the evil characters to be "nicer" because they are repeating the lessons their parents have taught them. Great parenting doesn't always translate into great storytelling.

The same goes for endings. The film *Titanic* is a great example. As the ship sinks, Jack (Leonardo DiCaprio) helps Rose (Kate Winslet) reach safety, but he succumbs to the frigid waters and dies. It is heart breaking. If polled, I bet that some audience members might have wanted him to live; however, he needed to die in order for the movie to achieve the maximum emotional influence. Yet writer/producer/director James Cameron gave a wink to the audience at the end when in a dreamlike state (or in death), Rose is reunited with Jack and all the other victims aboard a reincarnated ship. Cameron gave it to us both ways. That was a great ending!

During research on rough prototypes or pilots, it is also very important that the researcher be able to pinpoint specific strengths and weaknesses. In the movie and TV businesses, for example, it's critical to disentangle the appeal of the story's premise from the actual structure (beginning/middle/end), characters, character interactions, action elements, and humor. Audiences may dislike a movie because of one small element of humor or a character persona that could have easily been adjusted. I've also seen audiences love a TV pilot because of one small element of execution that, in the long run, would not be enough to sustain their interest. Good research will separate these elements and provide useful direction.

If you are an entertainment executive, be sure the prototype for the research is a great representation of the idea, and let the researchers know if you had considered options of where the story or product might have gone but did not. Good researchers will know how to insert your thoughts into the research in order to help you create the best possible result.

If you are the creator/writer, hopefully you will be invited to attend the study. There you can insert your two cents and provide ideas that might shore up any potential weaknesses. Once again, this research isn't perfect but it adds to your on-going insights. Judgment and audience research are both valuable tools.

Marketing Development

The marketing machine starts crunching when the product is still in the development process. Marketers begin developing options for how to "position" the product in the minds of the audience, which should be based upon key emotional benefits found in earlier research. Campaign ideas using the highest scoring positioning will begin to form, complete with executions targeting key audiences (primary and secondary segments). Different product names/titles are considered. If it's a film, the appeal of the actors, directors, and producers will be assessed (star power) to determine the degree to which they will be used in marketing campaigns. Marketing/advertising materials might include key art/visuals, taglines, ads/trailers, musical treatments, consumer promotions, and packaging. Media plans will be put together.

Before too long, research is often conducted to test alternate communication strategies and tactics across audiences. Researchers will want to determine which marketing options have the potential to generate awareness, interest, involvement, purchase, recommendations to friends, and even lead to repurchase (in some cases). The options that test well across a broad audience might run on network television, whereas those that play better against a narrow audience might appear on cable channels that cater to that audience.

If there's one gripe I have about this research phase, it is that *some* marketing departments don't provide enough marketing options to test. A toy company might test a hundred toy ideas to narrow down to the few they will introduce, but then they will only test one or two advertising campaigns. A studio might test many advertising options for a film, but not adequately test the consumer promotions or merchandise. A video game developer might select a marketing campaign with little or no research at all. That's crazy, especially since the money spent in developing a project is enormous. More marketing options, tested well, should be standard practice.

Studios often ramp up testing a variety of marketing approaches when test screenings of a film are not positive. The intent is to find a way to sell a dog. It's not always the best use of marketing dollars, but miracles do happen.

Too often, the marketing options sent into testing tend to be safe ones. They don't often rock the boat. I prefer to test a range of ideas from the tried and true to riskier approaches. The very purpose of research is to test boundaries to ascertain which can be broken in order to find richer, undiscovered territories.

Sales Potential

When the finished product is ready to go, some companies test it yet again to establish the final potential before it is launched. Researchers might test for sales, expected number of butts in theater seats, anticipated number of people who will tune in, etc.

This stage can be painful. If the idea got this far and passed all the other hurdles, everyone is hoping for a favorable result. If the opposite happens, it can mean several things: someone did not listen to a critical piece of earlier research, the final execution didn't come together as planned, or the environment has changed and consumers have moved on. This research helps, however, in determining if this project should be shelved before more resources are expended or to what extent further resources, especially marketing dollars, should be spent.

Introduction/Tracking

Both before and after the movie hits the screen, the TV show premieres, or the toys and video games hit the shelves, tracking studies can show if the marketing campaign is effective. These studies typically entail large-scale consumer surveys whereby hundreds and even thousands of consumers are questioned to determine how many people have heard of the product (awareness), what they think of it (image/perception), do they intend to participate (buy/watch), have they already (bought/ watched), do they intend to do it again (repeat), will they tell others to participate (word of mouth), and who exactly are those who have participated (audience). Each answer will help diagnose the product's strengths and weaknesses and pinpoint where in the process the communications plan broke down. This is where researchers become great diagnosticians.

If the entertainment doesn't have strong awareness, then you are not spending enough money on media (either via number of viewers reached or their viewing frequency), or the message carried by your media is too soft to break through.

If the entertainment has awareness and the key product/ story message is coming through but sales are sluggish, it often means that the audience is rejecting your message. Ouch! Marketing needs to be adjusted.

If the entertainment has strong awareness, the message is coming through, you get great sales the first week, but then interest plummets in subsequent weeks, it often means that the audience was unsatisfied with the product itself and they told a million of their friends to avoid it.

There are many other scenarios. If the entertainment is attracting an unexpected secondary audience, for example, you might target that audience more aggressively with media. If the product or marketing is fixable at this point, that is great. If not, then the learning becomes important for the next time around by feeding the insights back into the entire process.

When I was at Ogilvy & Mather, we often conducted post mortems on new launches. We would evaluate successes and failures, learn from them, write them up, and produce guidelines for what worked and what did not. Our spirit guide was founder David Ogilvy. He was an ardent observer of human nature, a lover of research, an intense creative, and he always looked for opportunities to learn and teach. His book *Ogilvy on Advertising* is a classic. In many ways, his efforts to learn, apply, and teach inspired me to do the same.

Methodologies

There are two basic types of research methodologies: qualitative (focus groups, one-on-one interviews) and quantitative (large-scale surveys). Qualitative research puts you face to face with consumers, helping you to probe deep into the strengths and weaknesses of ideas, to disentangle elements so that you know which are contributing to strengths and weaknesses, and to find solutions to any issues that arise. Qualitative research also gives you the opportunity to pitch ideas to respondents to gauge their reactions. Quantitative research provides a larger sample size and thus more projectable, reliable results. The downside is that the depth of information regarding strengths, weaknesses, and ways to improve are more limited because executives are not typically observing the respondents firsthand; therefore, they cannot toss in questions if issues arise. Some methodologies do use a combo approach.

Ideally, you should do the qualitative research first. Use it to fix or optimize your entertainment, and then send the refined version into quantitative research. However, it doesn't always happen in this way due to budget and time constraints.

The Kid in All of Us

If you are attempting to create a blockbuster for the kid in all of us, then the research steps just outlined need to be conducted across all audiences. It's important to ascertain the strengths and weaknesses across each segment while knowing where the most business lies. It is critical to know the core emotional need the entertainment satisfies and to identify the different emotional needs that the entertainment might satisfy in all audience groups. It's also important to know where the influence within family households originates. Are the parents more likely to recommend a certain product/

movie to their children, or are the children more likely to ask their parents if they can participate?

When conducting research with parents and children, it is not wise to assume that parents know what their children's preferences are. Raf Berardinelli is an experienced entertainment researcher who knows the importance of going directly to the source. This is especially true when trying to decipher whether entertainment appeals broadly to kids and their parents. Says Berardinelli,

> A mistake I have seen over the years is that adults will reference themselves when trying to decide what their children like. In my experience, you cannot self-reference. Parents will say, "I like this, so my child will like this." Self-reference research is not good, yet I have seen that over and over through the years. Unfortunately, parents don't always know what their children prefer, so researchers need to go to the source and ask all potential audiences directly.

Appeasing multiple audiences is always a balancing act. Ideally, the win-win solution is to adjust some aspect of your entertainment to entice an uncommitted segment but in ways that do not alienate a segment that has already bought into it. Providing shared emotional content is often the most powerful way to bridge the divide.

Research—Creative Partnership

There can be a natural clash of objectives and personas where researchers and creative types are concerned. Many researchers are numbers oriented. They tell us what is. Creative types are imagination oriented. They tell us what can be. Research people are sometimes required to inform creative types that their baby is ugly. Creative types sometimes feel compelled to rush to the defense of their ugly child. Parents can get aggressive.

The best partnership occurs when researchers are sensitive to the creative process and when creative types understand and appreciate the benefits of research. Said another way; it's invaluable when researchers can translate research findings into recommendations that truly aid invention. It's equally invaluable when creative types know how to use research to make their efforts better.

My Pet Peeves

I have met, hired, and fired researchers. I'm one of them, in addition to being a novelist. I guess it takes being a part of the family to know what's right and what's wrong. The majority of researchers I have known are really good at what they do. Others, not so much, even though they think they are. Beware of four types of researchers.

The Politician as Researcher: This is the most insidious. This person tends to be a politician who happens to do research. He uses research as a powerbase because information is knowledge. He covets numbers as a way to tell others where they failed. He doesn't offer insight as much as he offers a report card.

The Indecisive Researcher: This researcher is either not mentally equipped to make strong recommendations or is too afraid to. He provides options but doesn't take a strong point of view either way. You want researchers with opinions based upon an accurate read of the audience. He needs to have skin in the game.

The Know-It-All Researcher: There are some researchers who *think* they know it all. They know how to do all research, know everything about the consumer, and know everything about their industry. They don't. We are always learning because our audiences are always changing. People who think they have nothing more to learn eventually make tragic mistakes.

The Data Researcher: This researcher provides reams of data but few insights. He cannot bridge the divide that turns data into insights that aids creativity. You can't learn that; it's innate.

These "types" are not limited to the research department; they are found in all disciplines. The problem with their presence in the research division is that they are the channel to the consumer and the environment. They feed information throughout an organization.

If you find researchers who are smart, sensitive to the

marketing and creative needs, can translate data into insights, and are not politicians, indecisive, or know-it-alls, hire them fulltime, pay them well, and keep them happy. Get them involved early in the creative process to help you to develop, not just "test," your creativity.

Better Than a Coin Toss

In one study I helped to conduct many years ago, we estimated in a particular entertainment category that the research methodology employed accurately predicted in-market performance roughly 80 percent of the time. In 20 percent of the cases, entertainment was either unjustifiably killed or unjustifiably launched. Still, being able to predict with 80 percent accuracy is better than a coin toss. That's why research aids judgment but can't replace it.

Key Takeaway

Research can be a great friend to the creative process. When used properly, it can

- Provide insights on the environment and audiences in ways that lay the foundation for ideas to be born and nourished
- Help you to ascertain which of many ideas have the most potential and which should be killed early on
- Help you to determine the strengths and weaknesses of the idea once it is further developed, along with providing thoughts on any needed refinements
- Help you to select the most effective ways to market the final entertainment
- Help you to establish the final product's potential before launch
- Help you to ascertain in-market performance on measures of awareness generation, perception created, and actual sales achieved

I believe in putting up or shutting up, so I conducted some research on concepts of my own. These are coming up.

Chapter 13

Launch an Idea Quest

Our *idea quest* is relentless and it should be. Ideas are the lifeblood of success. It takes a tremendous amount of work to generate a large number of ideas, and then more work to find the precious few that are worth pursuing. It then takes luck and timing for those precious few to become blockbusters. Far fewer of these will cross over to become blockbuster franchises.

The probability that you will generate an idea that becomes a blockbuster is low. It always is. I have provided various tools and insights throughout this book to help you increase the odds. They are similar to ones that I have used for years to help companies in various industries generate and refine ideas. The objective of those tools and insights is to help you find interesting combinations that you might not have considered otherwise.

Once you generate numerous ideas, you have to be ruthless when evaluating them. Troublesome, embryonic ideas become much more problematic as they mature. It's best to separate those that have potential from those that don't. Thin the herd.

This chapter might very well be "a bridge too far," referring to my overly ambitious objective. The goal of this chapter is to demonstrate the evaluative process. It contains twenty story ideas that I have generated using the tools in this book. Some of these ideas were cited in earlier chapters; some are new. I will review each idea and cite the pros and cons. Then I will show you the results of research I conducted whereby I exposed the ideas to respondents across the country to get their reactions.

Let me be honest about the dangers of this chapter. You might think my ideas are poor and, therefore, disregard the wonderful advice I have given throughout this book. I have rarely met any two writers who liked each other's ideas. You might think that the consumers should have rated my ideas higher or lower, which will toss the value of my ideas or the research into jeopardy. I don't care if you like my ideas or if you think they should have scored differently. This chapter is about the process. That's where learning is found. If you have better ideas, I encourage you to develop and test them.

Once I drafted the ideas, I had several men and women of varying ages provide feedback. Think of it as qualitative research that helped me to fix some obvious flaws. But since no ideas are perfect any way, it still gives me room to critique them. This gives you an opportunity to *hear me think* as I pick apart each idea. The criteria I use are the principles in this book, namely, does the story hit an emotional cord(s), is it based upon contemporary culture or trends, are the characters relatable and aspiring, does it have broad appeal, does it have the potential to become a franchise, do elements lend itself to marketable artistry.

Each idea is in standard story format. (A story is about a specific character that has a burning need to meet an important goal and must overcome a great challenge or series of challenges to reach it.) The first sentence of each concept is the summary logline and the follow-up sentences are important details that get it closer to becoming an Intellectual Property Story Idea (IP Story Idea). I did not always add secondary characters because these are ideas and not yet treatments. Key elements that relate to emotional needs, iconic characters, etc. are in bold to help you follow my reasoning. I did not state an idea's style of execution (e.g., animated or live action) because in several cases that is up for discussion.

My hope is that this exercise will be insightful by demonstrating how to employ the principles I have discussed to generate and evaluate ideas. I don't know of any other book that offers up new ideas for criticism (and ridicule!), but I'll take the hit in hopes you find this useful. Plus, it gives you the opportunity to beat up my ideas. That should be fun.

If one of these ideas (or titles) has already been introduced somewhere in the universe, my apologies; I read and watch a lot of stories, but I can't keep up with all of them. It would be simply coincidental. I also added a comment section beneath each idea so that you can write your own assessment.

Be sure to think about whether any of these could become Single-Event Blockbusters, Linear-Franchise Blockbusters, or Multi-Category-Franchise Blockbusters. The ideas are presented in no particular order.

E.T. Search & Destroy: This is an action story about a **warrior** who **hunts and kills space aliens** but decides to **save** one instead. Doug Banister (code name: Cobra) is part of an elite **Special Ops team** whose mission is to search and **kill space aliens** that break through **Earth's defenses**. About to **break the record** for most kills, Cobra discovers that the alien he is supposed to kill is on a mission of peace—and *she's* **an exotic beauty!** He can't bring himself to kill her, so he decides to **help her safely back** to her spaceship. The rest of the team is given new orders—**track and kill Cobra before he can save the alien.**

Pros: Survival, rescue, and nurturing the alien with potential for romance are emotional drivers. Characters are relatable and aspiring. Aliens are pop culture. It could be a Linear Franchise (sequels) if Doug's new goal is to save aliens. It might be a Multi-Category Franchise if the sets, alien features, and weapons are unique and intriguing enough to lead to merchandise.

Cons: Might not bring in women/girls even with the female alien/romance angle. Doug needs a human story. Perhaps an alien killed his wife, which provided his motivation to be the most efficient "alien killer." He then meets the beautiful female alien who wants peace, making Doug reconsider his motivation to kill aliens, as he falls in love again.

Your Comments: _____

_____

_____

Nerds Rock: This is a comedy about **nerdy** young women who **transform themselves** into a **hot rock group** to be cool. Alberta and her two friends work at a **biotech** company and can't meet any hot guys. **Discouraged by their own geekiness** (they play in a polka band), they inject themselves with a virus that **mutates their genes** and turns them into a hot, new, **rebellious rock band that attracts tons of guys.** They get everything they want until they discover that the nerdy guys back at the biotech company weren't so bad after all.

Pros: Good emotional satisfaction with wish fulfillment, achieving rock star dreams, and potential romance. It has relatable and aspiring characters. Nice use of DNA/science trend and rock pop culture. If it's successful, might sequel by having the girls use their DNA skills to transform into other aspiring iconic characters (Linear Franchise).

Cons: It seems like it's been done before and not enough at risk. We might create new news if we use a real rock star in the lead role. Lady Gaga? It might skew too much toward girls/women. We might need to add a male lead. It might be funnier if the DNA came with more hilarious consequences, such as transforming them back and forth without their control. Don't see it as a Multi-Category Franchise because there's only limited potential for other lines of business unless there's original music.

Your Comments: _____

_____

_____

N.D.E.: Near Death Experience: This is an action drama about a super smart college student (physicist) who must find his way **back from the dead.** David, **afraid of death** since his mother was **murdered** by his stepfather, has a **near-death experience** and is momentarily **reunited** with his loving mom's **spirit** in heaven. After being snapped back to the living, David creates a **machine** that he hopes will **open the gates between our world** and heaven so that he can continue their relationship. A miscalculation lands him in a part of the **underworld ruled by** his evil stepdad who recently died. He **struggles to get back to the land of the living,** but he can only succeed with help from his mom's spirit who enters the underworld to **save her son** and **confront the man who killed her.**

Pros: It has emotional depth. Life and death struggles, love of family, and confronting your murderer are strong emotional drivers. Characters are relatable and empathetic. It's on trend with science and mysticism (near-death experiences). It is reminiscent of the 1990 film *Flatliners* but with a very different premise (familiar but different).

Cons: If it's successful it might be able to sequel (Linear Franchise), but it currently feels closed-ended. It doesn't have much to make it a Multi-Category Franchise. David feels very alone; he could use a female companion who accompanies him for a romance angle and bring in a female audience. It might be too dark for kids. Perhaps David can also be accompanied by his little sister who sneaks in just in time to be transported? That might raise the risk.

Your Comments: _____

_____

_____

Jennifer Crusoe: This is an adventure comedy about a shy personal assistant who must **come out of her shell to save the guy she loves** from island horrors. Jennifer is **secretly in love** with her famous **rock star boss**—Prince Adonis. He's adored by fans but hated by others because he's demanding and insensitive, and **he doesn't know that Jennifer loves him.** Jetting on their way to an Asian tour, Prince Adonis and Jennifer **crash near a dangerous island.** Prince Adonis is no match for **real terror**—violent storms, cannibals, and beasts. It's up to shy Jennifer Crusoe to take **control and save their lives** while Prince Adonis learns a lesson **about life and love.**

Pros: Survival and romance hit emotional cords. Pop culture is handled with rock star life style. Jennifer may be relatable as a shy girl who needs confidence and boldness. It's a combo of *Robinson Crusoe* and *The Devil Wears Prada.*

Cons: May be too familiar. Too small. Not exciting enough unless execution can save it. Don't see this as a Linear Franchise (sequels) or Multi-Category Franchise that can support lines of business. It might not bring in enough males.

Your Comments: _____

_____

_____

Kickboxer: This is an action adventure about Brandy, a short, **fearful** eighteen-year-old kickboxing student who must **save her sensei.** Brandy is learning the sport so that she can **protect herself** from the **bullies in the big city.** But she is **thrust into the world of spies** when Sensei Matt, her handsome kickboxing master and **secret CIA agent,** is kidnapped by a foreign government. Poor little fearful Brandy has to **step it up a notch** to save them both, kicking and punching her way out of trouble.

Pros: Emotional drivers of survival and facing your fears work. Possible romance. Character is relatable (trying to face fears of violence, a small person in a big world of troubles). If successful, it could be a sequel. Brandy could be pulled into the CIA, but that direction might destroy the premise.

Cons: Feels way too familiar, small, and not unique enough. It doesn't really connect with trends or culture. Not much here for a franchise.

Your Comments: _____

_____

_____

College Ops: This is an action adventure about three college siblings who become **warriors to rescue their mom** from the **battlefield.** Capt. Janice Peterson reenlists in the army in order to pay the college tuition for her three super smart children—Deb, Tommy, and Jed. She's **deployed into combat and is captured.** The government stalls her rescue, so the Peterson clan go on a **daring adventure into the heat of battle.** They are determined not to let their mother die the same way **their military dad did years before.** They have their mom's **bravery** and plenty of their **dad's old equipment!**

Pros: Good emotional drivers in survival, need to rescue mom (love), and empowerment with kids in adult role. It has relatable, aspiring, and empathetic characters. Audience could be broad given the range of characters. Terrorism/war is relatable.

Cons: Might be too close to the film *Iron Eagle,* but the mom/kid approach might make it different enough. It might be able to sequel, but the story feels too close-ended. Not much here for a Multi-Category Franchise. The college kids have no depth as yet; they each need a motivation and persona that conflict and unite. Not sure if this should be told from the standpoint of the mother or from the standpoint of the children. Need to decide whose story this is.

Your Comments: _____

_____

_____

Spellbound: This is an action adventure about Spella, a beautiful yet **evil young witch** who **turns good** to **save mankind.** Spella, her mother, and sister use **magic to enslave** the world. Led by Prince Mankato, mankind revolts but fails. Impressed by the prince's bravery, Spella **falls in love** with him and decides to **free mankind.** Chased by her evil mother and sister, Spella and Prince Mankato travel across **dangerous lands to destroy the source of her family's power.** Spella gradually **loses her beauty,** which was magic-made, and **becomes plain looking.** However, Mankato **loves her all the more for her natural beauty.** They destroy the magic source and discover that Spella is a **princess who was kidnapped by the witches as a baby.**

Pros: Strong romance driver, along with beauty, power, survival. It's on trend with magic. Characters feel relatable and aspiring. It's definitely a family film. It could sequel, though it feels a bit final at the moment. It might be a Multi-Category Franchise if it is executed with elements that make for merchandise. Spella's transformation from beauty, which was made from evil magic, to plainly attractive (natural beauty, princess-like) would make a great doll that transforms. It feels as if it would be animated.

Cons: It might skew too young, so it needs gritty realism and great risk to entice parents and adults.

Your Comments: _____

_____

_____

Dr. Stem Cell: This is an action adventure about Willow, a young woman **born with super powers** who must **prevent people from becoming mutants.** A sinister **scientist, Dr. Stem Cell,** illegally **created Willow in a test tube.** She was whisked away before birth to live atop a fortress monastery with a **secret society** aimed to **protect and teach her.** All is well for twenty years until Dr. Stem Cell begins to **turn the rest of the world into mutated beasts.** Willow is the only hope, but **she must find the courage** to leave the safety of her home and **master her powers.** But Dr. Stem Cell **knows how to destroy her**—because he created her!

Pros: Connects with emotional needs for power, mastery, control, and a life and death struggle. It uses science trend/culture. Character feels empathetic. If successful, it feels open-ended enough to sequel (Linear Franchise), but there's not enough here yet to be a Multi-Category Franchise.

Cons: Feels like a comic-book-derived franchise, which might make it hard to compete with ingrained comic book franchises. Fan boys will find too many familiar alternatives. Male audiences might not accept a female lead unless she's gritty and deadly. She needs a companion, possibly her master from the monastery who accompanies her until his demise.

Your Comments: _____

_____

_____

Buster & Whirl Girl: This is an action comedy about a **grandpa and granddaughter superhero team** who must **unite** to defeat evil. Buster is a cranky, sixty-five-year-old superhero who was forced to retire. His anger over retirement leads to his divorce. An ancient evil rises and kills most of the younger superheroes so Buster reluctantly joins forces with the only remaining hero left alive, a sarcastic, know-it-all sixteen-year-old girl named Whirl Girl who wants to prove herself. They don't get along until Buster discovers that she's the granddaughter he never knew he had. His old-fashioned tactics and her new style of fighting must work together to destroy evil.

Pros: Hits emotional chords for older audiences (want to be useful, esteem) and young audiences (want to prove themselves, esteem). Characters feel relatable and aspiring. It connects with trend of aging population with grandparents and grandkids. If successful, it could sequel (Linear Franchise). It might be a Multi-Category Franchise if elements of execution lead to merchandise.

Cons: It might feel too similar to other recent family superhero stories. Sounds animated and young, but a live-action version with a Billy Crystal-type character could be hilarious, bring in adults, and make it unique. It might skew toward girls. It could use a male character, perhaps Whirl Girl's twin brother, to give boys a relatable/aspiring character and create more compelling family dynamics/friction.

Your Comments: _____

_____

_____

3 Deadly Wishes: This is an action romance story about Geniella, a beautiful genie who must prevent her master from taking over the world. An overly trusting genie, Geniella falls in love with her human master, but he tricks her, steals her powers, and leaves her to die in the streets of modern-day Los Angeles. Now, she must prevent her master from fulfilling his three wishes, which will make him master of the world. Geniella's only two hopes are the one power she has left—shape shifting—and the aid of a skeptical yet handsome police detective.

Pros: Love lost and found is a strong emotional driver, as is survival and revenge upon a lover that betrayed you. It ties into the **magic** trend. It could attract a broad audience using the iconic genie and detective characters. Characters feel relatable and aspiring. It could sequel (Linear Franchise) if kept open-ended, and there's a possibility for a Multi-Category Franchise with merchandise such as genie dolls, magic carpets, genie bottle, and genie-inspired apparel. The genie-related elements make for fun marketing.

Cons: It might skew more toward girls so we need to make sure it has male cues. We might accomplish this by making the master truly evil, the genie truly edgy, and casting the police detective as a tough iron-man type who doesn't believe in fairytale genie crap.

Your Comments: _____

_____

_____

Honor among Elves: This is an action adventure about Tolari, an **elf** who is **believed to be a coward,** and his **brave efforts to save his son.** Tolari brought shame upon his family's name for wanting to make peace with the **Dwarf Kingdom.** Elves **deemed him a coward** for refusing to fight. Dwarf warriors suddenly **kidnap** Tolari's son to use him in a **blood sacrifice** to a **dragon** in three days. The fear for his son's life is greater than his desire for peace, so Tolari treks across the **Dreaded Desert of Endless Fears** to recover his son—no **matter the cost.**

Pros: Saving face and saving loved ones are strong emotional drivers. Has a *Finding Nemo* feel but with multiple twists. Characters feel relatable and aspiring. Not really connected to any trend, though elves are part of pop culture due to *The Lord of the Rings.* If it's successful it might be able to sequel (Linear Franchise), but it currently feels closed-ended (you find the son and you're done). The environments and iconography could lead to merchandise (Multi-Category Franchise).

Cons: There might not be enough room for this idea given the appeal of *The Lord of the Rings*. It might also be too male oriented, so it could use a female entry point. Perhaps Tolari needs to save his daughter who is a capable warrior in her own right. That could make it different and might not alienate boys if she is tough.

Your Comments: _____

_____

_____

Astro-NUT: This is a comedy about Glenn, a twenty-year-old **technical geek** working for **NASA.** He wants a chance to be a **great astronaut,** but his **weakling body gets him rejected** by the program every time. To his surprise, he's selected to **compete** to be two of five astronauts to go to Mars! The **competition and challenges** he undertakes are as difficult as they are hilarious. His small-town girlfriend and family are so **proud!** So is Glenn until he **discovers that he was selected because he is so** *average,* which gives NASA a "benchmark" to judge the success of the more skilled candidates expected to win. Glenn must **prove that even an average guy has the right stuff to reach the stars!**

Pros: Nice use of the underdog persona who has to compete with those more talented. Pride, success, winning. The character is relatable and empathic. It's on trend with space exploration. If it is successful, it could sequel (Linear Franchise). Sounds a bit like the 1967 film *The Reluctant Astronaut* starring Don Knotts, but it's different enough (familiar with twists). It could use a star that fits the average persona, like Jack Black. It could lead to fun space-age marketing and NASA tie-ins.

Cons: It doesn't feel like there's enough at risk. It needs to lead to a survival, life-and-death moment. It doesn't yet have a romance angle or much to make it a Multi-Category Franchise.

Your Comments: _____

_____

_____

Recycled: This is an adventure romance about a **jelly jar named Jerry** whose girlfriend takes him on a **dangerous journey** to the **recycling** center so that he can **live again.** You see, Jerry's days are numbered; he's almost empty, which means he's going to **be tossed in the trash (the family doesn't recycle)!** Poor Pam the peanut butter jar is heartbroken because **she loves him.** She and the other kitchen friends decide to take Jerry to a place rumored to bring old containers back to life. It's called **recycling!** The team goes on a **dangerous journey** to the **recycling center.** They accomplish their task but are sad to leave their friend. However, groceries arrive weeks later, bringing a newly filled Jerry back to his loved ones. **Jerry lives!**

Pros: Connects with the emotional needs for survival, love, romance, and friendship. Characters are relatable and empathic. The recycling theme is on trend. If successful, I can envision sequels (Linear Franchise) as well as a Multi-Category Franchise with a lot of merchandise opportunities and tie-in partnerships with packaged-goods manufacturers.

Cons: It feels as if it skews very young unless the story is made highly emotional or edgier.

Your Comments: _____

_____

_____

Malt Shop Rock: This is a musical comedy about Susie and Ted, sixteen-year-old twins living in 1952 who **don't always get along.** But they do agree on one thing; they want to be **famous songwriters and performers.** They are in the perfect place and time—Nashville in 1952, home to many rock sensations. They work after school at their dad's **malt shop** (Malt Shop Rock) and **perform on countertops** with their friends who work there. It's the perfect place because Malt Shop Rock is visited by **soon-to-be-famous music artists like Elvis Presley.** Susie and Ted need to sell just **one song to become famous** and **save their dad's malt shop** from going out of business.

Pros: It connects with the desire for fame and fortune.

The idea to save their father's malt shop is noble and adds emotional depth (even though it's cliché). The characters are aspiring. The 1950s theme and artists are on trend and could connect to multiple generations. It's open-ended enough for a sequel. The music and period iconography would lead to a Multi-Category Franchise. It might be smart to insert original songs that sound like they came from the 1950s. It lends itself to fun marketing.

Cons: Might be too tween and teen oriented, but that might not be bad if it does a great job penetrating that demographic. It could use romance, perhaps with Susie and a bad boy rocker or a young soon-to-be-famous Elvis. Should Susie be the one to inspire Elvis by inadvertently stepping on his blue suede shoes? Perhaps she's a muse for all the soon-to-be rockers.

Your Comments: _____

_____

_____

Mad Skills: This is an action adventure about Madison, a brilliant and brave college student who **experiments with different careers** by pretending to be someone else (**a great imposter**). Madison **feels trapped** by having to work at his dad's uniform store after he graduates, so he secretly "tries on" different jobs. He **impersonates a quarterback** to play one game in the NFL, **a doctor** to perform an operation, and **a pilot** to fly a jet fighter in battle. He **blogs** about his experiences and everyone wants to know who the **secret imposter** is. His parents just don't understand why he doesn't want to take over the family business until one of Madison's special skills **saves their lives!**

Pros: It connects with everyone's desire to discover what they should do in life. The character is relatable and aspiring. The story's emphasis on blogging is on trend. It could sequel if successful (Linear Franchise). It feels like the film *Catch Me If You Can* (criminal who uses skill to avert police) yet it's a very different approach.

Cons: It may lack appeal to women so a romance angle may be needed. It doesn't appear to have potential as a Multi-Category Franchise.

Your Comments: _____

_____

_____

Extreme Gene: This is an action adventure about an ultra-genius middle-school boy named Eugene (Gene for short) who **creates beasts out of common pets** to seek **revenge** upon those who belittle him. Gene's **only friends are his puny little pets,** but even they are laughed at by the popular kids. He decides to use his **expertise in genetics** to add eagle wings to his pet dog, a lion's head and fangs to his cat, and an alligator's mouth to his hamster. He wants **revenge upon the popular kids,** but when a real disaster strikes the school, he realizes that they must work together to save the students.

Pros: Being an underdog is emotionally relatable. The character is relatable and somewhat aspiring. A kid playing God is interesting—has a Frankenstein quality. The science is on trend. The animal transformations are fun/potentially dark. If it is successful, it might sequel because the story seems open-ended. It could lead to merchandise like toys and video games where kids can invent animals (Multi-Category Franchise).

Cons: Feels very young and not likely to attract adults in large numbers unless it's edgier/darker and a family/adult presence is added (should dad be a veterinarian?). Also, Gene might be the antagonist, and a new, more likeable protagonist might be inserted.

Your Comments: _____

_____

_____

Carnies: This is a comedy about a **pampered young wife,** Cornelia, and her two **selfish kids.** One day, Cornelia's husband decides to quit being a doctor in New York to **buy a carnival** in the Midwest to **satisfy his childhood dream.** Cornelia and the kids hate their new carnival life and the carnies (people who work at the carnival). Cornelia and the kids are **dragged through elephant poop, nearly stabbed by knife throwers, and are set ablaze by fire breathers.** But the family learns a lesson about what's really important in life and that **family comes in all shapes and sizes.**

Pros: Fish out of water story has potential. It is based upon a cultural icon (carnivals). It includes some hilarious moments. It might be a TV series along the lines of the 1965 show *Green Acres.* It could blossom into a Multi-Category Franchise given all the iconography associated with carnivals. It's familiar, yet different enough. Iconic carnival settings would make for fun marketing efforts.

Cons: Not sure where the emotional depth is yet. It needs to dig deeper. There's not enough risk. Why is Cornelia the way she is? What's her emotional journey? Perhaps this story should be told through one of the other family members.

Your Comments: _____

_____

_____

Growth Spurt Alert: This is a comedy about twelve-year-old **Rachel who becomes eighteen overnight,** thanks to a tube of **lipstick** mistakenly injected with **growth hormones.** It started when Rachel's parents gave her a box of **childish cosmetics** for her twelfth birthday. **Embarrassing.** She quickly discovers that **whenever she wears the lipstick, she transforms into an eighteen-year-old beauty.** Rachel secretly makes her **every wish come true,** including getting a job as a **fashion model,** but she discovers that being eighteen has **scary consequences.** By then, she can't reverse the process until help arrives from her twelve-year-old buddy Billy.

Pros: Fits with girl's emotional fantasies. While it is reminiscent of the film *13 Going on 30,* it uses cosmetics as the transformation device, which fits the circumstances. Girls use cosmetics to look older, so what if they really made you older? Might work best as a TV series in which the girl can transform back and forth, thus leading a secret double life. Character would be highly relatable and aspiring for girls. It could be a Multi-Category Franchise with cosmetic/fashions as the leading line of business.

Cons: The small to big transformation has been done before. It skews female and probably young (kid, tween, maybe teen). It might work best as a cable show for tween girls. It would need a male friend to gain a male audience. Not really on any particular trend.

Your Comments: _____

_____

_____

The Future, in 3-D: This is an action adventure about a **selfish, fib-telling twelve-year-old boy named Donny,** who **steals** a pair of **3-D glasses** from a movie theater and soon discovers that it allows him to **see future disasters before they strike.** At first, Donny feels **empowered** when the minor mishaps he foresees through his glasses come true to neighborhood friends. Then the **glasses reveal that a nuclear power plant is about to explode** that will kill thousands. Panicked, Donny sets out to warn the city but will anyone listen to the boy who cried wolf in the past?

Pros: Fits with our desire to see the future. Empowering. Using 3-D glasses as the centerpiece is on trend with common technology we all use (pop culture). That Donny learns a lesson about his moral character is transforming. It could sequel (Linear Franchise) as long as they hold onto the special glasses and if the glasses have other powers as well. It lends itself to a cool a back story regarding why that particular pair of 3-D glasses is special. Perhaps the pair is military developed or lost by an alien race, or perhaps a supreme being selected Donny for a special, long-term reason. It could be a TV series as well. 3-D glasses would create fun marketing efforts.

Cons: It needs to age up, possibly by providing a parent role or edgy execution. Need to insert more girl appeal—maybe give Donny a female companion. Other than selling 3-D glasses, not sure this has potential as a Multi-Category Blockbuster.

Your Comments: _____

_____

_____

E-Bomb: Low-tech bomb-squad detective Jake Dugan unites with his estranged, high-tech teenage son to stop a powerful Internet executive from sending e-mail encrypted e-bombs that kill her rivals. These bombs are killing high-profile executives, and no one realizes they are delivered via the Internet. Detective Dugan is called to investigate and soon realizes he needs the help of his son Ben. It's a fragile relationship as they each blame the other for the death of Brenda, Jake's wife and Ben's mother. They put their differences aside to solve the case. Tech wizard Ben figures out that the bombs were sent electronically as harmless looking e-mails and text messages that turn any device into a bomb once the message is downloaded. Old Jake and young Ben have to unite to catch a killer before the killer finds them—electronically.

Pros: It potentially has emotional depth with old school vs. new school, and the estranged nature of the father/son relationship. They yearn for reconciliation. E-bomb is on trend. Using the Internet as the basis for the story could lend itself to exciting Internet marketing efforts. The film could sequel.

Cons: There is not much here for a Multi-Category Franchise. It needs a female presence. It feels a bit dark; Ben's persona could be mischievous and sarcastic to lighten the mood. This would play well against his father's more serious personality.

Your Comments: _____

_____

_____

Notice that I did not try to "sell" each idea by using

words or phrases like "the most exciting adventure" or "the funniest comedy" or "an amazing action story." I don't want you to be influenced by the hype. Ideas need to be pristine so they can be evaluated on their merits. There will be plenty of time for hype later.

Of these twenty ideas, which ten do you think have the most potential? Make your list before you glance at my list. Tick, tock.

Okay. Here are my ten in no particular order. They each have issues that need to be addressed, but I subjectively felt that the pros outweighed the cons. I also wanted to test a range of ideas, some more "safe" and some more "out there."

- E.T. Search & Destroy
- N.D.E.: Near Death Experience
- Spellbound
- Buster & Whirl Girl
- 3 Deadly Wishes
- Astro-Nut
- Recycled
- Malt Shop Rock
- Mad Skills
- Carnies

So what's next? Film students, professional writers, studios, and outside production companies would select the ideas that they felt best about, if any, and begin initial development. That's exactly the wrong thing to do!

At this stage, it makes sense to obtain some audience input to gauge innate concept appeal before you commit. Creative types often shun this type of research and say that concepts are too sterile to test. While I agree that concept research can give a false read, it's more tragic to get no audience reaction before spending hundreds of thousands of dollars on scripts and millions of dollars on production. If you write a concept that explains the essentials and lace it with emotional drivers, consumers can provide a rough interest measure that you can use as input alongside your intuition and experience.

So that's what I did. I commissioned the Chicago-based C+R Research to conduct a nationwide study. The objective was to ascertain the appeal for each of the ten concepts on my short list. The concepts were exposed to four hundred people, ages eight to fifty-five, males and females. They were shown the concepts without my annotated pros and cons or any potential actors' names. Ideas have to stand on their own. The respondents were told that the stories might be the foundation for a movie, novel, or television show. I then asked them to rate each idea on a five-point scale: definitely be interested, probably be interested, might/might not, probably would not be interested, or definitely would not be interested. If this was for an actual assignment, I would have specified which medium (movie, novel, or TV) and had a more specific behavior-related scale (e.g., definitely would see the movie, probably would see the movie, etc.). However, for our purposes, I kept it general.

This kind of research can help you narrow the concepts down to fewer stronger ideas. You might wonder why I would bother with research when I have already applied key principles. First, not all the ideas fit all the principles yet. Even if ideas adhere to the principles, success is not guaranteed. It's how all the elements fit together that matters. Hence, research will tell us what audiences think of each idea's mosaic. As I said throughout this book, we need to be willing to kill small ugly ideas before they become big ugly productions. It's put up or shut up time.

The results are in Exhibit 39. Respondents had clear preferences. The results show the top two box percentage score (percent definitely or probably interested). I used the top two box scores because new ideas that are not based upon established franchises score much lower because there's no in-going strength. For highly successful established franchises, scores are higher and top box scores make more sense to review.

Exhibit 39: Audience Interest in Story Concepts

Percent definitely or probably interested.

Representative Nationwide Sample

		Total (400)	Males (199)	Females (201)	Ages 8-12 (99)	Ages 13-19 (101)	Ages 20-35 (100)	Ages 36-55 (100)
1	Mad Skills	45.8%	49.2%	42.3%	40.4%	51.5%	45.0%	46.0%
2	N.D.E.: Near Death Experience	45.0%	49.7%	40.3%	43.4%	49.5%	49.0%	38.0%
3	Carnies	39.5%	36.7%	42.3%	39.4%	34.7%	45.0%	39.0%
4	Astro-NUT	38.5%	47.2%	29.9%	40.4%	29.7%	39.0%	45.0%
5	E.T. Search & Destroy	38.3%	51.3%	25.4%	41.4%	30.7%	48.0%	33.0%
6	Spellbound	38.0%	32.2%	43.8%	47.5%	25.7%	41.0%	38.0%
7	3 Deadly Wishes	36.0%	31.7%	40.3%	39.4%	30.7%	39.0%	35.0%
8	Buster & Whirl Girl	34.8%	40.7%	28.9%	42.4%	24.8%	38.0%	34.0%
9	Malt Shop Rock	31.8%	32.7%	30.8%	36.4%	28.7%	34.0%	28.0%
10	Recycled	21.0%	19.6%	22.4%	26.3%	12.9%	34.0%	11.0%

Source: 2011 Study of blockbuster entertainment, conducted by C+R Research, Chicago, Illinois, exclusively for the book Creating Blockbusters!

Two ideas stood above the rest: *Mad Skills* and *N.D.E.: Near Death Experience*. These did very well. Nearly half of respondents would definitely or probably be interested. They were strong across a spectrum of ages and genders. Could these be seeds of blockbusters? If so, I'd want to circle back and revisit my subjective pros and cons to find ways to strengthen the ideas before they go further. In particular, they could both use a stronger female presence than they currently have. Both could be a Linear Franchise.

As I mentioned earlier, you could argue that these rough concepts could have been better. I encourage you to generate your own and test them. That's the fun of concept testing; it allows us to discover how high is up before we decide which ideas to pursue.

There's a group of ideas in the middle of the pack: *Carnies, Astro-Nut, E.T. Search & Destroy, Spellbound, 3 Deadly Wishes,* and *Buster & Whirl Girl.* They each have different issues. *Carnies* does okay across most segments but drops slightly in appeal among teens. It needs to be more relatable to that age group. A change could be to make one of the kids a teen and giving the overall idea an edgier execution. There needs to be more at risk.

With *Astro-Nut,* interest drops among the female audience so a strong female presence is needed (romantic comedy?). Interest also drops with teens. Perhaps casting the right astro-nut, like Jack Black, would fix this. But it also needs more at risk, perhaps there needs to be a life or death moment as I first suspected.

E.T. Search & Destroy is strong among males (the highest scoring idea!) but weak among females, which accounts for weakness across ages as well. The romance between the warrior and the female alien would need to be dialed up as I earlier suspected. Could this be another blockbuster?

For *Spellbound,* interest drops among males, so this would need to be tweaked. The idea does best among younger kids ages eight to twelve (highest-scoring idea with this segment) and adults ages twenty to thirty-five. I wonder if adults responded this way because they would like to bring their young kids, even those younger than eight years of age. This might be a mainstream animated fantasy adventure for younger kids and parents. If it was executed in an edgy way, we might entice some older audiences as well.

No audience is madly in love with *3 Deadly Wishes.* I would need to rethink this.

Buster & Whirl Girl needs greater appeal among a female audience. Kids ages eight to twelve like it, but I'm not seeing a lot of love elsewhere. I would need to rethink this.

Malt Shop Rock and *Recycled* are the two concepts that fell hard. *Malt Shop Rock* has sluggish appeal across the board. In the computer tabulations, however, I found one interesting data point. The kids who like it most are girls in the eight to twelve age group (not shown in chart). Perhaps this is a movie or TV series for a children's cable channel. I would bring this idea back into research among that audience to get more details. The music/franchise potential is too big to pass up without investigating it further. *Recycled* did not do well. It's interesting to note that the most hope is among adults ages twenty to thirty-five who might have very young kids at home. But it's a long shot.

With that brief assessment, I would give initial priority to *Mad Skills* and *N.D.E.* I would give heavy consideration to *E.T. Search & Destroy* and *Spellbound*, with the understanding that these ideas need to be refined. I'd revisit some of the rest and drop most of the others. After revisions are made, I might test them again to discover the best of the best.

If I were researching these concepts for a client, I would have upped the sample size for more reliable results; broken out heavy movie-goers instead of mainstream movie-goers, which are reflected in the chart; broken out parents of younger versus older children; obtained diagnostics regarding the likes and dislikes of each concept; and judged the results against "norms" for other concepts tested (within the same genre). I might have also tested all twenty ideas. Since I was doing this as an exercise for the book, I kept the research brief. Once I discovered the concepts with the most potential, I might have also added potential actors' names in another research stage to help with casting.

I'm willing to state that a great writer and director might be able to make any of these ideas successful. However, their chances of success are much better if they select ideas near the top of the list than if they select ideas near the bottom. That's because the ones at the top already have greater innate audience appeal. Unless entertainment executives routinely conduct this type of analysis before projects are green-lighted, they won't know which ideas have the edge.

Will the adoption of concept testing change how Hollywood runs? Nope. It will always be deal driven rather than consumer driven. However, if this type of research, applied consistently, can increase the success rate by only 5 percent, that's a huge sum.

Key Takeaway

It's critical to develop a large number of concepts based upon principles first, and then use research and judgment to narrow the options down to a precious few before you decide which to pursue further. The more critical you are along the way, the more beneficial it will be later.

Chapter 14

End Game

Wow. We have come a long way. The principles I outlined throughout this book are simple and will help you to invent, develop, and market blockbusters.

- **Principle 1:** Satisfy Deep Emotional Needs
- **Principle 2:** Align with Contemporary Culture and Trends
- **Principle 3:** Create Relatable, Aspiring, Memorable Characters
- **Principle 4:** Generate Compelling Story Ideas
- **Principle 5:** Add Broad Audience Appeal
- **Principle 6:** Build in Elements That Make It a Franchise
- **Principle 7:** Fix Common Execution Problems
- **Principle 8:** Create Marketable Artistry
- **Principle 9:** Apply the Ever-Cool Formula
- **Principle 10:** Use Research to Optimize Decisions
- **Principle 11:** Launch an Idea Quest

While this is a handy list, I hope you have discovered that the real learning is in the details. I included so many exhibits in the text to give you easy reference charts to flip to when needed. Some of my clients have hung them on their office walls. I encourage you to do the same. The more often you review this information and keep it within sight, the more likely you are to incorporate it into your thinking. The goal is to create the next blockbuster, one that entices the kid in all of us to come out from within and embrace the child-like fantasies we all share.

As I write these final words, it's December 31, 2011. Year-end box office figures identified the winners. The top ten films included offerings from *Harry Potter, Transformers, The Twilight Saga, Pirates of the Caribbean, Cars, Thor,* and *Captain America.* Their successes are due to their ability to connect with the kid in all of us via emotional fulfillment, culture and trends, franchise elements, ever-cool principles, and marketing artistry. These few paid most of the bills for the films that failed. Unfortunately, the failures still managed to decrease overall 2011 box office revenue and attendance. Even big stars could not help stories that the masses found uninspiring, such as those contained in *The Rum Diary* (Johnny Depp), *J. Edgar* (Leonardo DiCaprio), and *Larry Crowne* (Tom Hanks and Julia Roberts). Think of the potential if just a few more films satisfied the criteria for success. It would mean greater audience satisfaction and billions of added dollars for the entertainment industry.

Once again, my opinion smacks of commercialism. But allow me to ask which is the more powerful art. That which emotionally moves one thousand people or that which emotionally moves fifty million people? Any reasonable person would say the latter. In most cases, the number of people who are emotionally moved is best represented by measures of box office receipts, TV ratings, and the like. It's ironic, then, that when entertainment is loved by the masses, which leads to great financial success, some people discredit the art by calling it cheap and commercial. Artists of less successful efforts are often the most vocal critics, disparaging entertainment that achieved commercial success as though it was impure or crass. Yet the opposite is true. Commercial success is most often a direct result of more emotionally powerful works. How many people have an inexpensive copy of Disney's *The Lion King* in their home? Millions. How many people have an inexpensive copy of the *Mona Lisa* in their home? Probably not as many. *The Lion King* moves more people emotionally. That opinion will drive some art-purists crazy, but it's a fact.

I also wanted to use this final chapter to share insights that didn't quite fit into the structure of the book. I hope you find them useful.

Perseverance Matters

It's cliché but true. The benefits of perseverance are real.

Even top movie producers tell tales of how it took decades to get a film green-lighted. TV shows bounce from network to network looking for a home. It's not unusual for even best-selling novelists to have had their early novels rejected for years before they were published.

Stephen King's first full-length novel, *The Long Walk,* was rejected by Bennett Cerf/Random House. His later book *Carrie* was rejected roughly thirty times before it was sold to a publisher. The science-fiction novel *Dune* was rejected by twenty-three publishers, the novel *Gone with the Wind* was rejected by thirty-eight publishers, and the novel *M*A*S*H* was rejected by twenty-one publishers.

Every major studio rejected *Star Wars;* it was finally picked up by 20th Century Fox. Columbia passed on *E.T.: The Extra-Terrestrial* before it was produced by Universal. TV networks rejected *All in the Family,* which became a landmark series.

It's not just the creative works that get rejected, but the creators themselves. It's been reported that Walt Disney was fired by a newspaper editor because the editor believed that Walt lacked imagination and had no good ideas. Jerry Seinfeld froze and was booed off stage the first time he performed at a comedy club. A movie executive once told Harrison Ford that he didn't have what it takes to be a star. Steven Spielberg was rejected by the University of Southern California's film school.

My son, Matthew Del Vecchio, is a talented artist in the video game industry and has worked on games such as *Thor* and *007 Quantum of Solace.* According to him, "Great developers deliver a compelling story, believable characters, and the kind of action that gamers want, but the key ingredient is the passion of the developers themselves. Without the passion needed to create innovative games, nothing will succeed."

Passion provides perseverance.

Good Ideas Die and Bad Ideas Live

The entertainment industry reveals an unfortunate truth.

Good ideas die all the time because the people who have the authority to approve them do not. The opposite happens. Bad ideas get produced with astonishing ease, evidenced by the fact that so many TV pilots fail to attract large enough audiences, many films don't cover their costs, and many novels don't make back their advance. That suggests that while there are people like Steven Spielberg, George Lucas, and James Cameron who are able to pick winners and losers with surprising consistency, most people in the position to approve or deny projects don't have that ability (they just think they do).

It makes you wonder. How in the heck did executives get to a position of authority when they cannot pick winners from losers? I have seen people thrust into positions of authority because they have more political talent than creative talent. I have also seen people who were associated with a bigger winner, come into great demand and then never achieve another great success. Their perceived talent was accidental. I once heard an executive claim that when someone has a great success, he or she can ride that for about five failures until the industry wises up.

Mostly, though, I think good ideas die and bad ideas live because most creators and entertainment executives are not methodical enough. They don't routinely revisit core principles. Professional athletes tell us of the importance of practice and consistency. They routinely watch films of past games to figure out what works and what does not. They learn from their mistakes and successes to prepare them for the next game. That kind of commitment can go a long way in achieving consistent success.

Integrity and Competence Are Not Dead, Just Sleeping

I wrote a book on ethics many years ago titled *A Knight's Code of Business: How to Achieve Character and Competence in the Corporate World*. Introduced during the Enron debacle, my book discussed how corporate CEOs and rank-and-file employees can achieve honesty and integrity each and every day. I divided people you find in corporate America into four quadrants. The two key dimensions were moral character and competence. Employees with high competence and high moral character are Good Knights, those with high competence and low moral character are Evil Barons, those with low initial competence but strong moral character are Squires-in-Training, and those with low competence and low moral character are Henchmen who report to Evil Barons. It was a humorous way to address all the characters we find in corporate America. The book went on to explain all of the subtle situations we are placed in and how a Good Knight might approach them. I discussed duplicity, corporate aristocracy, fraud, larceny, insincerity, and even tomfoolery. Executives from across the nation provided insightful, real stories about the lack of integrity or competence. My own experience came from decades in corporate life, including a long stint on an advertising agency's executive committee.

My ethics book didn't sell. I'm willing to admit that my book may have been too whimsical for the topic, but I also think that a great contributing factor is that most people don't think they need a lesson on integrity and competence. They think they have enough already. It's always the "other guy" who they claim needs more. Yet we are all constantly put into delicate compromising positions where self-interests may trump company interests, where feeling entitled may trump feeling appreciative, where guarding one's own "turf" may trump company success, and when style may trump substance. You may love a screenplay that you just read, but upon finding out that your boss hates it, you might state that you hate it too in order to reflect your boss's opinion. While that is politically advantageous for your career, you are doing a disservice to the writer, your own judgment, and possibly the company that might have profited had the screenplay been a success. If you're a researcher at an entertainment company, you may have tested a TV pilot that is at the "norm" for past pilot's tested; but because you personally dislike it, you twist the results to a "glass half-empty" approach, omitting or including data to make your case. That's intellectually dishonest. Or perhaps you wine and dine your boss to get a promotion you covet while your peer works his butt off to do great work. You get the job through pandering and taking credit you didn't deserve and your peer loses the promotion because he was too busy doing his job to brown nose the boss.

As I said, my ethics book didn't sell. Here's the best example as to why; I sent signed copies of the book to a dozen college presidents. One of those copies was soon for sale on the Internet as a "signed by author" copy. The college president was more interested in the twenty bucks he was hoping to gain than the ethical principles listed in my book. That said it all.

I think that integrity and competence do matter. I have done things in my career that held me back and didn't do things that might have propelled me forward. But it's worked out okay. The quality of the work should trump all. The quality of the work should be put before self-interests, entitlements, and politics. Creating the most powerful blockbuster screenplays, video games, novels, toy lines, and so forth should be all that matters. Do that and careers fall naturally and successfully in place. Our efforts should be focused there and not on the myriad other political crap that turns employees into Evil Barons and Henchmen.

Beware of Ego Trumping Talent

I have worked with extremely creative people for thirty years, including some in advertising agencies who thought they were Picassos and some at studios who thought they were Spielberg. Ego is healthy. It tells us we have self-worth, but too much ego is bad. I noticed that as long as the value of a person's talent was bigger than the cost of his ego, he stayed gainfully employed. But as soon as the cost of a massive ego (in terms of the friction it created) outstrips the value of his talent, he gets fired.

This observation led me to create an ego to talent index. An index of one hundred puts you right on the border where ego is about the size of your talent. But once the index tops one hundred, you are in trouble because your ego is larger than the value of your talent. That's when the knives come out. I remember one case when an egomaniac creative finally didn't deliver, people came out of the woodwork to get this executive fired—and it worked. There's an expression that you should be nice to people on the way up because you will meet them again on the way down. That's what the ego to talent index is all about.

I think ego increases the most when talent begins to fade. I have seen this in aging executives who become more aggressive when their light dims. They try to browbeat associates into agreeing to their creative direction because their creativity isn't good enough to do it for them.

I also know many executives in large entertainment companies who are wildly talented and have no ego that I have ever detected. They have been in place for years. They are treasures to be kept happy and well paid.

Innovators and Procrastinators

Having been out there for three decades, I see material that repeats. A guy is an innovator, his talent does amazing things, the company flourishes, then he goes away, and those left in charge tend to maintain the company where it is instead of advancing it into the future.

This happened when Walt Disney passed away. The Walt Disney Company seemed stuck in the past for a while, doing the status quo instead of advancing. When Michael Eisner and Frank Wells took the helm, they recharged the animation studio and were responsible for launching the era of the Disney renaissance. Films during that period included *The Little Mermaid, Aladdin, Pocahontas,* and *The Lion King.* New theme parks opened. The Disney Channel expanded. When Robert Iger took the helm it expanded further, most notably with the acquisition of Pixar and Marvel Entertainment.

Innovators thrive on ideas and make things happen. Procrastinators sit on ideas out of fear or incompetence or both. The industry needs innovators.

Be Both a Student and Teacher of Your Craft

Years ago, at Ogilvy & Mather advertising, I was often asked to interview other departments' potential employees. I always asked the prospective new hire to "identify a couple great advertising campaigns and tell me what made them great." I didn't care which advertising campaigns they selected or the criteria they used. I just wanted to know if they had an opinion based upon some principles they had devised. I was always shocked by the number of senior advertising professionals who could not answer this simple question. It told me that they were not students of the craft of advertising. They never observed what led to success and what led to failure. Without a rudimentary knowledge, they are potential disasters. We never hired them. Be a student and teacher of your craft. It matters.

Ideas Need Champions

Many, many years ago, I ran my first ideation session for a studio. The objective was to generate movie ideas that would appeal to a kid audience. The entire production staff was there and included the president of development and a slew of internal producers. I began the session by presenting my knowledge of youth culture, the emotional needs that youth need to satisfy, and how that might be translated into stories and characters that are relatable and aspiring. I then divided the group into about four teams, gave them materials to help spark ideas, and set them loose. They generated dozens of great ideas and then presented the best of the best to the bigger team. They went back to their offices the next morning and started to put several of the ideas into early stages of development.

Six months later, a new studio president was installed, most of the executives from the ideation session were let go, and every idea from that session became an orphan. The ideas eventually died, mostly because they were created by the old team and the new team didn't want to nurture the old team's ideas.

Ideas need champions, no matter where they come from.

Blockbuster ideas need blockbuster champions. Being a champion requires more than just supporting an idea. They take measured risks. They consistently follow principles that work. They put the interest of the idea above self-interests. They seek advice from all parties before they make tough decisions. They don't foster fear. They foster the nonjudgmental exchange of ideas. They praise worthwhile attempts, no matter the outcomes. They learn from failure and are not stifled by one. They swing for the fence, but they know when a single is all that is needed to bring someone home. They love creativity but are strategists, marketers, and researchers at heart.

In a sense, this book is not really about creating blockbuster entertainment. It is about creating blockbuster champions—my end game all along.

I hope that you take to heart those pieces of advice that made sense to you, toss aside any of my advice that doesn't work in your particular circumstance, and add your own insights that do. An old professor of mine said that it was important for each of us to make our own contribution to knowledge. This is a part of mine.

Good luck.

Yours truly,
Gene Del Vecchio

Appendix

2011 Study of Blockbuster Entertainment
Study Overview: Research was conducted across the United States among users of entertainment ages eight to fifty-five. The objectives were to discover the following:

- The types of stories, characters, and character goals and challenges audiences like most
- The elements that audiences dislike about today's entertainment
- Audience reactions to ten potential story concepts for films, novels, and TV

Sample Size: Four hundred nationally, broken by age and gender as shown on the following page.

Method: Internet survey, balanced to represent US ethnicity, income, and geography.

Questions: Closed-ended questions, as shown on the following pages.

Timing: June 2011.

Research Company: C+R Research in Chicago, Illinois.

Entertainment Usage: In the past year, on average, respondents in this survey claim that they went to a movie theater nearly nine times and read eighteen books (non-text books). In a typical day, they claim to watch 3.6 hours of television.

Confidence Interval: For the total sample of N = 400, the data is accurate to within approximately +/- 4 percent at the 90 percent confidence level. Caution should be used at lower sample sizes.

Representative US Sample							
Total Sample Size = 400							
Total	Ages 8 to 12		Ages 13 to 19		Ages 20 to 35		Ages 36 to 55
N=400	N=99		N=101		N=100		N=100
Male = 199 Female = 201	Male	Female	Male	Female	Male	Female	Male	Female
Segment Size	50	49	49	52	50	50	50	50

Character Goals/Needs Desired by Audience

Q: When thinking of stories for movies, TV shows, and books that you personally enjoy, look at the entire list below first, and then pick as many as ten goals that you would want the main characters to achieve

Goals/Needs	Total (400)	Males (199)	Females (201)	Ages 8-12 (99)	Ages 13-19 (101)	Ages 20-35 (100)	Ages 36-55 (100)
Survive life and death situations	52.8%	53.8%	51.7%	48.5%	57.4%	48.0%	57.0%
Be brave	48.8	52.8	44.8	61.6	53.5	40	40
Fulfill full potential	45	38.2	51.7	44.4	51.5	42	42
Find love of family and friends	44.8	32.7	56.7	42.4	40.6	46	50
Stop evil	42.8	52.3	33.3	54.5	39.6	41	36
Get respect	39.8	33.7	45.8	41.4	39.6	44	34
Redemption	39.5	35.7	43.3	37.4	37.6	40	43
Be appreciated	39.3	38.2	40.3	41.4	38.6	39	38
Be creative	37.8	36.2	39.3	40.4	36.6	37	37
Find romance	36	22.1	49.8	19.2	42.6	40	42
Achieve mastery of some ability	35.8	44.2	27.4	41.4	40.6	27	34
Become a winner	35	41.2	28.9	45.5	36.6	27	31

Goals/Needs	Total (400)	Males (199)	Females (201)	Ages 8-12 (99)	Ages 13-19 (101)	Ages 20-35 (100)	Ages 36-55 (100)
Get freedom or independence	33.8	35.2	32.3	25.3	39.6	34	36
Get control of a situation	32.8	31.2	34.3	31.3	37.6	32	30
Increase his or her power	24.5	33.7	15.4	29.3	32.7	19	17
Get recognition	22.5	24.6	20.4	17.2	24.8	29	19
Get health back	19.8	13.1	26.4	24.2	16.8	18	20
Get to be rebellious	17.8	18.1	17.4	8.1	28.7	18	16
Get fame/glory	17	17.6	16.4	27.3	20.8	11	9
Get beauty and glamour	13.8	4.5	22.9	18.2	11.9	14	11
Get status/ rank	13.8	16.1	11.4	14.1	18.8	14	8

Source: 2011 Study of blockbuster entertainment, conducted by C+R Research, Chicago, Illinois, exclusively for the book Creating Blockbusters!

Character Transformations Desired by Audience

Q: When thinking of stories for movies, TV shows, and books that you personally enjoy, look at the entire list below first, and then pick as many as ten ways you would like to see main characters change.

Transformations	Total (400)	Males (199)	Females (201)	Ages 8-12 (99)	Ages 13-19 (101)	Ages 20-35 (100)	Ages 36-55 (100)
Weak to strong	52.8%	49.7%	55.7%	57.6%	56.4%	44.0%	53.0%
Helpless to survivor	44.0	42.7	45.3	39.4	47.5	37.0	52.0
Loser to winner	42.5	43.2	41.8	41.4	37.6	45.0	46.0
Coward to brave	40.0	42.2	37.8	49.5	36.6	31.0	43.0
No love to love	39.5	28.6	50.2	22.2	43.6	43.0	49.0
Boring to exciting life	39.0	40.2	37.8	45.5	39.6	29.0	42.0
No friends/family to friends/family	37.0	30.7	43.3	46.5	37.6	29.0	35.0
Selfish to selfless	35.5	32.7	38.3	40.4	31.7	25.0	45.0
Beginner to a master	35.0	38.7	31.3	40.4	37.6	37.0	25.0

Transformations	Total (400)	Males (199)	Females (201)	Ages 8-12 (99)	Ages 13-19 (101)	Ages 20-35 (100)	Ages 36-55 (100)
Evil to good	35.0	33.7	36.3	36.4	33.7	28.0	42.0
Poor to rich	33.5	36.7	30.3	38.4	30.7	32.0	33.0
Unpopular to popular	27.5	24.6	30.3	37.4	29.7	19.0	24.0
Not so smart to smart	26.8	28.1	25.4	26.3	29.7	20.0	31.0
Not in charge to in charge	26.0	28.1	23.9	23.2	26.7	29.0	25.0
Sick to well	25.5	19.1	31.8	26.3	27.7	19.0	29.0
Unknown to famous	23.0	24.6	21.4	26.3	25.7	26.0	14.0
Mortal to immortal	21.0	23.1	18.9	28.3	17.8	22.0	16.0
Ugly to pretty/handsome	19.8	11.6	27.9	22.2	21.8	19.0	16.0
Younger to older or from older to younger	15.5	14.6	16.4	21.2	15.8	16.0	9.0
Small to big or from big to small	12.3	12.1	12.4	16.2	15.8	12.0	5.0

Source: 2011 Study of blockbuster entertainment, conducted by C+R Research, Chicago, Illinois, exclusively for the book Creating Blockbusters!

Characters Fears Desired by Audience

Q: When thinking of stories for movies, TV shows, and books that you personally enjoy, look at the entire list below first, and then pick as many as fifteen fears that you would most enjoy seeing various main characters face.

Fears	Total (400)	Males (199)	Females (201)	Ages 8-12 (99)	Ages 13-19 (101)	Ages 20-35 (100)	Ages 36-55 (100)
Death	35.3%	35.7%	34.8%	29.3%	42.6%	40.0%	29.0%
Personal dangers/injury	35.0	35.2	34.8	27.3	31.7	37.0	44.0
War	30.3	41.2	19.4	29.3	30.7	34.0	27.0
Kidnapping	30.0	23.6	36.3	33.3	30.7	27.0	29.0
Losing friends, family or girl/boyfriends	29.0	27.6	30.3	27.3	32.7	31.0	25.0
Being Alone	28.5	22.1	34.8	22.2	28.7	26.0	37.0
Intimacy/romance	28.5	16.1	40.8	13.1	30.7	34.0	36.0

Fears	Total (400)	Males (199)	Females (201)	Ages 8-12 (99)	Ages 13-19 (101)	Ages 20-35 (100)	Ages 36-55 (100)
Rejection of friends, etc.	28.5	23.6	33.3	29.3	35.6	26.0	23.0
Getting lost	27.8	24.6	30.8	31.3	30.7	21.0	28.0
Losing all of their money	27.0	23.6	30.3	33.3	17.8	23.0	34.0
Public humiliation	26.3	22.1	30.3	36.4	23.8	21.0	24.0
Plane and car crashes	26.3	29.1	23.4	28.3	26.7	22.0	28.0
Terrorism	26.3	31.2	21.4	20.2	20.8	29.0	35.0
Monsters	26.0	34.2	17.9	26.3	24.8	29.0	24.0
Police	25.8	28.1	23.4	20.2	27.7	28.0	27.0
Fierce animals	25.5	29.1	21.9	31.3	19.8	24.0	27.0
Burglars/robbers	23.5	28.1	18.9	26.3	23.8	15.0	29.0
Criticism	22.8	19.1	26.4	22.2	27.7	22.0	19.0
Making big mistakes at school or work	22.8	21.1	24.4	37.4	18.8	17.0	18.0
Spiders or snakes	21.5	25.1	17.9	35.4	19.8	19.0	12.0
Gossip	21.3	12.1	30.3	29.3	22.8	18.0	15.0
Drug use	20.8	18.6	22.9	9.1	27.7	22.0	24.0
Strangers	20.0	15.1	24.9	22.2	20.8	19.0	18.0
Being alone in the dark	19.8	15.1	24.4	26.3	21.8	13.0	18.0
Public speaking	19.8	18.6	20.9	30.3	21.8	11.0	16.0
Failing at school or job	18.0	17.1	18.9	24.2	17.8	17.0	13.0
Germs and diseases	18.0	17.6	18.4	14.1	16.8	15.0	26.0
Taking hard tests	18.0	17.1	18.9	27.3	17.8	13.0	14.0
Getting beat up by bullies	16.0	15.1	16.9	22.2	16.8	14.0	11.0
Divorce	14.8	9.0	20.4	8.1	16.8	15.0	19.0
Heights	14.8	14.1	15.4	14.1	15.8	12.0	17.0
Doctors/dentists/injection	13.8	11.1	16.4	17.2	11.9	14.0	12.0
Insects/bugs	13.8	16.6	10.9	21.2	12.9	11.0	10.0
Being late to school	11.8	10.1	13.4	22.2	10.9	10.0	4.0

Source: 2011 Study of blockbuster entertainment, conducted by C+R Research, Chicago, Illinois, exclusively for the book Creating Blockbusters!

Iconic Characters Desired by Audience

Q: When thinking of stories for movies, TV shows, and books that you personally enjoy, look at the entire list below first, and then pick as many as ten character types that you like to see most.

Iconic Characters	Total (400)	Males (199)	Females (201)	Ages 8-12 (99)	Ages 13-19 (101)	Ages 20-35 (100)	Ages 36-55 (100)
Spy/secret agent	40.5%	43.7%	37.3%	50.5%	41.6%	27.0%	43.0%
Vampire, werewolf, monster	34.8	37.7	31.8	39.4	34.7	29.0	36.0
Wizard, witch, or genie	34.3	31.7	36.8	38.4	31.7	32.0	35.0
Adventurer, treasure hunter, pirate	33.3	38.7	27.9	25.3	33.7	38.0	36.0
Mom, dad, kid	33.3	21.1	45.3	44.4	26.7	30.0	32.0
Warrior, soldier	31.8	45.7	17.9	29.3	28.7	32.0	37.0
Mythic gods (Zeus, Odin, Hercules, Thor)	27.5	32.2	22.9	26.3	36.6	24.0	23.0
Scientist and inventor	25.3	31.7	18.9	19.2	27.7	24.0	30.0
Folklore creatures (elf, dwarf, ogre, fairy)	25.0	28.1	21.9	26.3	22.8	23.0	28.0
Bride/groom or boyfriend/ girlfriend	24.5	9.5	39.3	17.2	28.7	30.0	22.0
Ghosts/ spirits	24.3	26.6	21.9	28.3	25.7	18.0	25.0
Policemen and firemen	24.0	25.6	22.4	17.2	22.8	23.0	33.0
Rock star	23.5	18.1	28.9	35.4	21.8	17.0	20.0
Movie star	23.3	17.1	29.4	33.3	26.7	18.0	15.0
Dancer	22.8	8.0	37.3	37.4	20.8	22.0	11.0
Queen, princess, ruler	22.0	9.0	34.8	34.3	17.8	21.0	15.0

Iconic Characters	Total (400)	Males (199)	Females (201)	Ages 8-12 (99)	Ages 13-19 (101)	Ages 20-35 (100)	Ages 36-55 (100)
Teacher, principal, or student	20.8	13.6	27.9	24.2	23.8	17.0	18.0
Robots	19.5	27.6	11.4	27.3	17.8	13.0	20.0
Athlete or Olympian	18.8	19.6	17.9	25.3	21.8	15.0	13.0
King, prince, ruler	18.8	20.1	17.4	18.2	15.8	26.0	15.0
Martial arts master	18.5%	25.1%	11.9%	19.2%	17.8%	21.0%	16.0%
Space alien	18.3	26.6	10.0	17.2	17.8	18.0	20.0
Rich people/ billionaire	17.8	15.6	19.9	23.2	12.9	16.0	19.0
Medical doctors or veterinarians	16.8	9.0	24.4	19.2	13.9	17.0	17.0
Race car driver, daredevil	16.0	19.6	12.4	24.2	11.9	11.0	17.0
Cowboy or pioneer	14.3	15.1	13.4	14.1	13.9	12.0	17.0
Fashion design, model	14.3	4.5	23.9	26.3	14.9	12.0	4.0
Astronaut or pilot	13.8	21.6	6.0	11.1	12.9	13.0	18.0
Native peoples	11.8	12.6	10.9	5.1	10.9	13.0	18.0
Prize fighter	7.8	11.1	4.5	6.1	5.9	12.0	7.0

Source: 2011 Study of blockbuster entertainment, conducted by C+R Research, Chicago, Illinois, exclusively for the book Creating Blockbusters!

Gender Sensibilities of Audience

Q: When thinking of stories for movies, TV shows, and books that you personally enjoy, look at the entire list below first, and then pick as many as ten items and themes you enjoy seeing.

Distinguishing Male Themes	Males (199)	Females (201)
Battles	56.8%	21.9%
Weapons/gadgets	55.3	15.9
Power	44.2	26.9
Being tough	42.7	29.4
Winning	38.7	28.9
Gross stuff	25.6	11.4
Muscles	21.6	16.4
Distinguishing Female Themes		
Relationships and friendship themes	28.1%	62.7%
Romance themes	15.1	50.7
Being sweet/sassy	12.6	43.3
Beauty	10.6	37.8
Cuteness	11.6	34.8
Glamour/fashions	10.1	27.4
Playing nice to make friends	15.6	25.9
Nurturing/mothering	7.5	23.4
Other		
Funniness	49.7	63.2
Being mischievous/rebel	31.7	36.3
Playing hard to win	29.1	32.8
Getting along well with team members	27.1	25.9
Being the star of the team	18.6	14.4

Source: 2011 Study of blockbuster entertainment, conducted by C+R Research, Chicago, Illinois, exclusively for the book Creating Blockbusters!

Audiences Dislikes of Movies, TV Shows, and Books

Q: When thinking of stories for movies, TV shows, and books that you have seen or read, what, if anything, don't you like? You can pick as many as eight things.

	Total (400)	Males (199)	Females (201)	Ages 8-12 (99)	Ages 13-19 (101)	Ages 20-35 (100)	Ages 36-55 (100)
Relevancy Issues							
Didn't interest from start	44.5%	40.7%	48.3%	43.4%	45.5%	43.0%	46.0%
Characters not relatable or aspiring enough	22.8	18.6	26.9	14.1	28.7	26.0	22.0
It's more for someone else	22.0	22.1	21.9	18.2	25.7	24.0	20.0
Action/Excitement Issues							
The story was boring	59.3%	53.3%	65.2%	64.6%	59.4%	50.0%	63.0%
It was too slow	46.8	43.7	49.8	36.4	58.4	39.0	53.0
Not enough suspense	33.8	34.7	32.8	31.3	39.6	31.0	33.0
Not enough action	32.8	35.7	29.9	45.5	29.7	19.0	37.0
Humor issues							
Not funny enough	38.5%	40.7%	36.3%	47.5%	31.7%	33.0%	42.0%
Complexity Issues							
Too confusing	33.3%	30.7%	35.8%	47.5%	25.7%	31.0%	29.0%
Uniqueness Issues							
Not different enough	16.8%	18.6%	14.9%	16.2%	15.8%	20.0%	15.0%
Characters not different enough	14.0	14.1	13.9	16.2	12.9	17.0	10.0

	Total (400)	Males (199)	Females (201)	Ages 8-12 (99)	Ages 13-19 (101)	Ages 20-35 (100)	Ages 36-55 (100)
Other Issues							
It was just stupid	50.3%	45.7%	54.7%	46.5%	56.4%	43.0%	55.0%
It was too long	31.5	25.6	37.3	38.4	28.7	28.0	31.0
Little characters conflict	13.3	15.1	11.4	15.2	16.8	13.0	8.0
Not extreme enough	10.3	10.6	10	15.2	10.9	8.0	7.0
None of the above	7.0	7.0	7.0	6.1	5.0	12.0	5.0

Source: 2011 Study of blockbuster entertainment, conducted by C+R Research, Chicago, Illinois, exclusively for the book Creating Blockbusters!

Audience Interest in Concepts

Q: Next you will see ideas for new stories that might appear in movies, TV shows, or books. For each one, please tell us how interested you personally would be in seeing it (if a movie) or reading it (if a book).

Percent definitely or probably interested	Total (400)	Males (199)	Females (201)	Ages 8-12 (99)	Ages 13-19 (101)	Ages 20-35 (100)	Ages 36-55 (100)
Mad Skills	45.8%	49.2%	42.3%	40.4%	51.5%	45.0%	46.0%
N.D.E.: Near Death Experience	45.0	49.7	40.3	43.4	49.5	49.0	38.0
Carnies	39.5%	36.7%	42.3%	39.4%	34.7%	45.0%	39.0%
Astro-NUT	38.5	47.2	29.9	40.4	29.7	39.0	45.0
ET Search & Destroy	38.3	51.3	25.4	41.4	30.7	48.0	33.0
Spellbound	38.0	32.2	43.8	47.5	25.7	41.0	38.0
3 Deadly Wishes	36.0	31.7	40.3	39.4	30.7	39.0	35.0
Buster & Whirl Girl	34.8	40.7	28.9	42.4	24.8	38.0	34.0
Malt Shop Rock	31.8%	32.7%	30.8%	36.4%	28.7%	34.0%	28.0%
Recycled	21.0	19.6	22.4	26.3	12.9	34.0	11.0

Source: 2011 Study of blockbuster entertainment, conducted by C+R Research, Chicago, Illinois, exclusively for the book Creating Blockbusters!

Index